Hiking Yosemite National Park

Help Us Keep This Guide Up to Date

Every effort has been made by the author and editors to make this guide as accurate and useful as possible. However, many things can change after a guide is published—trails are rerouted, regulations change, techniques evolve, facilities come under new management, etc.

We would love to hear from you concerning your experiences with this guide and how you feel it could be improved and kept up to date. While we may not be able to respond to all comments and suggestions, we'll take them to heart, and we'll also make certain to share them with the author. Please send your comments and suggestions to the following address:

The Globe Pequot Press
Reader Response/Editorial Department
P.O. Box 480
Guilford, CT 06437

Or you may e-mail us at:

editorial@GlobePequot.com

Thanks for your input, and happy trails!

Hiking Yosemite National Park

A Guide to Yosemite National Park's
Greatest Hiking Adventures

Second Edition

Suzanne Swedo

FALCONGUIDES ®

GUILFORD, CONNECTICUT
HELENA, MONTANA
AN IMPRINT OF THE GLOBE PEQUOT PRESS

FALCONGUIDES®

Text design by Nancy Freeborn
Photos by Suzanne Swedo
Maps by XNR Productions Inc. © Morris Book
Publishing, LLC

ISSN 1554-4303
ISBN 978-0-7627-3055-1

Manufactured in the United States of America
Second Edition/Fourth Printing

For my sister Jo.

Contents

STANISLAUS
NATIONAL FOREST
(EMIGRANT
WILDERNESS AREA)

HUMBOLDT-TOIYABE
NATIONAL FOREST

To 395

Twin Lakes Rd.

To 395

54 57

52 56

53

51

INYO NATIONAL
FOREST

46 47 48 49

Hetch
Hetchy

Tuolumne R.

YOSEMITE

NATIONAL

PARK

50

120

45

37

20 22 38 41
42 43 44 55

34 35 18 36

Tuolumne Meadows
Visitor Center

39 40

120

19

32

21 33

Information
Station

13 14

120

16

Valley Visitor
Center

6 1 5

59

2

4 7 17 29 30 58

15

3

8 9 12

11

STANISLAUS
NATIONAL
FOREST

140

10

25 27 28

41

24

26

23

31

N

0   Kilometers   8

0   Miles   8

41

SIERRA NATIONAL

FOREST

Acknowledgments

Thanks to the many park rangers and other personnel and volunteers of the National Park Service in Yosemite who have been so generous with their time and assistance, especially Laurel Boyers and Dave Gansci, Linda and Alan Estes, and Deanna Petree. All have provided much valuable information and have helped to smooth the way. The biggest debt of gratitude is owed to wilderness ranger Mark Fincher, who knows everything there is to know about the trails of Yosemite, and who, during his busy summer season, reviewed the manuscript and made comments and suggestions that were always right on target. What a joy to work with people whose lives have been dedicated to caring for and sharing their love of the most beautiful place in the world! Also deeply appreciated are the support and assistance of June at the USDA Forest Service office in Oakhurst and of Penny Otwell, Lou Carter, Beth Pratt, and all the hardworking staff at the Yosemite Association, whose purpose it is to initiate and support interpretation, education, research, scientific, and environmental programs in Yosemite. For their aid and encouragement and plain good company in the field, thanks also to Joellyn Acree, Erica Crawford, Melinda Goodwater, Jane Magid, Sally McKinney, Celia Ronis, and Sandy Steinman, and for infinite patience and tolerance and caring, Rex.

Introduction

Yosemite National Park occupies the heart of John Muir's "Range of Light" in the Sierra Nevada. The name means "snowy range" in Spanish, and in winter more than 60 feet of snow may accumulate. Yet the Sierra has also been called the gentle wilderness, because extremes of temperature are not great and the hiking days of summer are comparatively dry and sunny. It is a land of amazing diversity. Elevations in Yosemite range from 2,000 to more than 13,000 feet, from the rolling oak woodlands of the western slope to the jagged mountain crest, where offspring of the great glaciers that carved the spectacular topography still lie in shady hollows above thousands of lakes. Then, to the east, the land abruptly drops away to the apparently endless sagebrush desert of the Great Basin. There are three groves of giant sequoia trees, the largest living things on earth, miles of forests and meadows, and a rich and varied collection of wildflowers, wildlife, and history galore. Then there is the incomparable valley itself, Yosemite, surrounded by massive granite domes and spires and booming waterfalls, and in the summer season, teeming with tourists.

Up to four million people visit the park each year. Most concentrate their activities in Yosemite Valley, a mere 1-by-7-mile corner of the park. Those who are willing to explore on foot, however, can expect a genuine, uncrowded wilderness experience. Yosemite's borders encompass almost 1,200 square miles, and almost 800 miles of excellent trails travel through some of the most dramatic and beautiful scenery on earth.

This book describes the best of them, how to find them, how to plan and equip yourself to tackle them, and what special, natural wonders to enjoy along the way.

Life in Yosemite

Yosemite is a hiker's paradise because of its wonderful diversity. The Sierra Nevada range is only about 400 by 70 miles in extent and is mostly gray granitic rock, yet every nook and cranny, every stream drainage or mountain peak, is different from the rest. The main reason for this variety is Yosemite's wide elevation range. Extremes of topography lead to extremes of weather, temperature, and soil. These in turn provide habitats for a wide variety of plants and animals. More than 1,300 species of flowering plants, 223 kinds of birds, and 77 kinds of mammals are found here. Summer days in the western foothills can reach 100 degrees Fahrenheit; winter nights at the crest of the range may be 30 degrees below zero. The foothills may receive as little as 15 inches of precipitation in a year, while the forests at 8,000 feet may get 65 feet. Still, the Sierra Nevada is a gentle wilderness to hike because 95 percent of its precipitation falls as winter snow. Summers are usually sunny and dry, and though thundershowers can be expected in July and August at higher elevations, they are usually of short duration.

The hiking season can begin as early as April in the western foothills between elevations of 2,000 and 4,000 feet. The rolling hills are covered with a mixture of shrubby chaparral and oak woodland, green and carpeted with flowers usually through May, becoming hotter and drier later in the season. As elevations increase, wispy gray bull pines appear on the hillsides, along with the showy white wands of California buckeye.

At 4,000 to 6,000 feet a mixed coniferous forest of ponderosa pine, Douglas fir, and incense cedar flourishes, along with live oaks, deciduous black oaks, and maples. Warm, moist pockets support three separate groves of giant sequoias. Yosemite Valley, at about 4,000 feet, is at its finest in May and June. Waterfalls pour over the cliffs and dogwoods and azaleas bloom along the streams. Mule deer, black bears, and several kinds of ground squirrels are active in spring, summer, and fall, along with a great variety of birds.

Lodgepole pine and red fir dominate at 6,500 to 8,000 feet. This is the zone of heaviest snowfall in winter. Moisture from the Pacific Ocean is wrung from the air and piled up here in deep snowdrifts that remain well into July. Forests are dark and deep with fairly open, bare floors, because little sunlight reaches the ground. Yet strange little parasitic and saprophytic plants, including several kinds of orchids, thrive here, nourished by dead and decaying material in the soil.

The subalpine zone from 8,000 to 10,000 feet is considered by some to be the beginning of the true High Sierra. The landscape is more open and rocky and the views are the finest. The sky is intensely blue because the air is thinner. Graceful mountain hemlocks stand tall at the lower end of this zone, but the lodgepole and whitebark pines near timberline are often gnarled and stunted, forced to hunker down to avoid howling winter winds. Belding's ground squirrels and marmots whistle in the meadows, and showy black, white, and gray Clark's nutcrackers squawk among the trees.

The region of high peaks and passes above timberline is true arctic-alpine country. The temperature is low, winds high, and the growing season short, so plants keep their heads low. Most of the alpine wildflowers are perennials that wait underground for the few short weeks of sunshine and freedom from snow. Beginning roughly in mid-July and continuing through August, they burst forth to carpet the high meadows and decorate the rock crannies with masses of color. Across the late-lying snowfields, rosy finches chase insects that have been blown upward from below. Pikas scurry among the rock piles, gathering food to see them through the winter.

Then at the crest, all at once, the mountains fall away to the Great Basin. On the steep eastern slope, mountain and desert species mix together. Sagebrush and pinyon pines appear. The very rock is different on the eastern side of the crest. Ancient red and white metamorphics remain above the much younger granite that underlies most of Yosemite. Many points along the crest reveal stupendous views of Mono Lake, the Owens Valley, and the White Mountains.

Geology

Yosemite occupies the central part of the Sierra Nevada, a 400-mile-long active dynamic classroom of geologic forces and features. The range was formed by the collision of vast plates of the earth's crust, lifting what had once been seafloor and offshore volcanic islands to become mountain peaks. Roughly 150 million years ago, huge globs of molten material called magma from beneath the earth's crust forced their way toward the surface, cooking the surrounding and overlying seafloor sediments to a new kind of rock known as metamorphic. Most of the molten material cooled and solidified beneath the surface to become granitic rock. Then, about 80 million years ago, mountain building ended for a time. For millennia rain and wind and weather washed away almost all of the overlying ancient seafloor to reveal the gray granite that gives Yosemite its distinctive appearance today. A few remnants of the old metamorphic rock can still be seen in a narrow belt low in the western foothills, and in another high on the Sierra crest, but more than 95 percent of the Sierra Nevada is granite.

About twenty-five million years ago, the range began to rise again, this time as a result of movement on the famous San Andreas Fault. North of Yosemite volcanoes erupted, blanketing the land in lava and ash. The entire range broke apart along its eastern border, the Sierra crest thrusting upward, the Owens Valley dropping down, so that the current range slopes gradually upward from west to east, till it reaches the crest, then drops away in a vertical cliff. Eventually the mountains gained enough height to block the flow of the moist winds that blow from the Pacific, which dropped their loads of rain and snow on the western flank of the range, cutting rivers and streams. The sediment washed away to the west, filling the great Central Valley of California with rich and productive soil. The land to the east, now deprived of water, became desert.

The movement of ice applied the finishing touches to Yosemite's scenery. About two to three million years ago, the climate of the earth cooled just a bit. Enormous ice caps formed over the poles and spread outward. While they did not reach Yosemite, the snows that did fall accumulated to great depths, then compressed to ice. The ice, under its own weight, began to flow down the previously cut stream courses, gouging them wider and deeper, scraping and polishing their bottoms and sides, sharpening the mountaintops into spires and horns, forming knife-edged ridges called arêtes and amphitheaters called cirques. The ice dug out basins in the rock, and when it melted, it left thousands of sparkling alpine and subalpine lakes, many of which over time filled in with silt to become flower-filled mountain meadows. The glaciers in Yosemite today are not remnants of the original ice flows. The global climate has warmed and cooled in cycles since then, and the glaciers have melted and re-formed in response. The current glaciers are only a few hundred years old, but they lie in the hollows created by their larger predecessors, and the weather processes that created them are still at work. The mountain-building processes are at work, too. The mountains are still being steadily, though not smoothly, uplifted. The Sierra is alive and growing. All along the eastern slope, hot springs steam and bubble along numerous faults, and earthquakes rattle local residents. As recently as 1872, an earthquake struck the Sierra to the south of Yosemite, lifting the mountains 15 to 20 feet in that area and devastating the small town of Lone Pine.

In Yosemite we can see the evidence of more than 600 million years of geologic history, and as the mountains build and erode away, witness the process as it happens.

History

The southern Sierra Miwok people, who hunted, fished, and gathered a rich variety of plant materials, especially acorns, inhabited Yosemite for more than 800 years. They conducted trade with the Piute from the east side of the mountains for obsidian for arrowheads, salt, and various foods. Both made beautiful baskets.

Yosemite was first seen by outsiders in 1851 when the Mariposa battalion chased a band of Indians led by Chief Tenaya into the valley. Shortly thereafter the native people were forced to leave their villages in the area. By 1855 the first tourists had arrived, followed by the first homesteaders. Stagecoach routes, then railroads, were built to reach the valley. Sheep and cattle were turned into the meadows to graze and trample the grasses, and loggers began to cut the trees. Fortunately, a few far-sighted individuals recognized the need for protection and set in motion the appropriate political machinery leading to President Abraham Lincoln's signing of the bill that placed Yosemite Valley and the Mariposa Grove under the protection of the state of California. In 1868 the legendary John Muir arrived in Yosemite and led the movement for federal protection.

Yosemite National Park was created in 1890. All parks were patrolled by the U.S. Cavalry until 1916, when their function was taken over by the National Park Service. Many trails and other facilities were constructed or expanded by federal agencies like the WPA (Works Progress Administration) and the CCC (Civilian Conservation Corps) during the Great Depression of the 1930s. After World War II, people and cars poured into the park in ever-increasing numbers. Now, Yosemite gets as many as four million visitors each year, forcing the National Park Service to walk a tightrope between two somewhat contradictory mandates. It must "conserve the scenery and the natural and historic objects and the wildlife therein . . . " and it must "provide for the enjoyment of the same in such manner and by such means as will leave them unimpaired for the enjoyment of future generations."

Providing access to the park and accommodations within so that everyone can enjoy them without disrupting and changing them forever is an ongoing challenge. Roads, trails, campgrounds, other lodging, emergency services, administration, and sources of supply, no matter how carefully planned and constructed, inevitably make an impact on the natural environment. Hikers can do their part by respecting park rules and practicing zero impact principles.

Zero Impact

While the primary aim of this book is to encourage people to experience and appreciate the beauty of Yosemite up close and on foot, the backcountry is heavily used, and the environment is fragile. To prevent further wear and tear on the land, each hiker must accept personal responsibility for his or her impact on the environment by practicing zero impact principles. You can do your part by reading and following the suggestions and regulations that you receive when you pick up your wilderness permit.

Guidelines for day hikers can be found in the Yosemite Guide, which is given to every park visitor at all entrance stations and at visitor centers and wilderness centers.

On the Trail

When traveling on trails, group size is limited to fifteen people (except at a few very heavily used trailheads such as Happy Isles, where the limit is ten.) Groups traveling cross-country are limited to eight people. All routes described in this book are on trails. Hiking on trails leaves the least impact on the land, so all the hikes in this book follow established trails. To prevent damage to the trails themselves, do not shortcut switchbacks. They have been built to retard erosion as well as to create a more comfortable grade for gaining and losing elevation. When the trail is wet or muddy, try to avoid walking alongside it, trampling vegetation and wearing a parallel trail. Many of Yosemite's meadows are scarred by a series of wide parallel ruts across the landscape that look like the work of vehicles. On the other hand, if you must cross a meadow with no conspicuous pathway, and are part of a group, spread out so that you do not create a new rut by numerous feet passing over the same route.

Good manners and consideration for others, not to mention safety, dictate that foot travelers yield to pack animals on the trail. Step off the trail and stand quietly until the last horse or mule has gone completely past. Bicycles or mechanized travel of any kind is prohibited in the backcountry (as are pets and firearms). Downhill hikers should yield to those heading uphill so that the climbers can maintain their rhythm and momentum.

Selecting a Campsite

Camping is prohibited within 4 trail miles of Yosemite Valley, Hetch Hetchy Reservoir, Wawona, Glacier Point, and Tuolumne Meadows, and within 1 mile of any road. Otherwise you may camp anywhere you choose in the Yosemite wilderness so long as you observe a few restrictions designed to reduce your impact on the land and on other campers.

Choose a site at least 100 feet from water and, whenever possible, 100 feet from the trail, or at least out of sight of passers-by. Pitch your tent or spread your tarp on sandy ground or pine duff, never on growing vegetation. In the afternoon sunshine, green meadows are deceptively inviting, but are cold, damp, and buggy at night. Use an established and designated campsite, one that has been used before, and do not modify the area in any way by digging trenches around tents, building new fire rings, or breaking limbs off trees.

Campfires

Campfires are prohibited above 9,600 feet in Yosemite and are discouraged even at lower elevations. If you must have a fire, keep it small and cozy, and take only firewood that is dead and lying on the ground. Do not remove branches from standing dead trees. They provide homes for dozens of different creatures and are important parts of the ecosystem. High-elevation fires are proscribed not because of wildfire danger, but because the 9,600-foot mark is the average timberline elevation in Yosemite, where vegetation grows slowly, and the few trees that manage to hang on to life near timberline are evergreens that do not drop much organic material on the ground. The soil needs protection from compaction that the litter on the forest floor supplies, especially where people are moving around and pitching tents. Compaction prevents the soil from absorbing vital water and oxygen, and removes the source of organic material that is returned to the soil as it decomposes.

Backpacking stoves are so light and efficient, and modern fabrics so warm, that fires are no longer needed for cooking or warmth, but for social atmosphere alone. As attractive as going "back to nature" seems, there are too many of us now, and too little truly wild nature left to afford an extravagant campfire. Keep it small if you must have it, and of course, make sure it is completely out when you leave.

Housekeeping

There is one simple rule for good housekeeping in the wilderness: Do not put anything in the water. That includes soap, food scraps, and fish guts. Biodegradable soap is not the answer. To biodegrade means to decompose; that is, to rot. Biodegradable soap does not poison organisms in the water like detergent can, but it does encourage the growth of bacteria that can upset the chemical balance of the water to the detriment of the organisms that live in it. Hot water and a little sand do fine for washing dishes, but if you must use soap, wash and rinse everything at least 100 feet from any water source. The same goes for your own body. A refreshing swim in a mountain pond won't do any damage, and you can surely survive a few days in the wilderness without contracting some dread disease if you do not use soap; but if you feel you must, wash and rinse at least 100 feet away from water.

Keep your camp clean of crumbs and other edibles. Learn to take just what you need to eat, and pack out your leftovers. At very popular campsites jays, squirrels, mice, and marmots have come to expect human food scraps and have acquired bad habits like snatching food from your hand or chewing holes in your pack or tent to investigate appetizing smells. In popular camping areas leave pack zippers and flaps open when you are asleep or away from camp so that varmints can crawl in to investigate and crawl back out again, without gnawing their way through the fabric.

Human waste disposal is one of the most difficult problems in the backcountry. There are simply too many of us concentrated in too few areas to avoid having a serious impact. The park service has constructed solar composting toilets at the most popular campsites in the park and encourages campers to use them. Otherwise, find a spot 200 feet from water where there is some organic material on the ground and dig a hole about 6 inches deep, then cover everything. Take extra plastic bags along and pack out your toilet paper. A teaspoon of powdered bleach in the plastic bag will prevent odors. Do not bury it. It is sometimes dug up again by animals and takes many years to decompose underground. Burning toilet paper is no longer recommended since the practice has started more than one serious fire.

Wilderness Permits

Wilderness permits are required year-round for all overnight trips into the Yosemite backcountry. They are not required for day hikes. The permits are free of charge.

Permits are issued under a quota system designed to prevent overcrowding and damage from overuse in popular wilderness areas. They are based on trailhead entry, not on final destination. Forty percent of the permits available for each trailhead can be picked up within twenty-four hours of your trip at wilderness centers throughout Yosemite on a first-come, first-served basis. The Yosemite Valley wilderness center, the Tuolumne Meadows wilderness center, the Big Oak Flat and Wawona visitor centers, and the Hetch Hetchy entrance station all issue permits. Reservations for the other 60 percent of the permits are available in advance by mail, but you must pick up the permit in person before your hike. There is a $5.00 per person charge for advance reservations. Reservations for trips between mid-May and to mid-October are accepted from two days to twenty-four weeks in advance. Call (209) 372–0740. You can request a reservation online at www.nps.gov/yose/wilderness/permits. You can also request a reservation by mail at Yosemite Association, P.O. Box 545, Yosemite, CA 95389. Mail requests and phone requests are processed simultaneously. For more information about permits, call (209) 372–0200.

If your hike begins outside Yosemite, obtain your permit from the Forest Service permit station nearest your entry point. All hikes described in this book that originate east of the park begin in the Hoover Wilderness. Trails north of Lundy Canyon are administered by the Bridgeport Ranger District of the Toiyabe National Forest. Permits are available from the USDA Forest Service Office in Bridgeport. Call (619) 932–7070. Trails south of Lundy Canyon are administered by the Mono Ranger District of the Inyo National Forest. Permits are available from the Mono Basin visitor center at Mono Lake near Lee Vining. Call (619) 647–6525. Hikes that begin to the south of the park are administered by the Sierra National Forest in North Fork and Oakhurst. Call (559) 877–2218.

The purpose of wilderness permits is not merely to maintain trailhead quotas. They help the National Park Service determine how much use each trail gets, so that priorities for trail maintenance and patrols can be established and funds allocated. They also allow a point of contact at which hikers can be informed of current trail conditions or any special regulations that might be in effect due to bear activity, fires, or any other emergency.

Wilderness permits are not a form of trail registration. Your itinerary is on file so that search and rescue teams have some idea of where to begin if you are reported lost, but it is up to you to leave word with someone at home who will contact the park service if you do not return when expected.

Bears

Black bear management has become such a serious issue in Yosemite that it deserves special discussion. All of Yosemite's bears are black bears, regardless of their color. The grizzly, the California state mammal, is now extinct in California. Black bears are neither as unpredictable nor as aggressive as grizzlies. No human has ever been killed by a black bear in Yosemite, but there have been numerous injuries, lots of property damage, and many vacations spoiled. The fault is not with the bears. For many years Yosemite bears were fed scraps from local hotels, to the delight of tourists who came to watch the evening show. When the practice was discontinued, the bears resorted to raiding garbage containers all over the park. When bear-resistant garbage containers were installed, the bears mastered the art of opening ice chests in campgrounds, and when bear-proof boxes were installed in campgrounds, the bears moved into the backcountry to feast on freeze-dried backpacker cuisine. At the same time, they discovered what culinary delights are to be found in vehicles left in parking lots. The National Park Service has tried tagging, relocating, and even killing hundreds of Yosemite's bears, to no avail. Current park policy is to attempt to change the behavior of the humans, not the bears. After all, we created the problem in the first place.

The best way to help save Yosemite's bears, your expedition, and your vehicle is to carry a bear-proof food canister in the backcountry and to store any food you must leave behind in the bear-proof boxes located in parking lots and at trailheads. Bear-proof canisters are not perfect; they are bulky, weigh two to three pounds, hold only a few days' food, and cost about $75. Still, the bears have not figured out how to get into them. *The Park Service requires the use of bear-proof canisters within 7 miles of any park road and anywhere above 9,600 feet.* For more information visit the Yosemite Web site (www.nps.gov/yose/wilderness). For one thing it lists the brands of bear canisters that have been tested and approved. You can rent one in locations all over Yosemite for only $5.00 for your entire trip (with a limit of two weeks). Once you learn to select and pack your food carefully, you can carry enough food for two people for several days. The alternatives are few. The counterbalance method of hanging food appears simple on paper, but it is very difficult to find a tree of the proper height with a branch of the proper diameter and to balance your food sacks perfectly. It should be considered a delaying tactic only. Bears are much stronger, more patient, more determined, and much more intelligent than you think. If you can get it up there, they can get it back down again. Attach pots and pans or other noise-makers to your food sacks so that when the bear goes to work you will have some warning and can chase it away.

Thousands of vehicles have been broken into in parking lots. Bears break windows, tear off doors, and tunnel through upholstery to reach the trunk from the inside. Do not store any food, garbage, anything that smells like food, or any containers that look like they might contain food like ice chests or paper bags, even if they are empty, in your car. Not even in the trunk. Do not assume that if food is sealed in plastic or foil and has not been opened that a bear cannot smell it. Their sense of smell is extremely acute, and they have learned that food comes in certain kinds of containers even if they can't read the labels or smell what's inside. They have been known to open cans of motor oil just to check. All parking lots, campgrounds, and trailheads in Yosemite have bear-proof food storage boxes nearby. Use them.

The National Park Service considers proper food storage to be your responsibility. Don't expect sympathy if you lose your food. You are liable for a fine for not storing it properly.

A Few Words of Caution

Weather Patterns

While most Sierra summer days are clear and sunny, high mountains create their own weather. Hikers must be prepared for anything. Snow can fall at any time of year, including July and August, though it is not common. Afternoon thundershowers, sometimes accompanied by violent hailstorms, can build with amazing rapidity on summer days that begin without a cloud in the sky. They are usually of short duration, but long enough to drench and chill an unprepared traveler. Never set out without rain gear. Lightning can be a serious hazard on open ridges above timberline. If a storm threatens, head downhill to the cover of timber as quickly as possible. If you're caught in an exposed area with no time to descend, get away from your pack or any metal equipment and squat until the danger passes—do not sit.

Drinking Water

In spite of the clear and sparkling appearance of Yosemite's lakes and streams, water from even the most remote of sources has been found to contain *Giardia lamblia,* a microorganism that causes diarrhea and other intestinal upsets. It is not life threatening for normal healthy adults, but it is debilitating and persistent and must be treated with antibiotics whose side effects may be equally unpleasant. The symptoms do not appear for more than a week after exposure, so victims sometimes do not associate their malady with their wilderness experience. Treat all water with a water filter guaranteed to remove giardia, with iodine, or by bringing it to a rolling boil. Iodine is lightweight, convenient, and effective if fresh, but some people are allergic and some object to the taste.

If you decide to wade, always overestimate the depth and strength of the current.

Wild Animals

Injuries caused by bears in Yosemite are almost invariably due to human ignorance or carelessness. Take care to avoid moving between a mother and her cubs, and do not try to touch or feed a bear or to reclaim food the bear has already taken from you. More injuries are caused by deer than by bears in the park since people are more likely to approach a deer and risk being sliced by sharp hooves when the animal is startled.

Mountain lions have been spotted in Yosemite, but they are very shy, and attacks are extremely rare. If you should encounter one, do not run or you might be mistaken for prey. Hold your ground, wave your arms to make yourself appear larger, and shout. Then congratulate yourself on being given the gift of a glimpse of a beautiful animal in its native habitat.

You'll find rattlesnake habitat at lower elevations where there is plenty of brush to provide cover for small animals like rabbits, squirrels, and mice. Rattlers are most active at dawn and dusk and blend beautifully with their surroundings. They prefer to save their venom for catching their prey and do not strike at people unless they feel threatened. Stay alert and watch your step. The chances of being bitten are extremely slim, and snakebites are rarely fatal.

Stream Crossings

This is one hazard that is not exaggerated, unlike perceived threats from wildlife. Most of the larger streams in Yosemite have sturdy bridges across them, but in exceptionally wet years, even some of these get washed away. Be sure to research trail conditions in advance if your proposed route involves a major river crossing. More frequently, it is the smaller creeks swollen with snowmelt early in the year that are most dangerous. Some have rock or log crossings that must be managed with great care. A stout stick is a great stabilizer. Be sure to plant it upstream so that rushing water does not grab it and pull it out from under you. Always unbuckle your pack straps so that if you should fall in, you can free yourself from being dragged and held underwater.

If you decide to wade, always overestimate the depth and the strength of the current. Sierra streams are so clear they are usually deeper and swifter than they seem. Do not wade through water higher than your knees. The recommended method is

Trail ducks, also called cairns, mark many of Yosemite's trails.

to remove your socks and cross in your boots, which will give you temporary protection against the numbing cold and more stability on underwater obstacles. Do not try to cross barefooted. Seek out the widest part of the stream, even though the temptation is to pick a narrower spot to make the crossing quicker. The widest spot is usually the shallowest, slowest, and safest. If you are not sure whether you can cross safely, you can try again early in the morning when the snow upstream has begun to melt in the morning sun. Do not take chances. You can always return.

Losing the Trail

Yosemite trails are much more defined, well marked, and better maintained than those you will find in most other wilderness areas. Still, some are used more regularly than others and are easier to follow. High water, avalanches, rockslides, and fast-growing meadow vegetation and brush can obscure a clear trail in a single season. Watch for trail blazes on the trees, made by cutting away the outer bark, usually in simple geometric shapes at approximately eye level. In open rocky places, watch for cairns, also known as ducks, which are piles of rocks that indicate the presence of a trail. Stay alert for sawed logs, metal tags, sometimes even plastic strips. If you become confused, go back to a point where you were absolutely certain of your location, and start over. If you feel you are hopelessly lost, stay put and wait for help.

How to Use This Guide

The purpose of this guide is to help you choose and plan a day hike or backpack in Yosemite best suited to your time, energy, experience, and personal preferences. It offers a preview of what you are likely to see and experience along your chosen route: geological features, historical sites, trees, birds, flowers, and mammals. It helps you anticipate places where the trail is faint, where it is clear, where and when rivers and streams are special sources of delight, or where they may be obstacles to travel.

Trail descriptions are intended to be used along with U.S. Geological Survey topographic maps, available at wilderness outfitting and sporting goods stores, at visitor centers and shops in Yosemite, and through the USGS at P.O. Box 25286, Federal Center, Denver, CO 80225; (800) USA–MAPS; or online at www.mapping.usgs.gov.

Each trail description begins with a summary of the hike. A statistical section follows for quick reference to more specific characteristics of the hike.

Total **Distance** is described in miles. The mileage is one-way for a loop, in which you return to the place where you started without retracing your steps; or a shuttle hike, in which you begin at one trailhead and end at another, requiring two vehicles, a shuttle bus, or another driver to pick you up or deposit you at either end. Round-trip mileage is provided for an out-and-back hike, in which you return to the trailhead the same way you came.

The **Difficulty Rating** is bound to be interpreted differently by hikers in varying degrees of physical condition, including their adaptability to high elevation. In general, "easy" trails can be negotiated by anybody who can walk. "Moderate" trails are of greater length or involve some elevation gain and loss; they may challenge those who are not accustomed to much physical activity. "Moderately strenuous" hikes are for experienced hikers or those who are very physically fit. "Strenuous" hikes will challenge the most experienced and energetic of hikers.

The **Seasons** heading refers in most cases to the only time that trails are open and safe to use at all. The hiking season in Yosemite is all too short. Most trails are passable only on skis, snowshoes, or with special winter climbing equipment for most of the year. More specific times to visit areas especially noteworthy for their seasonal displays of wildflowers or fall colors or flowing waterfalls will be mentioned here.

Facilities refers to sources of supplies or contact with emergency services nearest the trailhead.

Permits are discussed in the special section on wilderness permits on page 7.

Miles and Directions point out landmarks on the trail, often trail junctions. The distances are based on the official National Park Service measurements, but the park service cautions hikers to be aware that trails have been rerouted over the years to avoid obstacles like rockslides or washouts or to protect fragile vegetation in boggy meadows. The signs marking these trails have not always been corrected. Sometimes new signs have been added to one end of a trail but not to junctions along the way, so you will find that the miles don't always add up. Still, I have walked every trail in this book and have found none of the stated mileage between points to be inaccurate by more than a quarter mile.

This book uses **Elevation Profiles** to provide an idea of the elevation changes you will encounter along each hike. This, in turn, will help you understand the difficulty of the hike. In the profiles, the vertical axes of the graphs show the total distance climbed in feet. In contrast, the horizontal axes show the distance traveled in miles. It is important to understand that the vertical (feet) and horizontal (miles) scales can differ between hikes. Read each profile carefully, making sure you read both the height and distance shown. This will help you interpret what you see in each profile. Some elevation profiles may show gradual ascents and descents to be steep and steep ones to be gradual. Elevation profiles are not provided for hikes with little or no elevation gain.

The maps in this book that depict a detailed close-up of an area use elevation tints, called hypsometry, to portray relief. Each gray tone represents a range of equal elevation gain and loss. The darker tones are lower elevations and the lighter grays are higher elevations. The lighter the tone, the higher the elevation. Narrow bands of different gray tones spaced closely together indicate steep terrain, whereas wider bands indicate areas of more gradual slope.

Maps that show larger geographic areas use shaded, or shadow, relief. Shadow relief does not represent elevation; it demonstrates slope or relative steepness. This gives an almost 3-D perspective of the physiography of a region and will help you see where ranges and valleys are.

Legend

— – – Park Boundary

⇒⟨395⟩⟨ U.S. Highway

—⟨120⟩— State Highway

———— Other Paved Road

════ Gravel Road

==== Unimproved Road

------ Trail

·········· Shared Trail

▬▬▬ Highlighted Route

⬬ Lake/Large River

〜〜 River/Creek

⌇⌇ Intermittent River/Lake

⁕ ⁕ Marsh/Swamp

○⌐ Spring

⫽ Waterfall

⊰⊱ Bridge

▲ Campground

●–● Gate

🐎 Horse Trail

🛏 Lodging

▲ Mountain/Peak

◘ Overlook/Viewpoint

🅿 Parking

)(Pass

🛆 Picnic

■ Point of Interest

🚩 Ranger Station

🚶 Trailhead

+ UTM grid tick

The Valley Floor

Yosemite Valley is one of the natural wonders of the world. Almost vertical walls rise up to 4,733 feet above the valley floor, where the Merced River winds its way through flower-filled meadows and shady forests. The famous profile of Half Dome dominates the east end and El Capitan the west. Some of the world's highest waterfalls pour from the cliffs. It is a mecca for hikers, climbers, photographers, fishermen, rafters, cyclists, and just plain tourists from everyplace on earth. While it covers only about 7 square miles of a national park that sprawls over 1,200 square miles, the majority of visitors stay in the valley, and indeed, many believe that Yosemite Valley and Yosemite National Park are one and the same. Do not expect a wilderness experience in Yosemite Valley, but don't assume that hiking there is not worthwhile just because it's popular. The valley's attractions draw so many sightseers because they are well worth seeing, but there are also many beautiful, quiet, out-of-the-way corners to enjoy on foot and in solitude.

Spring and fall are the best times to hike the valley. The crowds and traffic are heaviest in summer and temperatures can be uncomfortably hot for strenuous hiking. Springtime is more pleasant; the waterfalls are full, and the wildflowers are blooming. In fall the air is clear and brisk and the changing colors of the oaks, dogwoods, maples, and willows are spectacular.

All hikes on the valley floor are day hikes because no camping is allowed outside established campgrounds. Permits are not necessary, but it's a good idea to drop by the visitor center and the wilderness center for information about trail conditions and weather reports. You can help reduce traffic and pollution in the valley by parking your car in the lot across Northside Drive from Yosemite Village, or at Camp Curry, and using the shuttle buses that run every ten minutes and go to most valley trailheads.

If you are planning a backpack that originates in the valley, you can pick up your wilderness permit at the wilderness center, between the Ansel Adams gallery and the post office in Yosemite Village. You can also get a parking permit there to display in your window in the backpackers' parking lot just east of Curry Village. The other lots are for day use or for lodge or tent cabin guests only. If you arrive the day before your trip, remember that all accommodations—campgrounds, lodges, and hotels— are usually full and require reservations many months in advance. Camp 4, formerly known as Sunnyside, a walk-in campground on the north side west of Yosemite Lodge is your best bet. Be sure to stow all food, food containers, garbage, and ice chests in the bear-proof containers in the parking lot any time you leave your car.

The valley is open year-round and can be reached from the west via Highway 41 from Fresno, Highway 140 from Merced, and Highway 120 from Manteca. In summer Highway 120, the Tioga Road, is open all the way through the park to the east side of the Sierra near Lee Vining on U.S. Highway 395. There is a $20 fee per car to enter the park from any direction. Remember: *There is no gas in Yosemite Valley.*

Contact Yosemite at (209) 372–0200 or visit the park's Web site, www.nps.gov/yose, for more information.

1 East Valley Floor

This is a leisurely, flat loop hike with views of North Dome, the Royal Arches, and Yosemite Falls, where you can visit Happy Isles Nature Center and the infamous 1996 rockslide, and stroll along sometimes boisterous, sometimes tranquil stretches of the Merced River.

Start: Raised wooden deck in front of Curry Village.
Distance: 2.6-mile loop.
Approximate hiking time: 1 to 4 hours.
Difficulty: Easy.

Seasons: Year-round.
Nearest facilities: Curry Village; snacks, water, and toilets at Happy Isles.
Permits: None.
Map: USGS Half Dome quad.

Finding the trailhead: Board the Yosemite Valley shuttle bus from anyplace in the valley and get off at Curry Village.

The Hike

From the raised patio area in front of the bustling Curry Village snack bar/grocery/bike rental complex, look beyond and above the enormous parking lot to towering North Dome and the Royal Arches, serene and indifferent to the hubbub below. Then follow the paved footpath eastward past a line of tent cabins fronted by a row of large, brown steel bear-proof boxes for nighttime storage of food, toothpaste, and other aromatic bear-tempting articles.

If you set out before 9:00 A.M., a good idea in midsummer when valley temperatures climb into the 80s, you are likely to pass a row of bleary-eyed tent cabin guests brushing teeth, applying deodorant, and generally preparing for the day. A few hundred yards beyond the tent cabins and the toothbrush brigade, a driveway turns right into a parking lot for backpackers. Go into the lot, turn left, and walk to the southeast end. Take the unmarked but wide and obvious trail into the shady ponderosa pine and incense cedar forest.

Pass a little A-frame structure used for ranger/naturalist talks, and at 0.9 mile reach a swampy area known as The Fen. Here a boardwalk runs through a lush growth of water-loving horsetails, sedges, and fragrant mints. An interpretive panel tells about the living things inhabiting soggy places like this one. The trail crosses a paved path at 1 mile just before meeting the Merced River. To the right is the Happy Isles Nature Center, with wonderful exhibits and books inside. Behind the building you can see the rubble and smashed trees left by the 1996 rockslide that killed a hiker. Now head downstream and follow the riverside path to the shuttle bus stop on the road where you will find restrooms and a snack bar.

The hike crosses the road and continues downstream along the north bank of the Merced. Take a tiny detour and walk out onto the bridge over the road for views

East Valley Floor

Hypsometry

7500

3500
Elevation in Feet

To Mirror Lake

4,180,000

275,000

Merced River

Tenaya Creek

Stables

Upper Pines Campground

Shuttle Stop 16

The Fen

Happy Isles Nature Center

To Vernal Fall

4,179,000

275,000

274,000

Lower Pines Campground

P

Backpackers' Parking

Curry Village

START

Merced River

273,000

4,180,000

N

0   Kilometer 0.25

0   Mile   0.25

Glacier Point 7,214 ft.

273,000

4,179,000

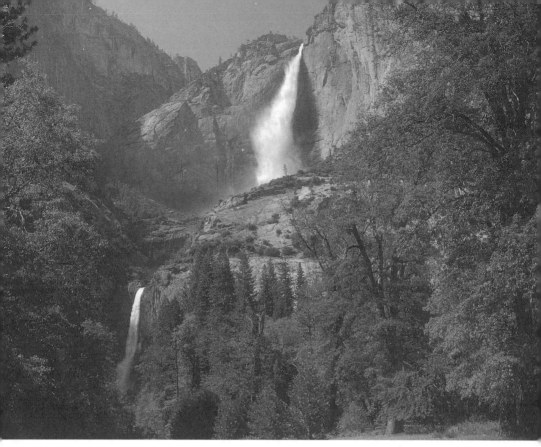

Stop for a view of Yosemite Falls from the east valley floor.

of the river, which rushes toward the bridge in noisy white-water rapids, then emerges more quietly from the other side. The view of North Dome over the river on the downstream side is a photographer's favorite.

Once you have crossed the road, you leave the crowds behind and follow a path through incense cedar and pine, streamside alder and dogwood. Big, showy white azaleas perfume the air in May and June. The river changes character at every turn, sometimes gurgling busily, sometimes green and placid, occasionally splitting to flow around wooded islands. This section of the trail is shared by horses and mules because it connects their stables to the John Muir Trail. Remember to step off the trail to let them pass, since pack animals always have the right-of-way.

At 2 miles the stable area appears across the road on the right, and simultaneously Upper Yosemite Fall comes into view ahead. Turn left here and cross back over the Merced on the road using Clark Bridge. Pass between the entrances to Upper and Lower Pines Campgrounds. A sign on the right directs you to Curry Village. Shortly thereafter you will spot the cabins for Curry Village employees straight ahead. Just beyond the cabins and to the right (west) you'll find the Curry Village parking lot and the end of the hike.

Miles and Directions

0.0 Curry Village parking lot trailhead.

0.1 Backpackers' parking lot.

0.9 The Fen.

1.0 Happy Isles Nature Center.

1.1 Happy Isles Bridge on the shuttle bus road.

2.0 Stables.

2.6 Curry Village.

2 West Valley Floor

This end of Yosemite Valley is surprisingly quiet and unvisited, except near popular attractions like Bridalveil Fall and El Capitan Meadow. If you start fairly early in the morning though, you can have even these busy spots to yourself. Dogwoods and maples are especially beautiful at this end of the valley, blooming and fragrant in spring, blazing with color in fall, and the beaches along the Merced River invite sunning and swimming in summer.

Start: El Capitan Bridge near the center of the valley.
Distance: 6.5-mile loop.
Approximate hiking time: 3 hours to all day.
Difficulty: Easy.
Seasons: Spring, summer, and fall.

Nearest facilities: Everything you need, except gas, at Curry Village and Yosemite Village.
Permits: None.
Maps: USGS El Capitan and Half Dome quads.

Finding the trailhead: From Yosemite Village, take Northside Drive (one-way westbound) to El Capitan Drive and turn left (south). From any of the west-side park entrances take Southside Drive (one-way eastbound) to El Capitan Drive and turn left (north). Park along the road on either side just west of the El Capitan Bridge.

The Hike

The route begins beside an apple tree at the west end of the bridge over the Merced River. Upstream to the north is the 7,569-foot monolith of El Capitan, downstream are the Cathedral Rocks and Cathedral Spires. Set off upstream (northward) alongside the quiet, green river on a path of partly eroded asphalt, following the curve of the river as it swings eastward and parallels the road for a short distance. This curve is called the Devil's Elbow. In midsummer, the water level drops to reveal a sandbar in midstream, popular with swimmers and sunbathers. Where a fence ends at 0.3 mile, cross Northside Drive, and make a sharp hairpin

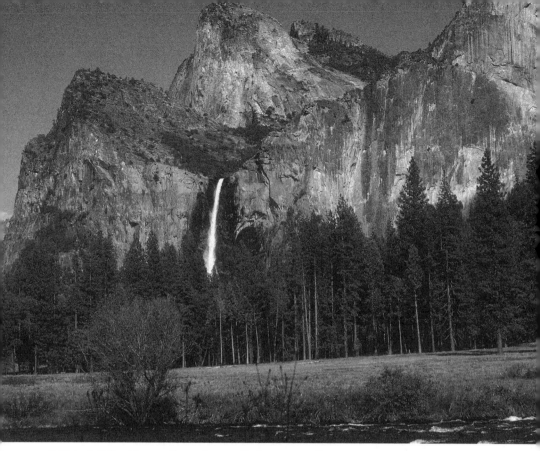

Bridalveil Fall spills over the southern wall of Yosemite Valley.

turn back westward. The trail sign across the road says EL CAPITAN 0.4 MILE. As you walk westward, the famous North American Wall of El Capitan looms directly overhead. It was named for a patch of darker-colored mineral in the granite that is shaped like the North American continent. You are close enough here to see, without binoculars, the figures clinging to the rock above and hear them shouting back and forth. As you approach the nose of El Capitan, you cross several spur routes used by climbers to reach the base of the wall. Two of these have signs (in four languages) setting out rules and warnings for climbers. At the second climber warning sign at 0.6 mile, the trail sign says BRIDALVEIL FALL 3.7 MILES. Some distance beyond, another sign says exactly the same thing: BRIDALVEIL FALL 3.7 MILES. Continue straight ahead past both signs along the trail that parallels the road. If the season is early spring and Ribbon Creek is flowing fast and deep, cut downhill (left) to the road and walk along the shoulder to get across the dangerous part of the stream. Ribbon Creek falls over the cliff just west of El Capitan as Ribbon Fall, and like Bridalveil across the valley, dissolves into a mist toward the bottom in early summer and dries out entirely by mid-July.

West Valley Floor

Rejoin the trail beyond the creek. The blackened lower trunks of the trees are signs of prescribed burns. The trail comes almost all the way out to the road at an open place close beside the Merced where there is a good view of Bridalveil Fall. On the north side of the road, an interpretive panel explains glacial features and the origin of the waterfall. The trail ducks back into the forest of white fir, incense cedar, black oak, and a few ponderosas, and presently passes to the right around Black Spring, where water-loving cattails, horsetails, and willows thrive in the muck. It's a wonderful place to pause and listen to the songs of blackbirds and warblers. The trail comes to the road again at a spot called Valley View, one of the most popular photo stops in the valley as evidenced by a turnout and some pit toilets.

At 2.7 miles, cross the road and the river on the Pohono Bridge. Turn upstream (east) and walk between Southside Drive and the river past a gauging station. This must be one of the loveliest corners of Yosemite, especially in May and October when the dogwoods are in bloom or turning red. The Merced quickens its pace, and its racing over the rocks masks the sound of nearby traffic. There are two springs here on the right side of the road, Fern Spring and Moss Spring; in May the trail is muddy, but the moisture allows the growth of some beautiful pink bleeding hearts or frilly white false Solomon's seal lilies.

The trail hugs the riverside for a time, then emerges into sunshine next to Southside Drive, skirting Bridalveil Meadow. Across the road, a sign marks the site of the famous confab between John Muir and Teddy Roosevelt about the protection of land in the national park system. In mid-to-late season when Bridalveil Creek is low, you can follow the trail along the Merced, but earlier in the year you must leave the trail where it once again nears the road and walk along the shoulder to get over Bridalveil Creek. It is at this point that Southside Drive and the Wawona Road/Highway 41 come together. Backtrack just a few feet on Highway 41 to visit Bridalveil Fall at 4.1 miles. Bridalveil flows over the southern wall of Yosemite Valley through a defile between Cathedral Rocks and the Leaning Tower, but before it reaches the bottom 620 feet below, the wind catches, tatters, and flings the droplets into graceful lacy patterns.

Leave the Bridalveil Fall area on a wide beaten path and continue east, parallel to Southside Drive. Turn right at the junction that directs you to Curry Village. Climb over the Bridalveil Moraine a bit above the road and walk along a tumble of mossy rocks to get a great view of El Capitan across the valley. To your right the cliffs loom impossibly high and straight over your head. The trail leads you back down beside the road where you can see the back of El Capitan Meadow beyond, then swings away again through a stand of Douglas fir and incense cedar. At the signed junction at 5.8 miles, turn left (north). Cross Southside Drive at the Cathedral picnic area turnoff and follow the trail through a dense growth of baby ponderosa pines. The trail finally meets the El Capitan Road on the east side of the bridge. Cross the bridge to your car.

Miles and Directions

0.0 El Capitan Bridge.

0.3 Northside Drive.

0.6 El Capitan spur 2.

2.7 Pohono Bridge.

4.0 Bridalveil Fall parking lot.

4.3 Southside Drive.

5.8 El Capitan junction.

6.5 El Capitan Bridge.

3 Glacier Point via the Four Mile Trail

The Four Mile Trail is really 4.6 miles long because it has had to be rerouted since its original construction. It is a steep, steady uphill-and-back pull to Yosemite's most famous viewpoint. It's a great workout where the ever-changing perspective of the valley floor will keep your mind off your thudding heart and straining lungs. You can even reward yourself with a snack and a cold drink at the top.

Start: Four Mile Trailhead at the foot of Sentinel Rock.
Distance: 9.2 miles out and back.
Approximate hiking time: 4 to 8 hours.
Difficulty: Strenuous if you push yourself.

Seasons: Late spring, summer, and fall. Closed in winter.
Nearest facilities: Curry Village and Yosemite Village.
Permits: None.
Map: USGS Half Dome quad.

Finding the trailhead: Drive east on one-way Southside Drive to the parking area on both sides of the road just beyond the Sentinel Beach/Yellow Pine picnic areas. Watch carefully for the trailhead sign on the right—if you miss it, you'll have to drive all the way around the valley to get back. You can also use the Yosemite Valley shuttle bus, if you don't mind walking an additional mile each way. The nearest bus stop is at Yosemite Lodge. From there, follow the bike path across Swinging Bridge, turn right, and walk 50 yards to the trailhead. For an easier hike, take the shuttle bus to Glacier Point and hike downhill to the trailhead.

The Hike

An interpretive panel with historical information about the early days of tourism in Yosemite marks the beginning of the trail. Towering overhead is the vertical flat slab of Sentinel Rock beneath which the asphalt trail begins its switchbacking ascent among huge mossy boulders, shady live oaks, laurels, and maples. Mariposa lilies, catchfly, and alum root line the path, which soon crosses a little creek lined with thimbleberry, lupine, and monkeyflowers. The route works gradually eastward as it

The Merced River winds through Leidig Meadow, as viewed from the Four Mile Trail.

climbs. If you begin your hike by 8:00 A.M., watch for hang gliders suspended in air right beside the trail on their way to the landing area in Leidig Meadow. Still climbing, the trail comes even with Yosemite Falls, roaring across the valley in spring and early summer. About midway, you arrive at a short spur trail to Union Point where Tenaya Canyon, North Dome, Clouds Rest, and Half Dome appear briefly, then disappear as the trail heads in a more southerly direction. The switchbacks become a bit less short and steep and the way becomes sunnier and more open. At last, the trail loses a bit of elevation, rounds a shoulder, crosses a tiny rivulet, then makes a short climb to top out at Glacier Point. Enjoy the stupendous views of the park from the Glacier Point, then return the way you came. Descend carefully; the loose gravel over smooth granite can be slippery.

Miles and Directions

0.0   Four Mile Trailhead.

2.3   Union Point.

4.5   Glacier Point Snack Bar.

4.6   Glacier Point.

9.2   Four Mile Trailhead.

Glacier Point via the Four Mile Trail

A FIERY WATERFALL

Until 1968 Glacier Point was the site of the infamous firefall. The bark of hundreds of the magnificent old red firs from the nearby forest was set ablaze just after dark on summer evenings. After an elaborate ceremony of ritual calls between Glacier Point and the valley below, the glowing coals were raked over the cliff to form a fiery waterfall in the dark. It was a popular attraction, of course, but one more suited to an amusement park than to Yosemite. The lichens and other organisms inhabiting the rock face were seared away and the beautiful old forest was threatened. In 1968 the National Park Service ended the practice.

4 Happy Isles to the Top of Nevada Fall

If you have time for only one hike in Yosemite, whether you want to spend the day on the trail or take only a short stroll, this loop (or part of it) is the one. It's what Yosemite is all about: massive granite cliffs, classic glacial features, and views of at least four of the valley's biggest and best waterfalls. It climbs along the course of the Merced River as it plunges over the steps of the Giant Staircase in Nevada Fall, then Vernal Fall, before resuming its flat, meandering course over the floor of Yosemite Valley.

Start: John Muir Trailhead at Happy Isles.
Distance: 5.8-mile lollipop loop.
Approximate hiking time: 3 hours to all day.
Difficulty: Moderate.
Seasons: May to June for spectacular water-falls; October to early November for foliage. Closed in winter.
Nearest facilities: Snacks, toilets, and water at the trailhead.
Permits: None.
Map: USGS Half Dome quad.

Finding the trailhead: Board the Yosemite Valley shuttle bus from anyplace in the valley (Curry Village has parking nearest the trailhead), and get off at Happy Isles.
Special considerations: If you'll be hiking the Mist Trail in springtime, carry rain gear, or at least choose a warm day. You're sure to be drenched by the spray.

The Hike

The big sign at the trailhead marks the beginning of the John Muir Trail, showing mileage to various points all the way to trail's end at Mount Whitney, about 211 miles to the south. The first part of the trail was paved at one time, but the asphalt has washed away in places over the years, so it's sometimes rough and rocky. Don't expect a true wilderness experience here. This is a popular spot for good reasons, but the farther you go, the more solitude you'll find. It's popular not only because it is spectacular, but because it's one of the few routes out of the valley to the high country.

The trail climbs gently through black oak and pine forest among enormous lichen-draped boulders up along the north bank of the Merced. A little spring trickles out of the rocks a few hundred yards up on your left. Don't drink the water without purifying it. The trail steepens gradually as you climb, but you'll want to stop frequently anyway to enjoy the roaring river through openings in the trees. In about a half mile, across the Merced to your right, tucked back up in Illilouette Gorge, Illilouette Fall pours 370 feet down the Panorama Cliff to meet the Merced River. The trail suddenly descends to the Vernal Fall Bridge at 0.8 mile where dozens of visitors will be taking photos or staring in open-mouthed wonder at 317-foot Vernal Fall upstream. There are restrooms, a water fountain, and dozens of freeloading Steller's jays and ground squirrels near the bridge. For their health and your safety, do not feed them.

▶ **The falls of the Giant Staircase are well named: Vernal is Latin for "springtime," Nevada is Spanish for "snowy."**

Cross the bridge to the south side of the Merced, and turn left (upstream). The crowd will soon thin noticeably. At 0.9 mile, the Mist Trail leaves the John Muir Trail to the left. To follow the loop clockwise, take the left fork, and return on the John Muir Trail. Where a sign says FOOT TRAIL ONLY, TOP OF VERNAL FALL VIA MIST TRAIL .3 MILES, get out your rain gear. The Mist Trail climbs steeply over big wet stone blocks. The thunder of the falls is almost deafening in early season; morning sunlight through the spray has a diffuse, mystical quality, and there's always a rainbow or two if the sun is shining. At the top of the falls is an oak-shaded bench where you can shake off excess water. Beside this bench, the Merced pauses to collect itself in the deceptively quiet Emerald Pool before crashing over the cliff. A long, slanting ramp called the Silver Apron tempts the sweaty hiker to ride this water slide into the pool. Don't do it! In an instant you'll be washed over the rim to the rocks 320 feet below. There are several warning signs along the riverbank reminding hikers to keep away from the edge and out of the water. Some who have ignored the warnings have been killed.

At 1.5 miles, cross the bridge at the Silver Apron back over the Merced and begin climbing steeply again along its north shore, sometimes through a light mist from

◀ *The Merced River plunges over Nevada Fall, first step in the Giant Staircase.*

Happy Isles to the Top of Nevada Fall

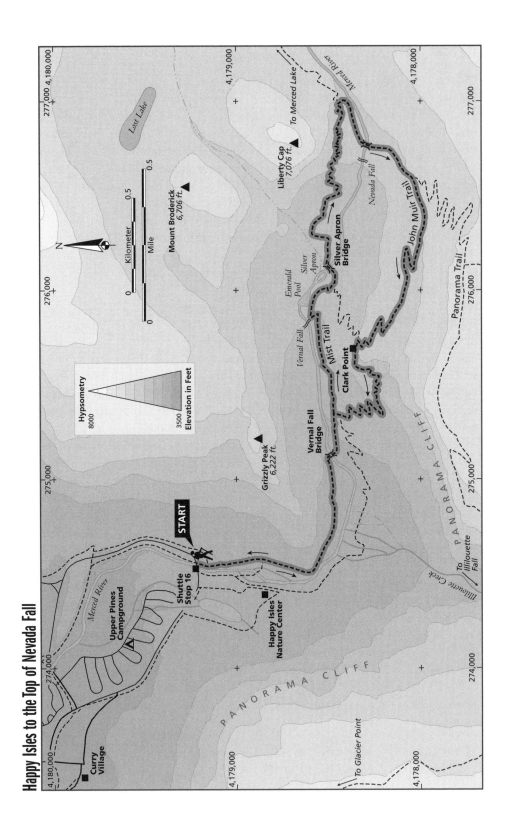

Nevada Fall in early season. Another set of switchbacks brings you out onto a sunny bench above the falls where you'll meet the junction with the John Muir Trail; follow the trail, turning right (south) toward Yosemite Valley. There are plenty of viewpoints with protective railings where you can watch Nevada Fall rush over the lip and drop 594 feet. It's a perfect place for sunbathing and picnicking. Keep an eye on your lunch! The local squirrels and jays will make off with it if your attention wanders for even a moment.

After gaping awestruck at the roaring water, cross the bridge and follow the slope upward a short distance to pass the junction with the Panorama Trail at 2.7 miles. It takes off to the left toward Illilouette Fall, Glacier Point, and beyond. Your trail to the right is cut into the side of the cliff beneath a weeping rock overhang that gently drips onto the trail. Delicate ferns and columbines are tucked into the cracks. Continue to descend on well-graded switchbacks, enjoying views of Upper Yosemite Fall across the valley to the northwest, until you reach Clark Point. This is where the hiker who is heading upward on the John Muir Trail catches the first jaw-dropping view of Nevada Fall with Mount Broderick and Liberty Cap looming above. There is a lateral trail here that cuts back downhill to the Mist Trail, but if you want to stay dry this time, keep left and stay on the John Muir Trail. Just before you reach the Vernal Fall Bridge again, you'll pass the junction to the Mist Trail at the point where you went up, then another junction for horses only that leads back to the stables. You cross the Vernal Fall Bridge at 5 miles and return to Happy Isles the way you came.

Miles and Directions

0.0 Happy Isles Trailhead.

0.8 Vernal Fall Bridge.

0.9 Mist Trail junction.

1.5 Silver Apron Bridge.

2.5 Top of Nevada Fall.

2.7 Panorama Trail junction.

5.0 Vernal Fall Bridge via John Muir Trail.

5.8 Happy Isles Trailhead.

5 Mirror Lake–Tenaya Canyon Loop

This short, easy loop day hike leads to one of the most isolated corners of the valley, though you have to get there by way of a favorite picnic and wading spot for families. If you head out early in the morning, though, you can complete the entire hike in solitude.

Start: Trailhead at Mirror Lake shuttle bus stop.
Distance: 4.2-mile loop.
Approximate hiking time: 2 to 4 hours.
Difficulty: Easy.
Seasons: Accessible year-round, but finest in May and June.

Nearest facilities: Everything you need (except gas) in Yosemite Village and Camp Curry.
Permits: None.
Maps: USGS Half Dome and Yosemite Falls quads.

Finding the trailhead: Board the Yosemite Valley shuttle bus from anyplace in the valley. (Curry Village has parking nearest the trailhead.) Get off at Mirror Lake.

The Hike

To hike the loop in a clockwise direction, skirting the west shore of Tenaya Creek and Mirror Lake and returning along the eastern shore, follow the sign to Mirror Lake along the paved road (no longer in use except for bicycles). Continue across the Tenaya Creek Bridge past the interpretive panel on the right, which tells about the Yosemite flood of January 1997. That year an unseasonable thaw sent runoff from a wetter-than-normal snowpack raging through the valley, gouging out the streambed and raising the water level as much as 20 feet above normal. It washed out roads, bridges, campgrounds, and housing, and closed down the park. There are other interpretive exhibits along this hike that are worth pausing to scan, since they illustrate Mirror Lake's remarkably rapid transformation into meadow.

Just beyond the first panel, you can leave the road and follow a signed footpath to the left or continue on the road. The road is the more scenic route since it follows the creekside. Both road and trail rise slightly, passing through a quiet forest of ponderosa pine, white fir, Douglas fir, incense cedar, and dogwood. At 1 mile, the forest opens to reveal tranquil Mirror Lake, reflecting Half Dome above it. Mount Watkins provides the backdrop to the north. There are sandy beaches along the lakeshore for picnics and wading.

The majority of visitors stop here, but those who continue on upstream will discover one of the more isolated, less hectic corners of Yosemite Valley. The forest floor is deeply carpeted with pine needles and bracken fern. Wild ginger, incongruously tropical looking in this setting, sprawls along the ground. Look for its weird, three-petalled purplish green flowers hidden beneath the big, shiny, heart-shaped leaves.

Mirror Lake–Tenaya Canyon Loop

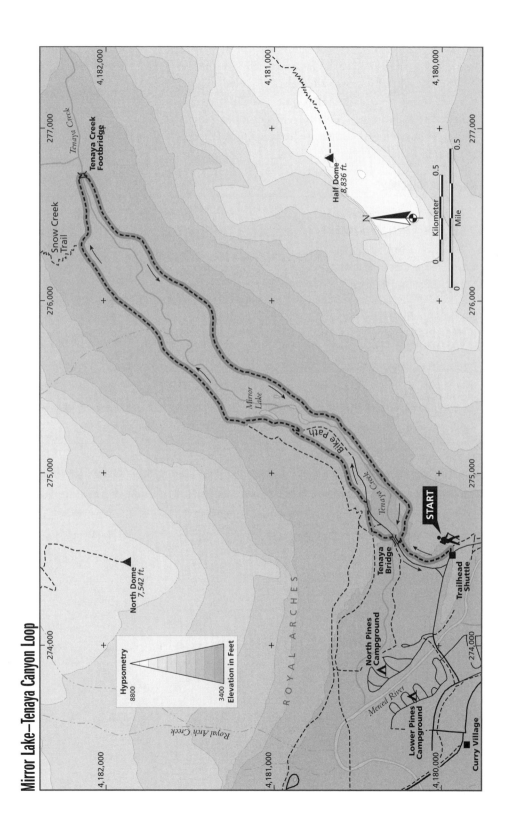

There are dozens of species of butterflies in patches of sunlight, and you can often hear canyon wren songs echoing off the cliffs upstream. A trail junction appears at 2.1 miles marking the Snow Creek Trail, which climbs steeply up out of Tenaya Canyon to the rim of the valley. Just past the big trail sign, cross the bridge over Tenaya Creek and return downstream along the eastern shore. Your trail meets the road again just where it crosses the Tenaya Creek Bridge, within a few hundred yards of the shuttle bus stop.

Miles and Directions

0.0 Mirror Lake Trailhead.

1.0 West end of Mirror Lake.

2.1 Snow Creek Trail junction.

2.4 Tenaya Creek Footbridge.

4.2 Mirror Lake Trailhead.

A VANISHING LAKE
Mirror Lake was created when a rockslide dammed up a section of Tenaya Creek, which promptly went to work to reclaim its original course. Every spring it washes tons of silt down the canyon to refill the lake basin, extending fingers of earth out into the water. These fingers invite colonization by water-loving plants such as sedges and willows, which soon come alive with the songs of red-winged blackbirds. Mirror Lake is well on its way to becoming Mirror Meadow. Eventually, as the basin fills in and dries out, trees will move in, and soon the land will again be a conifer forest with Tenaya Creek running through it, perhaps leaving the canyon as though Mirror Lake had never been—at least until the next rockslide. For years the park service periodically dredged the lake, slowing the natural succession from lake to forest in order to preserve the popular reflection, but the practice was finally discontinued.

6 Yosemite Falls

You can do this one as a steep up-and-back day hike or spend the night near the top of Yosemite Falls. Although the view back down into Yosemite Valley is good part of the way up, you don't get more than a glimpse of the falls themselves until you're on top. If you go when Yosemite Creek is full of snowmelt, the experience of standing just beside the very lip of the upper fall as it roars past you out into space is unforgettable and worth almost any amount of hard climbing.

Start: Upper Yosemite Falls Trailhead at Camp 4.
Distance: 7.6 miles out and back.
Approximate hiking time: 3 hours to all day as a day hike, or overnight as a backpack.
Difficulty: Strenuous.
Seasons: Late spring and early summer are best.

Nearest facilities: Yosemite Lodge and Yosemite Village.
Permits: None for a day hike; available in advance or from the wilderness center in Yosemite Village for a backpack.
Maps: USGS Half Dome and Yosemite Falls quads.

Finding the trailhead: Take the shuttle bus from anywhere in Yosemite Valley to Yosemite Lodge, then walk to the northwest end of the lodge buildings to Northside Drive. Cross the road to Camp 4 (formerly Sunnyside Campground). A sign in front points the way to the Upper Yosemite Fall trailhead, marked by another, larger sign with information about the history of the trail and mileage to various points.

The Hike

Begin climbing immediately up rocky switchbacks, winding your way among house-size boulders shaded by canyon live oak, ponderosa pine, and incense cedar. Slowly more and more of the flat valley floor comes into view through the trees. At 1 mile, you reach an overlook protected by iron railings known as Columbia Rock, where you'll probably need a breather. The trail ascends a few soft gravelly switchbacks, then descends for a short distance, crosses several little rivulets, rounds a cor-

ner and suddenly reveals 1,430-foot Upper Yosemite Fall, booming like thunder early in the summer. The refreshing mist supports little moss-and-fern gardens growing among the rocks. Over the roar of the falls, listen for the sweet descending notes of the canyon wren's song.

The trail now ascends very steep, rough stairsteps past the top of the lower falls and all of the middle falls (675 feet). Notice the trickles of water seeping out of the cracks between the layers of exfoliating (peeling) granite. Partway up the upper falls, the trail ducks behind a ridge, concealing the falls from view until you reach the top. Climb the sunny gully densely clothed in scrub oak, except where a huge pile of talus has spilled into the gully. Above the rock pile you can see a white scar on the cliff above where the darker, lichen-stained rock broke away in 1980 and killed three hikers. This part of the trail can be hot. As you near the top of the gulch, firs, Jeffrey pines, and a refreshing springtime trickle make a rest at the Yosemite Creek junction at 3.6 miles welcome. Follow the right fork for a few yards, then follow signs to the overlook, an area filled with weirdly sculpted rocks and twisted Jeffrey pines and an iron railing at 3.8 miles. Directly across the valley, the upside-down bowl of Sentinel Dome rises alone and to the west of Glacier Point. Farther in the distance is Mount Starr King, also somewhat rounded and isolated from the surrounding ridges. Farther beyond, beautiful Mount Clark and the Clark Range define the horizon.

Upper Yosemite Fall pours through a notch just to the left (east) of, and below, the overlook. Do not try to scramble down over the slippery rock to get a closer look. Instead, retreat back down off the overlook and walk around the base of the rock to pick up a narrow trail. This trail ends in an iron-railed walkway to a platform from which you can stand in the spray and watch Yosemite Creek rush out over the lip and crash down the cliff.

You can return the way you came, or if you are planning to spend the night, return to the main trail and follow it a little farther upstream. Do not camp in the trampled and overused forested spot just ahead. Camping within one-quarter mile of the rim is prohibited. If you continue north along the ridge a short distance, you will find several good campsites.

Miles and Directions

0.0 Upper Yosemite Falls Trailhead.

1.0 Columbia Rock lookout.

3.6 Yosemite Creek junction, turn right.

3.8 Yosemite Falls overlook, turn right again.

7.6 Return to Upper Yosemite Falls Trailhead.

In winter Upper Yosemite Fall's frozen spray forms a cone of ice at its base.

Yosemite Falls

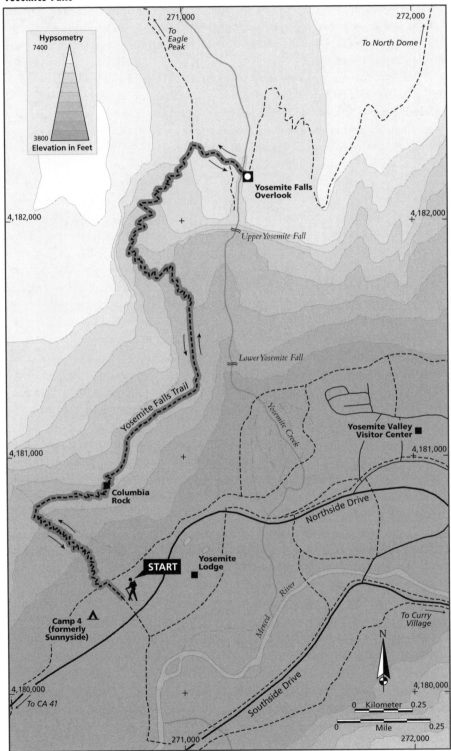

7 Half Dome

Half Dome is *the* symbol of Yosemite, its summit the goal of just about everybody who has ever donned a pair of hiking boots. It is a grueling workout, especially if you do it in one day, but if you spend the night in Little Yosemite Valley and tackle the peak first thing the second morning, you'll have a better chance of avoiding the traffic jams that sometimes build up at the base of the cables. The cables? The last 400 feet are over what feels like nearly vertical (though the angle is probably more like 45 degrees), smooth, exfoliating granite, so a series of horizontal bars about 5 feet apart, flanked by chains with which to pull yourself up, are the only way to get there without technical climbing equipment. It sounds scary but it is done by kids and grandmas and everybody in between. Because of its popularity, wilderness permits are snapped up quickly.

Start: John Muir Trailhead at Happy Isles.
Distance: 16 miles out and back.
Approximate hiking time: One long day or overnight.
Difficulty: Strenuous as a backpack, *very* strenuous as a day hike.
Seasons: All summer, whenever the cables are up. (They are removed when the going gets icy.)

Nearest facilities: Everything you need, except gas, in Yosemite Village and Camp Curry.
Permits: None for a day hike; available in advance or at the wilderness center in Yosemite Village for overnight.
Maps: USGS Half Dome and Yosemite Falls quads.

Finding the trailhead: Board the Yosemite Valley shuttle bus from anyplace in the valley and get off at Stop 16, Happy Isles. If you are backpacking, leave your car in the backpackers' lot near Curry Village.

Special considerations: This hike is not for acrophobics. Get a weather report before you start. If there is even the slightest chance of a thunderstorm brewing, turn back immediately. There have been several deaths by lightning on the mountain.

The Hike

From the big trailhead sign marking the beginning of the John Muir Trail, climb gently on an eroded asphalt path through black oak and ponderosa pine forest among enormous lichen-draped boulders. In about a half mile, across the thundering Merced River on your right, watch for 370-foot Illilouette Fall tucked back in its deeply cut gorge in the Panorama Cliff. The trail steepens briefly, then suddenly descends to the Vernal Fall Bridge at 0.8 mile. Upstream, Vernal Fall is perfectly framed by maple, alder, and various conifers as it drops 317 feet over the lower step of the Giant Staircase. There are restrooms, drinking water, and lots of people here.

Cross the bridge to the south side of the river and turn left, upstream. Pass a lateral trail on the right for horses only that leads back to the stables, then meet the Mist Trail junction at 0.9 mile. This is an alternate route to the top of Nevada Fall that is not recommended for backpackers since it is steep, slippery, and wet. The Mist Trail is best done as a day hike. Continue climbing on the John Muir Trail as it switchbacks relentlessly uphill. There are plenty of excuses to stop and rest on the way. Across the valley to the northwest you can see Upper Yosemite Fall and, to the northeast across the river gorge, the rounded backside of Half Dome. Shortly beyond, 594-foot Nevada Fall comes into view. This heart-stopping panorama is finest at Clark Point (2.3 miles) where a lateral trail cuts over to the Mist Trail, nearer to the river. Continue to ascend the John Muir

▶ In earlier days, it was possible to camp on the summit of Half Dome, but camping is now prohibited to protect the rare Mount Lyell salamanders that shelter under the rocks on top. This is probably just as well because there are no sanitary facilities on the summit and you can't dig holes in solid granite.

Trail on well-graded switchbacks, eventually passing beneath a dripping rock overhang decorated with delicate hanging gardens of ferns, columbines, monkeyflowers, and other water-loving species. At 3.3 miles the Panorama Trail leading back to Glacier Point joins this one from the right (south). The trail drops a bit, hops a couple of little creeks, then emerges into a wide sunny expanse of granite at the top of Nevada Fall. Here, at 3.5 miles, a footbridge crosses the river. Cross the bridge and follow the north shore of the river to a junction with the upper end of the Mist Trail at 3.8 miles. Continue upstream, climbing the well-defined trail over inlaid rocks. The way soon levels out and passes from sunlight into shade, and the Merced changes from a rushing, raging torrent to become quiet, dark, and deep.

At 4.3 miles, you reach a turnoff to the Half Dome Trail, but ignore it and keep right, going on to Little Yosemite Valley. If you are backpacking, you'll be going there anyway, and the earlier turnoff is steeper, if shorter, and does not save much time. Little Yosemite Valley, at 4.8 miles, is a busy place, especially for bears. There are bearproof boxes in the campground, but you should be carrying a canister anyway. There is also an architecturally elegant two-story solar composting toilet. The National Park Service has constructed two communal fire rings for campers to share. Please do not scar this already overused area by building another one.

Head north out of Little Yosemite Valley, passing a junction with the shortcut trail and climbing steeply, first along Sunrise Creek, continuing generally northward and upward to the Half Dome Trail junction at 6 miles. Leave the main trail here. About a half mile farther along the wide and dusty path, keep an eye out for a small spur trail to the right (east) where there is a spring. *This is your last source of water.* The trail

◀ *Majestic Half Dome has cables to help negotiate the last 400 feet to the summit.*

Half Dome

Hypsometry

Elevation in Feet

8500 — 3500

Clouds Rest Trail

John Muir Trail

Sunrise Creek

Half Dome Trail

Little Yosemite Valley

Merced River

Half Dome
8,836 ft.

Lost Lake

Mount Broderick
6,706 ft.

Liberty Cap
7,076 ft.

Mist Trail

Nevada Fall

Mirror Lake

Tenaya Creek

N

Kilometer   0.5   0   0.5
Mile   0.5   0   0.5

Merced River

North Pines Campground

Upper Pines Campground

Lower Pines Campground

Curry Village

Happy Isles Nature Center

START

Vernal Fall Bridge

Vernal Fall

Clark Point

Panorama Trail

Illilouette Creek

To Illilouette Fall

swings west to reveal a view of Half Dome to the left and Clouds Rest to the right. Across the way are Basket Dome and North Dome. The trail swings a little farther south now and faces the huge, sparsely timbered shoulder of Half Dome. A sign warns hikers not to proceed if bad weather threatens. Believe it! Now you switchback steeply on sometimes slippery gravel up and over the crest of a shoulder to at last come face to face with the famous—or infamous—cables. Grab a pair of gloves from the pile if you haven't brought your own, and haul yourself up the last 400 feet to the summit at 8 miles.

The top of Half Dome flattens out considerably and is furnished with flat, oddly weathered granite slabs. When you have recovered from your climb, wander around to take in the 360-degree panorama. Below, Yosemite Valley is spread out like a map, with El Capitan at its west end. North Dome and Clouds Rest flank smooth, bare Tenaya Canyon. Farther east, Merced Canyon points toward the Cathedral Range, and the colorful Clark Range is visible to the southeast. If you are day hiking, you'll have to tear yourself away after only a short visit to make it back to the valley before dark. You can vary your trip back by taking the Mist Trail down to Happy Isles.

Miles and Directions

0.0   Happy Isles Trailhead.

0.8   Vernal Fall Bridge.

0.9   Mist Trail junction.

2.3   Clark Point.

3.3   Panorama Trail junction.

3.5   Top of Nevada Fall.

3.8   Upper end of Mist Trail.

4.3   First Half Dome turnoff.

4.8   Little Yosemite Valley.

6.0   Half Dome Trail.

8.0   Summit.

16.0   Return to Happy Isles.

The South Rim of Yosemite Valley

All of the south rim trails begin along Glacier Point Road, which cuts off from Wawona Road (Highway 41) at Chinquapin, a junction about 14 miles from Yosemite Valley at 6,000 feet. The drive itself is beautiful, beginning among ponderosa and sugar pines, climbing through a red fir forest at almost 8,000 feet, then dropping to 7,200 feet at Glacier Point, 16 miles away. Glacier Point is an extremely popular overlook 3,000 feet above the valley floor; it offers the best views of Half Dome, the valley, and indeed, most of the park accessible by road. Almost all of the hikes beginning from this road have spectacular views of the valley, too. There is a snack bar, gift shop, phones, and toilets, along with an amphitheater for nighttime astronomy programs, and an area from which hang gliders are launched before 8:00 A.M.

It was also the site of the infamous firefall. The bark of hundreds of magnificent old red firs from the nearby forest was set ablaze just after dark on summer evenings. Then the glowing coals were raked over the cliff to form a fiery "waterfall" in the dark. The spectacle was magical to see, but the lichens and other organisms inhabiting the rock face below were seared away and the beautiful old forest was threatened. The National Park Service ended the practice in 1968.

The only accommodations anywhere on Glacier Point Road are at first-come, first-served Bridalveil Creek Campground. There is no place to stay overnight near the trailhead if you arrive late on the day before your hike, and you must get your wilderness permit for a backpacking outing down in Yosemite Valley or at Wawona.

The road is open all the way to Glacier Point spring through fall, but in winter it's plowed only as far as the ski area at Badger Pass. There are plenty of bears around. Do not leave ice chests or food in your car. All trailheads have bear-proof boxes for food storage.

A hiker's shuttle bus runs daily from the valley during the summer. You can get a schedule and fares at the visitor center, or call (209) 372–1240. Reservations are necessary.

8 Taft Point and the Fissures

Taft Point is the westernmost of several overlooks into Yosemite Valley from the south rim accessible by only a short hike. Don't miss it, even if you have already been to Glacier Point. In place of rounded domes and polished rocks, this section of the valley wall displays jagged, broken granite crags and soaring spires, as well as a new perspective of Yosemite Falls. On the way, you can peek down into the fabulous Fissures, cracks in the cliff that are only inches wide, but *thousands* of feet deep. You can look through them all the way to the valley floor. One glimpse is as good as a thrill ride.

Start: Taft Point/Sentinel Dome Trailhead.
Distance: 2.2 miles out and back.
Approximate hiking time: 2 to 4 hours.
Difficulty: Easy.
Seasons: Spring, summer, or fall, whenever Glacier Point Road is open.

Nearest facilities: Snacks, toilets, phones, and water at Glacier Point.
Permits: None.
Map: USGS Half Dome quad.

Finding the trailhead: Drive 13 miles up Glacier Point Road from Chinquapin. Parking and the marked trailhead are on the left.

Special considerations: The Fissures have not been defaced by protective railings and warning signs; you won't see them until you are very close, so this hike is not recommended for unrestrained small children. It's an upside-down hike, downhill to get there, uphill to get back. Allow extra time for the return trip.

The Hike

The trail begins in a sandy opening in mixed pine and fir forest. Turn left at the trailhead sign. (The right fork goes to Sentinel Dome.) Pass through a flat, fairly open stretch past a big outcrop of almost pure white quartz on the right, then swing south and start downhill where the forest closes in. At 0.4 mile the Pohono Trail joins yours from the right. Continue straight ahead, now on the Pohono Trail, ignoring the inaccurate trail sign that says you have only come 0.2 mile. The forest deepens and a little creek you will soon hop across nourishes a colorful garden of water-loving cow parsnip, senecio, corn lily, knotweed, and shooting stars. All at once the trail emerges from the shady forest onto open rock and steepens. The flower-filled gully on your right abruptly narrows, deepens, and drops through a notch that sends the little creek plummeting toward the valley floor.

Descend carefully down the rocks past low patches of manzanita and the occasional Jeffrey pine. Stay alert here. At 0.9 mile you will reach the first of several fissures, not visible until you are standing on their rims. They are narrow, deep cracks in the granite, perhaps 30 to 40 feet long, extending inward from the edge of the cliff. Peering over the side, you can see that they slice completely through the rock,

Glimpse the Yosemite Valley floor several thousand feet below through one of the Fissures.

Taft Point and the Fissures; Sentinel Dome

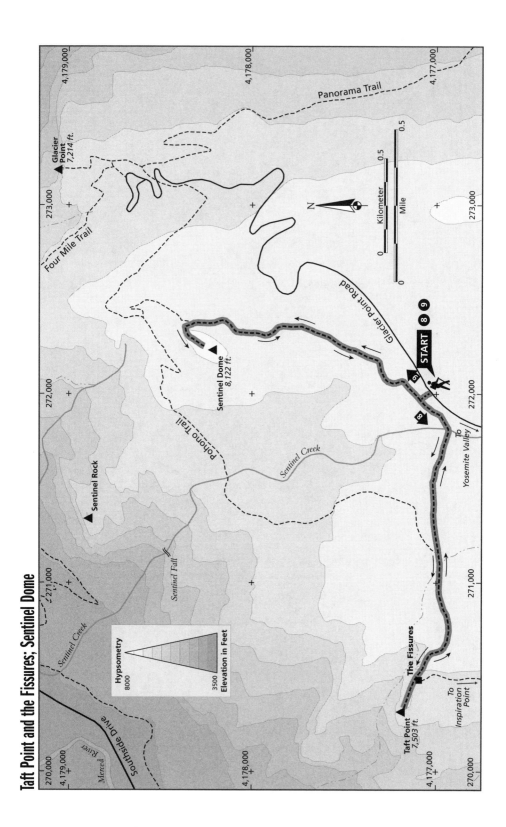

Glacier Point 7,214 ft.

Panorama Trail

Four Mile Trail

4,179,000

4,178,000

4,177,000

273,000

N

Kilometer

0.5

0

Mile

0.5

0

Glacier Point Road

START 8 9

9

8

Sentinel Dome 8,122 ft.

Pohono Trail

Sentinel Creek

To Yosemite Valley

Sentinel Rock

Sentinel Fall

Sentinel Creek

272,000

271,000

Hypsometry

8000

3500

Elevation in Feet

Southside Drive

Merced River

The Fissures

Taft Point 7,503 ft.

To Inspiration Point

270,000

4,179,000

4,178,000

4,177,000

revealing a stomach-lurching glimpse of the floor of Yosemite Valley several thousand feet below.

Once your internal butterflies have settled, proceed toward a slightly rising point of the cliff that leans out over the valley like the prow of a ship with a protective iron railing around it. This is Taft Point (1.1 miles). A look over the edge is guaranteed to reawaken the butterflies. Directly across from the point are the Three Brothers, the highest of which is Eagle Peak. To the left (west) is the massive face of El Capitan, to the right (east) is Yosemite Falls. Wander westward along the rim to see the dramatic knife edges and needlelike spikes of Cathedral Spires.

When you are ready to return, descend the slight hill to a trail junction. The left fork returns to the trailhead and parking, the right one heads westward along the Pohono Trail toward Inspiration Point.

Miles and Directions

0.0 Taft Point/Sentinel Dome Trailhead.

0.4 Pohono Trail junction.

0.9 The Fissures.

1.1 Taft Point.

2.2 Taft Point/Sentinel Dome Trailhead.

9 Sentinel Dome

Here's your chance to climb one of Yosemite's famous domes with minimal expenditure of time and effort. The view from the summit is everything you would expect, a 360-degree sweep of almost the entire park.

See map on page 48

Start: Taft Point/Sentinel Dome Trailhead.
Distance: 2.2 miles out and back.
Approximate hiking time: 2 to 4 hours.
Difficulty: Moderate.
Seasons: Spring, summer, or fall, whenever Glacier Point Road is open.
Nearest facilities: Snacks, toilets, phones, and water at Glacier Point.
Permits: None.
Map: USGS Half Dome quad.

Finding the trailhead: Drive 13 miles up Glacier Point Road from Chinquapin. Parking and the marked trailhead are on the left.
Special considerations: The dome is steep and slippery so wear good sturdy shoes for this one. Smooth-soled sandals invite accidents.

From Sentinel Dome you can see North Dome, Basket Dome, and Half Dome all at once.

The Hike

The trail begins at a sign in a sandy opening in the forest that directs you to the right (northeast). (The other fork goes to Taft Point and the Fissures.) Follow the rough and rocky path as it crosses a brook, then undulates gradually upward, slowly revealing the top of the dome. Soon it curves to the left (north) and proceeds more steeply over smooth and featureless rock. Stenciled metal signs keep you on course. At 0.4 mile an old, partly paved service road joins the trail from the right. Continue around the base of the dome on your left. When you have reached the "back," or more gradually sloping side of the dome at 0.6 mile, a trail splits off to the right and heads down to Glacier Point.

Turn left just past this point and head up the steep open slope on an indistinct trail of sorts. Don't worry if you lose the path; the only way to go is up. At the summit are the remains of the gnarled Jeffrey pine that was once the subject of innumerable photographs and postcards. The tree died in 1977, but remained standing and still beautiful until it toppled in 2003.

When you have caught your breath, make a slow circle around the summit. To the east Yosemite Valley, flanked by the Cathedral Rocks on the left and El Capitan on the right, stretches toward the coast. If the great Central Valley is free of smog (a rare occurrence) you can see all the way to the Coast Ranges. Moving clockwise, the entire length of Yosemite Falls comes into view, and in early summer you can hear its roar from here. Farther east is smoothly rounded Basket Dome and North Dome and, beyond them, Tenaya Canyon, with the sheer face of Half Dome glowering over it. Clouds Rest is just beyond Half Dome, and far behind it lies the Cathedral Range. Farther east the Merced River Canyon and Nevada Fall appear, then come Mount Clark and the colorful Clark Range, providing a backdrop for the rounded tops of Mount Starr King. The lower, forested country to the south closes the circle.

When you are ready, descend very slowly and carefully, avoiding loose sand and gravel whenever possible, and return the way you came. Take care to follow the metal signs directing you to the parking lot.

Miles and Directions

0.0 Taft Point/Sentinel Dome Trailhead.

0.4 Service road.

0.6 Glacier Point Trail junction.

1.1 Top of Sentinel Dome.

2.2 Taft Point/Sentinel Dome Trailhead.

10 McGurk Meadow

A short out-and-back day hike to one of Yosemite's "bloomingest" wildflower meadows.

Start: McGurk Meadow Trailhead on Glacier Point Road.
Distance: 1.6 miles out and back.
Approximate hiking time: 1 to 2 hours.
Difficulty: Easy.
Seasons: All summer, whenever Glacier Point Road is open, but flowers are best in July.

Nearest facilities: Food, water, and phones at Glacier Point.
Permits: None.
Maps: USGS El Capitan and Half Dome quads.

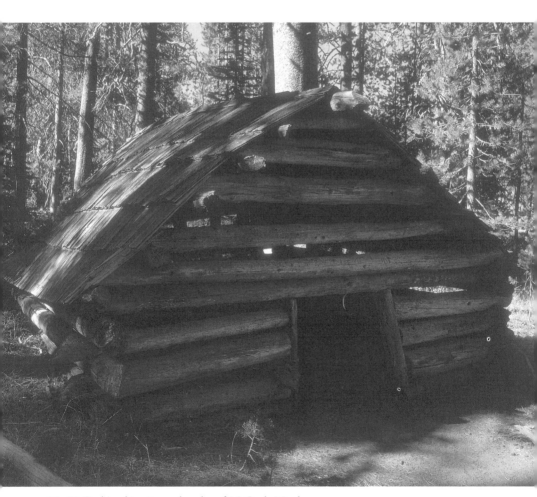

Mr. McGurk's cabin sits on the edge of McGurk Meadow.

McGurk Meadow

Bridalveil Creek

4,174,000 268,000 269,000 4,174,000

To
Pohono Trail

McGURK MEADOW

Hypsometry
7200

6600
Elevation in Feet

Cabin ■

4,173,000 4,173,000

To
Yosemite Valley

P

START

Glacier Point Road

Bridalveil Creek

Bridalveil

4,172,000 4,172,000

To
Glacier Point

**Bridalveil Creek
Campground** ⛺

N

0 Kilometer 0.25

0 Mile 0.25

To
Wawona

4,171,000 4,171,000
268,000 269,000

Finding the trailhead: Drive east about 8.5 miles up Glacier Point Road from Chinquapin. The trailhead is on the left just before you reach the entrance to Bridalveil Creek Campground. It's easy to miss. The campground is on the right (south) side of the road. The easiest way to find the trailhead is to drive to the campground entrance, turn around, and head back the way you came. Park in the first turnout on the right. The trailhead sign is about 100 feet beyond.

The Hike

The path descends through a quiet lodgepole forest where the wildflower show gets under way at once as currants, strawberries, lupines, and larkspur flourish alongside the trail. Just before you emerge from the forest to enter the meadow, watch for an old log cabin on the left. It was built by a Mr. McGurk in the late nineteenth century, but he had to abandon it when it was determined that he did not, in fact, own the land thereabouts.

The meadow is threaded by a little brook and spangled with wildflowers of every kind and color: shooting stars, lungworts, corn lilies, monkeyflowers, paintbrush, and dozens of others. This is actually a long narrow finger that extends eastward from the main part of McGurk Meadow. The larger section of meadow is much too soggy for comfortable hiking, but the path that skirts this section runs along the edge of the forest so that you can enjoy the flowers without getting your feet wet. Such a meeting of forest and meadow as this is the best sort of environment for wildlife watching, especially during morning and evening hours. When meadow once again gives way to forest, retrace your steps to the trailhead. If you want a little more exercise, you can continue your stroll northward downhill for about another half mile to meet the Pohono Trail. Just remember that you'll eventually have to climb back up again.

11 The Pohono Trail

The Pohono Trail skirts the entire south rim of Yosemite Valley from Glacier Point to Tunnel View. The rolling, up-and-down route takes you to a series of overlooks—Taft Point, Dewey Point, Crocker Point, Stanford Point, and Old Inspiration Point—that will change the way you perceive familiar landmarks even after you have returned to the valley floor. The view of Bridalveil Fall from above is worth the (nonexistent) price of admission all by itself. Strong hikers could do this one as a day hike, but if you hurry, you're likely to miss the good stuff. It's an easy overnight backpack with camping at Bridalveil Creek, the only really practical spot with reliable water.

Start: Panorama/Pohono Trailhead at Glacier Point.
Distance: 13.8 miles one way.
Approximate hiking time: Dawn to dinnertime as a day hike (7 to 8 hours), 2 shorter days as a backpack.
Difficulty: Strenuous as a day hike, moderate as a backpack.
Seasons: All summer, though creeks are dry by mid-August.

Nearest facilities: Everything you need (except gas) in Yosemite Valley; snacks, toilets, phones at Glacier Point; phones and toilets at Tunnel View.
Permits: None required for a day hike; available in advance or in Yosemite Valley or at Wawona for overnight.
Maps: USGS El Capitan and Half Dome quads.

Finding the trailhead: Follow Glacier Point Road to its end 16 miles from Wawona Road at Chinquapin, or take the shuttle to Glacier Point. If you are driving, park in the upper level of the Glacier Point parking lot, then walk directly toward Half Dome along the fenced path to the trailhead sign. Bear-proof boxes are tucked into the far corner of the upper lot.
Special considerations: This is a shuttle hike. You'll need to leave one car at Tunnel View and drive or get a ride to the trailhead at Glacier Point, or you can take the hiker's shuttle bus from the valley. (Call 209-372-1240 for reservations.)

The Hike

Take a minute to recover from the overwhelming immensity of the panorama at Glacier Point before setting off. To the left is North Dome, capping the graceful Royal Arches; in the center is Half Dome, the monumental symbol of Yosemite. Tenaya Canyon stretches away to the northeast, and to the west runs the Merced River Canyon, down whose Giant Staircase flow Nevada and Vernal Falls.

From the trailhead turn right (east) to find the Panorama and Pohono Trail junction at 0.1 mile. Keep right and at 0.2 mile, cross Glacier Point Road, then ascend a few switchbacks beneath white and red firs to 0.4 mile where a dirt road leads to a ranger residence on the left. Continue right on the trail that parallels the road for a short time. At 1 mile, meet the junction with the Sentinel Dome Trail, where a half-mile detour (one way) takes you to the top.

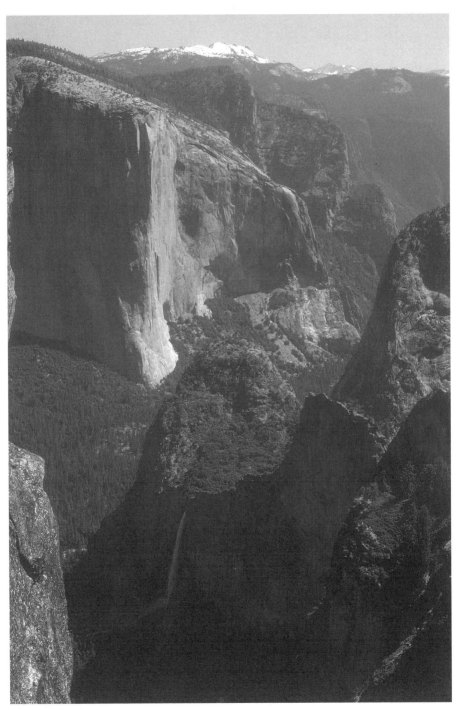

Get a different view—from above—of Bridalveil Fall from the Pohono Trail.

To continue on the Pohono Trail, go straight (southwest) along the valley rim. Watch for Yosemite Falls across the valley as the route climbs, levels, then descends on switchbacks. You can catch occasional glimpses of Sentinel Dome pushing up out of the forest uphill on your left. Cross Sentinel Creek, often dry later in the year, and wind through the forest over gently rolling terrain until you reach a junction at 2 miles with a spur trail that goes back to Glacier Point Road. The forest deepens and a little creek you will soon hop across nourishes a colorful garden of water-loving cow parsnip, senecio, corn lily, knotweed, and shooting stars. All at once the trail emerges from the shady forest onto open rock, and steepens. The flower-filled gully on your right abruptly narrows, deepens, and drops through a notch that sends the little creek plummeting toward the valley floor. Descend carefully down the open rock past low patches of manzanita and the occasional Jeffrey pine. As soon as the path begins to level a bit, watch for the Fissures, cracks in the cliff that are only inches wide but thousands of feet deep. There is a sign, but by the time you reach it, you will already have skirted several of them. They are not visible until you are standing on their rims. Shortly beyond, a short spur trail on your right takes you a few yards uphill to Taft Point, surrounded by an iron railing. This, the first in the series of marvelous valley overlooks, directly faces Eagle Peak and the Three Brothers.

Return to the Pohono Trail and continue west, first over open rock, then into forest, dipping down to meet Bridalveil Creek at mile 4.7. Just across the footbridge are a few small campsites, the best choice for camping on this route. A short distance beyond, at 5 miles, go straight ahead at a junction with a trail heading south to meet Glacier Point Road via McGurk Meadow. Another two or three minutes' walk takes you past a second McGurk Meadow cutoff. The trail rises and falls through the forest, crossing a few more creeklets that dry out by midsummer, then ascends to Dewey Point at 8.7 miles. You can scramble out to the very top to a granite aerie from which, laid out before you, is a panorama of almost the whole of Yosemite park. To the west you can see the Wawona Tunnel parking lot, your end point, and beyond it, Cascade Creek Falls. Directly across the valley, Ribbon Fall drifts down in early springtime, and just beyond that, El Capitan. You can hear climbers' shouts from here if the wind is blowing in the right direction. Mount Hoffman is on the horizon to the east, marking the geographic center of Yosemite. If the day is clear you can see Mount Conness on the northern park boundary. Tenaya Canyon, heading straight for the Cathedral Range, cuts the sheer granite at the base of Clouds Rest and Half Dome, partly hidden behind Sentinel Dome.

Return to the trail, which now alternates between forest and open spots with chinquapin, pinemat manzanita, ceanothus, and huckleberry oak—spiny shrubs unfriendly to hikers in shorts. The trail dips to pass Crocker Point at 9.3 miles. Be sure to detour the short distance out to the point, for from here you can look down upon Bridalveil Fall shooting over the cliff between the Leaning Tower and Cathedral Rocks.

The Pohono Trail

Curry Village

Glacier Point 7,214 ft.

START

Sentinel Dome 8,122 ft.

Southside Drive

4,180,000

4,178,000

272,000

Sentinel

Creek

Glacier + Point Road

272,000

To Yosemite Valley

4,176,000

Yosemite Lodge

Taft Point

The Fissures

270,000

4,178,000

Northside Drive

Eagle Peak 7,779 ft.

270,000

To Bridalveil Creek Campground

Merced River

Cathedral Spires

Cathedral Rocks

Bridalveil Fall

Bridalveil Creek

El Capitan 7,569 ft.

268,000

Ribbon Creek

Pohono Trail

268,000

Dewey Point

Crocker Point

Stanford Point

266,000

Hypsometry
8000
3500
Elevation in Feet

266,000

Fireplace Creek

264,000

Tunnel View

Artist Creek

Inspiration Point

Old Inspiration Point

To Fresno

4,180,000

4,178,000

264,000

4,176,000

N

Kilometer
0   1

Mile
0

The trail dips again and hops an ephemeral creek lined with willow, currant, monkeyflower, and wild geranium. It reaches Stanford Point at 10 miles, then veers away from the valley rim and climbs a rise through a garden of lupines to reach willow-choked Meadow Brook. This little creek drops over the cliff as delicate Silver Strand Falls, seldom seen past late June. The trail rises, then drops, more steeply now, to Artist Creek, dry in summer, then continues on a knee-pounding descent through shady forest to Old Inspiration Point at 12.7 miles. You can see the remains of the asphalt road that led to this original Inspiration Point years ago. Descend rocky switchbacks to 13.2 miles, where a trail cuts off to the right (east) toward Bridalveil Fall. Continue straight ahead down the rough path to the Wawona Road and the parking lot at Tunnel View.

Miles and Directions

0.0 Panorama/Pohono Trailhead at Glacier Point.

0.1 Panorama/Pohono Trail junction, turn right.

0.2 Cross Glacier Point Road.

0.4 Cross dirt road leading to ranger residence.

1.0 Sentinel Dome Trail.

2.0 Taft Point Trail.

4.7 Bridalveil Creek crossing.

5.0 McGurk Meadow/Bridalveil Creek Trail cuts left, continue straight ahead.

5.1 Second McGurk Meadow/Bridalveil Creek Trail also cuts left, continue straight ahead.

8.7 Dewey Point spur.

9.3 Crocker Point spur.

10.0 Stanford Point spur.

12.7 Old Inspiration Point.

13.2 Bridalveil Fall turnoff, keep left.

13.8 Tunnel View parking lot.

12 The Panorama Trail–Glacier Point to Nevada Fall

The name of the trail says it all. It follows the southeastern portion of the valley rim above Happy Isles, crossing Illilouette Creek at the top of Illilouette Fall to the (usually) sunny flat where Nevada Fall launches itself over the cliff into Yosemite Valley. The Giant Staircase is in sight most of the way, as well as occasional glimpses of Yosemite Falls back to the west. You get five famous waterfalls in one hike.

Start: Panorama/Pohono Trailhead at Glacier Point.
Distance: 10.4 miles out and back.
Approximate hiking time: 6 to 8 hours.
Difficulty: Moderate.
Seasons: All summer, whenever Glacier Point

Road is open, but it's best early in summer when all the falls are flowing.
Nearest facilities: Glacier Point has toilets, phones, water, and snacks.
Permits: None.
Map: USGS Half Dome quad.

Finding the trailhead: Follow Glacier Point Road to its end 16 miles from Wawona Road at Chinquapin, or take the shuttle from Yosemite Valley. (Call 209-372-1240 for reservations.) If you are driving, park in the parking lot, then walk directly toward Half Dome along the fenced path to the trailhead sign. There are bear-proof boxes in the far corner of the upper parking lot.

The Hike

Take a minute to recover from the overwhelming immensity of the panorama from Glacier Point before setting off. To the left (northwest) is North Dome, capping the graceful Royal Arches; in the center is Half Dome, the monumental symbol of Yosemite. Tenaya Canyon stretches away to the northeast, and to the west runs the Merced River Canyon, down whose Giant Staircase flow Vernal and Nevada Falls.

From the trailhead sign, turn right (east) to find the Panorama and Pohono Trail junction at 0.1 mile. The Panorama Trail heads left (south) toward Illilouette Fall. The first mile of trail switchbacks downward through an area burned in 1987. Fragrant ceanothus and chinquapin with its spiny green fruits line the path. This is a good place to listen for the booming call of the blue grouse in spring and early summer.

At 1.2 miles, a trail coming from Mono Meadow joins this one from the south. Keep left (northeast) and continue to descend into Illilouette Gorge. Shrubs give way to forest and the rush of Illilouette Creek becomes audible. Other hikers have worn a little turnout to the left of the trail to get a look at the fall, which is just out of sight from the trail itself. This is the only way to see Illilouette Fall from any direction because it is tucked so tightly back into the notch. Just before the trail reaches the bridge over Illilouette Creek, you might spot what appears to be an idyllic

Vernal and Nevada Falls flow down the Giant Staircase
through the Merced River Canyon.

The Panorama Trail—Glacier Point to Nevada Fall

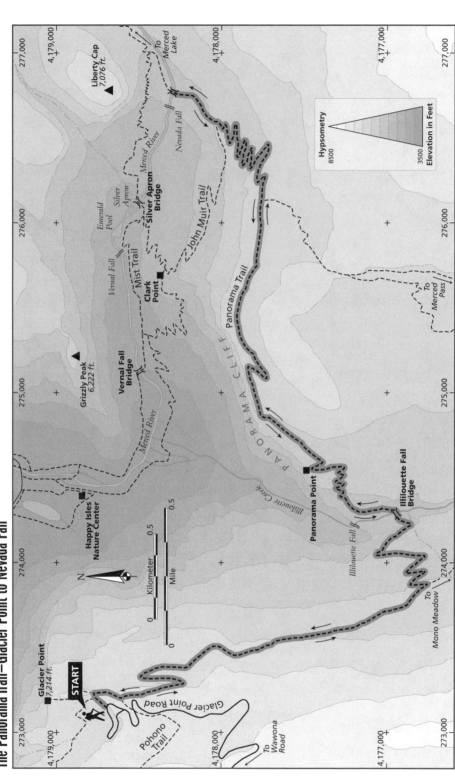

campsite on the right, but camping is not permitted here. It's too near the water, too near the trail, and too near the road. It's a nice spot for a rest and a snack, though. Cross the footbridge over the creek at 2.1 miles. The fall is not visible from the footbridge, but the creek cascades down in picturesque wedding cake fashion, and in springtime, the blooms of western azaleas lining the banks perfume the air.

From the bridge the trail climbs fairly steeply up out of the gorge, then follows the brow of the Panorama Cliff. There is no sign to mark Panorama Point, but it is the obvious place to step off the trail a few yards to the left to take in the view. You can get a good look at the notorious rockslide of 1996 that damaged much of Happy Isles. Yosemite Valley winds off to the left and Yosemite Falls are just visible on the far side. Soon the trail winds far enough around the hill to reveal spectacular 584-foot Nevada Fall, and shortly after that, reaches a junction at 4 miles. Here, a trail heads right (south) through a badly burned area, eventually to rejoin Illilouette Creek several miles upstream from Illilouette Fall. The Panorama Trail stays left and switchbacks down fairly steeply past several little rills and mossy rock gardens to meet the John Muir Trail coming up from Yosemite Valley at 5 miles. Follow the signs to the right to the top of Nevada Fall at 5.2 miles.

Join the crowd there picnicking, sunbathing, and watching the Merced River shoot over the lip of the sheer cliff. Be sure to stay behind the protective rails and away from the slippery edges. The river has claimed several lives here. You can continue on down the John Muir Trail to Yosemite from here (if you have a ride back up to Glacier Point), or you can return the way you came.

Miles and Directions

0.0 Glacier Point Trailhead.

0.1 Panorama/Pohono Trail junction, turn left.

1.2 Mono Meadow Trail junction, keep left.

2.1 Illilouette Fall Bridge.

4.0 Illilouette Creek Trail junction, keep left.

5.0 John Muir Trail junction, turn right.

5.2 Top of Nevada Fall.

10.4 Glacier Point Trailhead.

THE BLUE GROUSE

Male blue grouse find a territory to their liking then sit on a limb and hoot, hour after hour, day after day, sometimes for weeks at a stretch, hoping to encourage a mate and discourage competitors. Their call is like the sound made by blowing over the mouth of a bottle. Later in summer, watch for processions of little striped balls of fluff following their mothers (adults are about the size of small chickens), pecking in the duff or crossing the trail. They are only visible when they are moving, blending with the underbrush when they freeze. If you come too close they explode around you in a flurry of frantic flapping, but will wait until the last moment before breaking cover.

The North Rim of Yosemite Valley

Hikes on this side of the valley start later in the year than those on the south because the snow lasts longer in the shady hollows and valleys, and many of the streams are too fast, too wide, and too deep to cross safely until well into July. Because of the deep gorges cut by these streams, along with differences in the nature of the rock that makes up the cliffs, north rim trails cannot skirt the valley rim as closely as the south rim trails do. There are many breathtaking views from the tops of landmarks like El Capitan and North Dome, but the trails sometimes retreat through forest back toward Tioga Road for several miles between one scenic point and the next. Furthermore, many of the south rim overlooks can be reached in a relatively short day hike, while most of the north rim trails are very strenuous as day hikes and may be more enjoyable as overnighters. For these reasons, the north rim is not so heavily used as the south, providing more opportunities for solitude (and for obtaining wilderness permits). The nearest source for permits for these hikes is the Big Oak Flat Entrance Station; they are also available at Tuolumne Meadows and Yosemite Valley.

All of the hikes in this section are reached from Highway 120, known as the Big Oak Flat Road west of Crane Flat, and Tioga Road to the east. There are several first-come, first-served campgrounds off the road: Porcupine Flat, Tamarack Flat, Yosemite Creek, and White Wolf. The Hodgdon Meadow Campground at the Big Oak Flat entrance and the Crane Flat Campground require reservations. White Wolf has a High Sierra Camp as well, for which reservations many months in advance are needed.

The nearest (minimal) source of supplies is the gas station at Crane Flat. Both Tuolumne Meadows and Yosemite Valley have more, but the valley is almost an hour away, and Tuolumne Meadows is even farther. There is no gas in Yosemite Valley.

13 Tioga Road to the Top of Yosemite Falls

This is an easier but much longer way to reach the top of Yosemite Falls than climbing straight up from the valley floor. The mostly forested up-and-down trail follows along Yosemite Creek, hopping or wading several of its tributaries to where the creek, compressed between narrow walls, gathers speed and force and shoots out over the north rim into the valley in a series of steps totaling 2,425 feet. You can stand very close to the edge where the falls begin and, if the water is high, get soaked and half-stunned by the spray and the roar. There is camping nearby.

Start: Yosemite Creek Trailhead on Tioga Road.
Distance: 16 miles out and back from Tioga Road, 13 if you start from the campground.
Approximate hiking time: 8 to 14 hours.
Difficulty: Moderate.
Seasons: Summer and fall, best after June when the snow is gone and before August when the falls dry up.
Nearest facilities: Crane Flat.
Permits: None for a day hike; available in advance or from the wilderness center in Yosemite Valley or Tuolumne Meadows.
Map: USGS Yosemite Falls quad.

Finding the trailhead: On Tioga Road (Highway 120), drive about 20 miles east of Crane Flat, 26 miles west of Tuolumne Meadows. There is parking on both sides of the highway. The Ten Lakes Trail departs from the north side, the Yosemite Creek Trail from the south. The trail begins at the west end of the parking area.
Special considerations: You can save 3 miles and some elevation gain and loss as well as one potentially difficult stream crossing by parking in the Yosemite Creek Campground and beginning your hike from there. The road to the campground cuts off to the south from Tioga Road several miles to the east of the parking area.

The Hike

From the trailhead sign, descend through lodgepole pines to cross Yosemite Creek, which can be difficult in early season when the water is high. Then descend more gradually until you reach the Yosemite Creek Campground at 1.5 miles. Follow the paved road all the way through the campground, over the bridge across Yosemite Creek, and past the campground entrance. Just after crossing another smaller branch of the creek, turn left at a sign marked TRAIL JUNCTION, and leave the road and the campground at 2.2 miles.

The trail wanders through fairly flat forest, then climbs over a rocky shoulder marked with ducks where the route is obscure. Some handsome junipers grow from cracks in the rock. Shortly after dropping from this shoulder, a trail cuts back to the right (northwest) at 3.7 miles, heading toward Lukens Lake and White Wolf. Continue straight ahead (south) and cross a tributary of Yosemite Creek. There are a few campsites here. Gradually, the smooth rounded granite walls force the trail and the

From Eagle Peak you can see where Tenaya Canyon and Merced Canyon meet in Yosemite Valley.

creek into a narrow defile, and the lovely aquamarine water races over the rock in hypnotizing swirling patterns. Then the valley widens and the creek and trail meander more slowly through the forest where more good campsites can be found. Cross Blue Jay Creek carefully on rocks that are sometimes slippery, then cross two wide, sandy flats, reenter the forest and meet the Eagle Peak Trail in a ferny glen at 7.5 miles. (See Option.) Descend a slot that crosses a couple of bumps to reach the Yosemite Falls junction at 8 miles. This is where you will meet a steady stream of sweating, gasping hikers laboring up from the valley floor.

Follow the signs to the overlook a short distance to the east for a spectacular view, then retreat a few yards to find a path heading right (east) that rounds the point of the overlook. A series of steep and slippery steps cut into the cliff drops onto a platform protected by iron railings. The thunderous roar, the drenching spray, and the dizzying drop over the falls are exhilarating, but not for the faint of heart or the acrophobic.

If you plan to spend the night, retrace your steps to the main trail and follow it back upstream before pitching your tent. The area just at the top of the falls is trampled and overused, and camping within 0.25 mile of the rim is prohibited anyway.

Tioga Road to the Top of Yosemite Falls

Miles and Directions

0.0 Yosemite Creek Trailhead.

1.5 Yosemite Creek Campground. Follow the paved road through the middle.

2.2 End of campground, leave the road and turn left.

3.7 Lukens Lake junction, continue straight ahead.

7.5 Eagle Peak junction, continue straight ahead.

8.0 Yosemite Falls, turn left to the overlook.

16.0 Return to the Yosemite Creek Trailhead.

Options: Eagle Peak

Eagle Peak, at 7,779 feet, is the highest of the Three Brothers. From its summit you can see just about all of the park, from the star attractions of Yosemite Valley to distant landmarks like Mounts Lyell and Maclure, the Clark Range, parts of the Cathedral Range, and all the way to Mount Conness. Beginning at the Eagle Peak Trail junction at the top of Yosemite Falls, head back northwest toward the Tioga Road, climbing up a steep gully in deep shade to top a rise, then turning left at a signed trail fork. You slosh through ferns and soggy ground, climb steeply to an open grove where you cross Eagle Peak Creek, skirting the edge of more damp meadows, then turn left at the fork with the El Capitan Trail. The sign says Eagle Peak is 0.3 miles ahead, but it's more like 0.6. There's a little scramble up a pile of weathered granite to reach the very top, but you can see almost as much from the ridge just below the summit if you have no head for heights. This option adds about 6 miles and more than 1,000 feet gain to the Yosemite Creek hike, but the view is well worth every calorie and drop of sweat you'll expend to get there.

14 Porcupine Creek to North Dome

North Dome is one of the most photographed features of the park, especially from the Happy Isles Bridge with the Merced River in the foreground. It is smooth and rounded, more symmetrical than Half Dome, crowning the exfoliating Royal Arches. This is probably the best full-day outing on the north rim, and it is a popular one. The views are everything you would expect from such a vantage point, and as a bonus, you get to see the famous granite arch atop Indian Ridge, accessible only to foot (or horse) travelers.

Start: Porcupine Flat Trailhead.
Distance: 8.8 miles out and back.
Approximate hiking time: 6 to 9 hours.
Difficulty: Moderate.

Seasons: Summer and fall.
Nearest facilities: Tuolumne Meadows.
Permits: None.
Map: USGS Yosemite Falls quad.

Finding the trailhead: On Tioga Road (Highway 120), drive 14 miles west of Tuolumne Meadows or 23 miles east of Crane Flat. The trailhead and parking area are on the south side of the road.

Special considerations: Allow more time than you think you will need for this hike. There are lots of ups and downs, and the rock is sometimes slippery. Wear good boots and take your time.

The Hike

From the trailhead sign at the east end of the parking area, head downhill to meet the eroded remains of an old road and follow it on down until you reach Porcupine Creek at mile 0.7. If the water is high, there is a log crossing just upstream. Continue through red fir and lodgepole forest, climbing slightly, to a junction at 1.5 miles. Your trail goes straight ahead. A few feet beyond this, another sign directs you straight ahead again to North Dome and Yosemite Falls. At yet another fork, you keep left toward North Dome. The right fork goes down to Yosemite Valley via Yosemite Falls. (This series of forks shows as a single four-way junction on the topo.) Wind steadily uphill, partly through forest, partly over open rock lined with manzanita, until you reach the top of Indian Ridge at mile 2.7. A short detour cuts off to the left (northeast) to a very unusual rock arch, a geologic feature seldom seen in granite. There is nothing else like it in Yosemite, so don't miss it.

The main trail follows the top of Indian Ridge toward the south, drops sharply off to the left, then picks up the ridgeline again. Here, in an open rocky space, another short spur trail goes right (south) for a stupendous view and your first look at the bald rounded top of North Dome just below. Yosemite Valley stretches away to the right, flanked by Sentinel Rock and El Capitan. To the left, Half Dome looms

This arch on Indian Ridge is unusual because it's made of granite.

impossibly huge just across the gorge and Clouds Rest rises even higher in smooth curves farther back along the same ridge. The bare dome rising out of the trees behind Half Dome like a whale snout surfacing is Mount Starr King.

Return to the main trail and make your way carefully down the slickrock to a junction at 3.9 miles. Turn left and head south down toward North Dome. At first you drop down the east side of the ridge crest, and while it may appear that you are heading the wrong direction, this *is* the trail. Some people do not return to the main trail and instead, following the spur, shortcut straight down the smooth rock face directly above North Dome—but this way is slippery. The trail is safer. It passes Basket Dome to a timbered saddle, then back up the smooth exfoliating crown of North Dome, reaching the summit at 4.4 miles. North Dome's position above the confluence of several major drainages makes it one of the finest viewpoints in Yosemite. From left to right Tenaya Canyon, Merced Canyon, Illilouette Gorge, and Yosemite Valley itself fan out in all directions. When you have run out of film and/or time, return the way you came.

Porcupine Creek to North Dome

Miles and Directions

0.0 Porcupine Creek Trailhead.

0.7 Porcupine Creek crossing.

1.5 Four-way junction.

2.7 Indian Ridge.

3.9 North Dome spur trail.

4.4 Summit.

8.8 Return to trailhead.

15 The North Rim

This is an overnight shuttle route that follows the north rim of Yosemite Valley from west to east, beginning near Big Oak Flat Road, skirting the tops of El Capitan, Yosemite Falls, and North Dome, and dropping into the valley at Tenaya Canyon above Mirror Lake. It is a cooler, longer, slightly later-season trek than the south rim route, with breathtaking views of the valley.

Start: Trailhead near the Foresta turnoff on Highway 120, Big Oak Flat Road.
Distance: 30 miles one way.
Approximate hiking time: 3 days.
Difficulty: Moderate to strenuous.
Seasons: Summer and fall.
Nearest facilities: Everything you need except gas in Yosemite Valley. There is gas at Crane Flat.
Permits: Available in advance or from the wilderness center in Yosemite Valley and the Big Oak Flat Entrance.
Maps: USGS El Capitan, Half Dome, and Yosemite Falls quads.

Finding the trailhead: From the junction at the west end of Yosemite Valley, drive 4 miles north on Big Oak Flat Road (Highway 120). There is trailhead parking on the left (south) side, just beyond the Foresta Road turnoff. The trail begins on the other side of the road.

Special considerations: Ask about trail conditions in early season. Snow lies in the shady gullies well into summer, and some of the creek crossings are dangerous at high water. You will need two cars to complete the hike, one to leave at the trailhead, the other at the backpackers' parking lot in the valley.

The Hike

Climb the chaparral-covered slope that is recovering from the 1990 Foresta fire, staying alert for rattlesnakes. You soon cross to the north side of the ridge where millions of young ponderosa pines jostle one another for growing space and sunlight. The forest floor, newly opened by fire, hosts a colorful display of wildflowers, especially showy wild irises. Birding is exceptional here too, because of the number of desirable nesting sites in the hollow, burned-out trees. Leaving the burned area behind, you cross several tributaries of Wildcat Creek, blooming with dogwoods and azaleas, and continue on to Tamarack Creek, which might be tricky to cross at least until midseason. Huge leaves of Indian rhubarb, twice the size of dinner plates, line the creek, and when they are in bloom, their flowers seem to poke up right through the center of the leaves.

A little farther on, cross a small branch of Cascade Creek and reach the now abandoned Old Big Oak Flat Road at 4 miles. Turn right. The left fork leads back up to Tamarack Flat Campground and Tioga Road. Cross the main branch of Cascade Creek on a bridge and continue down the road to 4.7 miles, where the road is blocked with a pile of logs diverting you to the left (north) at a signed junction. The trail turns back on itself for a short time and begins a stiff climb up a forested slope to follow a ridgetop, climbing steadily to Ribbon Meadow. This area is almost too thickly forested to rightfully be called a meadow, but it is boggy (and buggy) enough early in the year to deserve that designation. A little way beyond is Ribbon Creek, where there is some camping if the creek is still flowing. Cross the creek, then follow the trail as it cuts back north around the edge of El Capitan Gully, down which there is a stomach-lurching view of the valley. You can see El Capitan ahead of you now. A junction with the spur trail to the top of El Capitan appears at 9.7 miles. The view from the top is all you would expect from such a height, but don't go too near the downward-sloping edge. Return to the main trail at 10.3 miles, descend to the turnoff to Eagle Peak, at 11.8 miles, and climb to the top, scrambling up a pile of granite boulders at the summit. At 7,779 feet, this is the highest of the Three Brothers, and from here you almost see the entire park. Descend to the main trail again at 12.6 miles.

Continue north over mushy ground alongside Eagle Peak Meadows to meet the Yosemite Creek Trail at 14 miles. The trail descends through forest to another junction at 15.3 miles. This is where you'll meet the sweating, panting hikers toiling up from the valley floor to the top of Yosemite Falls. Turn left (southeast) and follow the signs to the overlook, an area of sculpted rocks and twisted Jeffrey pines, to an iron railing. Directly across the valley the upside-down bowl of Sentinel Dome rises alone to the west of Glacier Point. Farther in the distance is bullet-shaped Mount Starr King, standing isolated from the surrounding ridges. Now retreat a few yards to find a path heading right (east) that rounds the point of the overlook. A series of steep and slippery steps cut into the cliff drops onto a platform protected by more iron railings. The thunderous roar, the drenching spray, and the dizzying drop over

◀ El Capitan rises majestically above the Merced River.

The North Rim

the falls are exhilarating, but not for the faint of heart or the acrophobic. Return to the trail and cross Yosemite Creek on a footbridge just above where the creek plunges over the rim. Continue upstream on switchbacks over mostly open rock to Yosemite Point, immediately above Yosemite Village. You can just glimpse Yosemite Falls back to the right. There is camping not far away if you want to spend the night here. Go back to the main trail and follow it northward (upstream) as it parallels the west side of Yosemite Creek. There are several sites within the next half mile.

To continue your journey along the rim, leave Yosemite Point, climbing steeply at first, then beginning an up-and-down progress through fir forest, crossing Indian Canyon Creek. Just before Lehamite Creek at 17.7 miles, a side trail cuts off to the left, returning to the Tioga Road. Your trail continues straight ahead, gaining elevation gradually at first, then more steeply, finally laboring up rough switchbacks to the crest of Indian Ridge. Half Dome rears up in front of you, impossibly enormous at such close range. You can see the bald pate of North Dome below you. Cross over the ridge, following ducks, to a spur trail at 19 miles. Don't miss the experience of descending to the top of North Dome, where Yosemite Valley stretches off to the west, Illilouette Gorge heads south, Merced Canyon comes in from the east, and Tenaya Canyon from the northwest.

Return to the main trail at 20 miles, then climb steeply up the slick rock along the east side of the crest of Indian Ridge. Partway up is another spur trail leading to another overlook above North Dome. Continue up the ridge to a saddle where another detour cuts off to the right (northeast) to a very unusual rock arch, a geologic feature seldom seen in granite. There is nothing else like it in Yosemite. Back on the main trail, descend through alternating manzanita and forest to a junction at 22.1 miles. Turn right (east) toward Mirror Lake. Descend slowly until you near the main branch of Snow Creek, where you pass a junction with a lateral trail leading northwest across a footbridge (at mile 25.6). Keep right (south) and drop sharply downhill to meet the Snow Creek Trail at 25.6 miles. Continue south down some very steep switchbacks beside wonderful exfoliating granite with hanging gardens fed by seeps of water coming from between the layers, to Tenaya Canyon at 27.9 miles. Turn right (west) and follow Tenaya Creek to Mirror Lake, at 29 miles. From here you can follow the road for a mile back to the backpackers' parking lot or ride the shuttle bus back to Curry Village.

Miles and Directions

0.0 Trailhead.

4.0 Old Big Oak Flat Road, turn right.

4.5 Cascade Creek, cross on the bridge.

4.7 Leave the old road and turn left onto trail.

9.7 El Capitan spur.

10.3 Return to main trail from El Capitan.

11.8 Eagle Peak spur.

12.6 Return to main trail from Eagle Peak.

14.0 Upper Yosemite Creek junction.

15.3 Lower Yosemite Creek junction.

17.7 Lehamite Creek, continue straight ahead.

19.0 North Dome spur.

20.0 Return to main trail from North Dome.

22.1 Upper Lehamite Creek junction, turn right.

25.6 Snow Creek Bridge, turn right.

27.9 Tenaya Canyon.

29.0 Mirror Lake.

30.0 Mirror Lake shuttle bus stop.

16 Tuolumne Grove

The Tuolumne Grove, one of three giant sequoia groves in Yosemite, is not as heavily visited as the Mariposa Grove and does not have a tram tour through it, so you can enjoy the beauty and serenity of the forest away from the sounds of "civilization," especially if you make this easy out-and-back hike early in the morning.

Start: Tuolumne Grove Trailhead.
Distance: 2 miles out and back.
Approximate hiking time: 1 to 3 hours.
Difficulty: Easy.
Seasons: Spring, summer, and fall, whenever Tioga Road is open.

Nearest facilities: Gas, phones, and snacks at Crane Flat.
Permits: None.
Map: USGS Ackerson Mountain quad.

Finding the trailhead: From Yosemite Valley, drive 16 miles north on Big Oak Flat Road to Crane Flat. Turn right on Tioga Road (Highway 120) and drive less than a mile to the Tuolumne Grove parking area on the left.

The Sequoia gigantea *trees in Tuolumne Grove are among the largest living things on earth.*

Tuolumne Grove

The Hike

The route through the grove follows an old road now closed to vehicle traffic. It passes through a closed gate and descends in a beautiful old forest of white fir, Douglas fir, sugar pine, and incense cedar. This last, with its smooth red bark, is often confused with the giant sequoia, but the first of these will not appear for about a half mile. In spring exquisite white dogwoods bloom in openings in the forest. The first huge sequoia, with an interpretive panel beside it, appears on the left. A sign to the right directs you to the Tunnel Tree. This tree was already only a stump when the tunnel was cut through it in 1878, but dead or alive, it gives you an eerie feeling

▶ All the giant sequoias in the world are confined to a narrow band of country only 15 miles wide and 260 miles long, between 5,000 and 7,000 feet in elevation along the western slope of the Sierra Nevada. They are clustered together in seventy-five separate groves where conditions of temperature and moisture suit them best. There are three groves in Yosemite.

to look straight up to the sky while you're inside. Beyond the Tunnel Tree is a picnic area that used to be a parking lot when cars were allowed into the grove. A nature trail begins here on the right across a little bridge. It has a series of excellent interpretive signs explaining the natural history of the trees: how they reach their great ages of 3,000 years; how they are adapted to survive repeated fires; how they depend on fire, insects, and squirrels to reproduce; and more. The nature trail returns to the road at the picnic area, from which you now climb back up to the trailhead.

Miles and Directions

0.0 Tuolumne Grove Trailhead.

0.1 Closed gate.

0.9 Tunnel Tree.

1.0 Picnic area in Tuolumne Grove.

2.0 Return to trailhead.

The High Sierra Camps

These are a series of five backcountry camps with tent cabins that offer dorm-style sleeping, linens, meals, and showers (except at Vogelsang and Glen Aulin). They are about a day's hike apart, and a popular trip is to make a loop of all of them, though each is within a day's walk of a trailhead and may be visited individually. They range in elevation from 7,200 feet at Merced Lake to 10,100 feet at Vogelsang and occupy some of the most beautiful settings in Yosemite. The largest, Merced Lake, accommodates sixty people; the smallest, Glen Aulin, holds thirty-two. You can hike the camps on your own, or as part of an organized, naturalist-led group. The High Sierra Camps offer a wonderful way to see some of Yosemite's finest backcountry without carrying a pack, but of course, they are extremely popular. They are operated by DNC Parks & Resorts, the concessionaire, and reservations are granted by lottery. Lottery applications are accepted from September 1 to December 1 for the following summer, and the lottery is held in mid-December. Call (559) 253–5674.

Each of the High Sierra Camps provides good camping for backpackers with solar toilets and bear-proof boxes nearby. Snacks and emergency supplies are available at the camps during limited hours each day, which vary from camp to camp. Even if you are backpacking, these camps are very popular and permit quotas are filled early. The surest way to see them is to go early or late in the season.

This section will describe hikes to each of the camps from their nearest trailhead, then will describe the loop in a counterclockwise direction, beginning at Tuolumne Meadows—since the first camp on the loop, Glen Aulin, is downhill from here, you have extra time to adjust to the higher elevations.

17 Merced Lake High Sierra Camp

Merced Lake is the site of the largest of the High Sierra Camps and the farthest from any trailhead. The hike up the Giant Staircase along the Merced River allows you to experience the river in its many moods and to appreciate the power of the glaciers that carved and polished the canyon. Expect lots of company; it's a popular route.

Start: Happy Isles/John Muir Trailhead.
Distance: 26.8 miles out and back.
Approximate hiking time: 2 to 4 days.
Difficulty: Strenuous as a 2-day trip, moderate if you take longer.
Seasons: Mid-June to September.
Nearest facilities: Everything you need in Yosemite Valley. There are toilets and snacks at Happy Isles.

Permits: Required; available in advance or from the wilderness center in Yosemite Valley. *NOTE:* Because this trailhead gets so much use, group size is limited to ten people, rather than the usual fifteen.
Maps: USGS Half Dome and Merced Peak quads.

Finding the trailhead: Park in the backpackers' lot east of Curry Village. You can take the shuttle bus from Curry Village to Happy Isles, or walk from the parking lot, turn right (east) at the entrance and follow the well-marked path to Happy Isles. This will add 1 mile each way to your hike. From the shuttle bus stop, continue on the paved road over the Happy Isles Bridge, then turn right, following the river upstream to the big sign that marks the beginning of the John Muir Trail.

The Hike

The sign at the trailhead shows mileage to various points on the John Muir Trail all the way to Mount Whitney, 211 miles to the south. You will have plenty of company, especially at the beginning of this hike, since it is one of the starting points of the High Sierra Camps Loop, as well as the jumping-off point for the John Muir Trail and the climb to Half Dome.

The trail climbs gently on an eroded asphalt path through black oak and ponderosa pine forest among enormous lichen-draped boulders. In about a half mile, across the thundering Merced on your right, watch for 370-foot Illilouette Fall tucked back in its deeply cut gorge in the Panorama Cliff. The trail now steepens briefly, then suddenly descends to the Vernal Fall Bridge at 0.8 mile. Upstream, Vernal Fall is perfectly framed by maple, alder, and various conifers as it drops 317 feet over the lower step of the Giant Staircase. There are restrooms, drinking water, and lots of people here.

Cross the bridge to the south side of the river and turn left, upstream. Pass a lateral trail on the right for horses only that leads back to the stables, then meet the Mist Trail junction at 0.9 mile. This is an alternate route to the top of Nevada Fall,

The Merced River slides over the Bunnell Cascade.

which is not recommended for backpackers since it is steep, slippery, and wet. Continue climbing on the John Muir Trail as it switchbacks relentlessly uphill. There are plenty of excuses to stop and rest on the way. Across the valley to the northwest you can see Upper Yosemite Fall. To the northeast across the river gorge, the rounded backside of Half Dome comes into view along with Mount Broderick, Liberty Cap, and finally, 594-foot Nevada Fall. This heart-stopping view is finest at Clark Point (2.3 miles), where a lateral trail cuts over to the Mist Trail, nearer to the river. Continue to ascend the John Muir Trail on well-graded switchbacks, eventually passing beneath a dripping rock overhang decorated with delicate hanging gardens of ferns, columbines, monkeyflowers, and other water-loving species. At 3.3 miles the Panorama Trail leading back to Glacier Point joins this one from the right (south). The trail drops a bit, hops a couple of little creeks, then emerges into a wide sunny expanse of smooth granite at the top of Nevada Fall. Here, at 3.5 miles, a footbridge crosses the river. There are plenty of viewpoints with protective railings where you can watch the falls rush over the lip. Please stay behind the railings and heed the warning signs. Hikers have slipped on the slick rock and been washed over the falls.

Merced Lake High Sierra Camp

This is a perfect place for lunch or a snack, but please do not share your food with the pan-handling squirrels and jays.

Cross the footbridge and follow the north shore of the river to 3.8 miles. There is an outhouse here, and just beyond, the junction with the upper end of the Mist Trail. Continue upstream, climbing the well-defined trail over inlaid rocks. The way soon levels out and passes from sunlight into shade, and the Merced changes from a rushing, raging torrent to become quiet, dark, and deep.

▶ Watch for brilliant red snowplants and the taller, drabber, brownish pinedrops on the forest floor where little sunlight comes through. These live on decaying material in the soil, so they have no need of green leaves and can survive in deep shade.

At 4.3 miles, your trail parts company with the John Muir Trail, which heads off to the left (northeast) toward Half Dome while you continue straight. After slogging through heavy sand for a half mile, another lateral trail at 4.8 miles takes off to the left to join the John Muir and Half Dome trails. Ahead is Little Yosemite Valley, your first camping opportunity. (NOTE: Camping is prohibited for the next 2 miles beyond Little Yosemite Valley.)

It's a busy and popular place, especially for bears. There are plenty of bear-proof boxes for food storage, but you should be carrying a canister anyway. There is also an architecturally elegant two-story solar composting toilet. The National Park Service has constructed two communal fire rings for campers to share. Please do not scar this already overused area by building another one.

Beyond Little Yosemite Valley the trail continues through level forest for a little more than a mile to where steep granite walls close in, pinching shut Little Yosemite Valley and forcing the river to pick up speed and vigor. It cascades noisily for a short time before slowing and widening out once again through Lost Valley, severely burned in a recent fire. Climb out of the valley, passing below the enormous dome of Bunnell Point across the river, where the water pours over the long slippery slide of Bunnell Cascade and is finally crossed on a footbridge to the south side. Climb switchbacks blasted out of the smooth granite, then pause to wipe away the sweat and enjoy the sight and sound of the river roaring through its spectacular rocky gorge.

Descend once again, cross back over the river, and soon enter Echo Valley, another badly burned-over flat where several creeks flow in to join the Merced. At 11.4 miles, where Echo Creek flows into the valley, a trail to Sunrise High Sierra Camp cuts off to the north. Soon the Merced begins to race beside the trail again as you climb the final mile to Merced Lake. There is a stock gate at the west end of the lake at 12.7 miles. Be sure to close it behind you. Skirt the lakeshore until you reach the High Sierra Camp at 13.4 miles. The backpackers' camp is a short distance beyond. Campers may use the water tap at the campground, but are asked to use the toilets at the backpackers' campground. You can buy emergency items and snacks during posted hours at the High Sierra Camp. Less than a mile beyond the camp is a ranger station, open all summer. From here you can return to Yosemite Valley or continue north to Vogelsang High Sierra Camp to continue the loop.

Miles and Directions

0.0 Happy Isles.

0.8 Vernal Fall Bridge; cross the bridge, turn left.

0.9 Mist Trail junction, keep right.

2.3 Clark Point, continue straight ahead.

3.3 Panorama Trail junction, keep left.

3.5 Cross the footbridge over Nevada Fall.

3.8 Upper end of the Mist Trail, keep right.

4.3 John Muir Trail junction, continue straight ahead.

4.8 Little Yosemite Valley.

11.4 Echo Valley, keep right at Sunrise Trail junction.

12.7 West end of Merced Lake.

13.4 Merced Lake High Sierra Camp.

26.8 Return to Happy Isles.

18 Vogelsang High Sierra Camp

This overnight loop to the highest of the High Sierra Camps may be hiked in either direction, approaching Vogelsang from the west via Rafferty Creek, or from the east via the Lyell Fork and Evelyn Lake. If you have only one night to spend, you can make an out-and-back hike of 13.4 miles via Rafferty Creek, but this area really deserves more time, at least three days. It will be described here in a clockwise direction, that is, via Lyell Fork, returning via Rafferty Creek, because the ascent is more gradual.

Start: John Muir Trailhead at the Dog Lake parking lot.
Distance: 19.1-mile lollipop loop.
Approximate hiking time: 2 to 4 days.
Difficulty: Moderate.
Seasons: Late June to September.

Nearest facilities: Food, gas, and phones at Tuolumne Meadows.
Permits: Required; available in advance or at the Tuolumne Meadows Wilderness Center.
Maps: USGS Vogelsang Peak and Tioga Pass quads.

Finding the trailhead: From the west, drive Tioga Road (Highway 120) eastward past the Tuolumne Meadow visitor center, store, and campground, all on the right. Cross the bridge over the Tuolumne River. After about a mile, turn right at the entrance to the wilderness center. Follow the road as it curves around to the left for about a half mile to the Dog Lake parking lot on the left. You might see broken glass on the asphalt where bears have broken into cars containing improperly stored food. Leave ice chests and all food in the bear-proof boxes provided. You can also ride the Tuolumne Meadows shuttle bus to the Dog Lake Trailhead.

The Hike

Cross the road south of the parking lot to the John Muir Trailhead sign. Follow the trail southeast to the footbridge over the Dana Fork at 0.2 mile. Ignore the cutoff back to the lodge and cross the bridge, then turn left and follow the river upstream. At 0.3 mile is another cutoff to the left to Gaylor Lakes. Keep right here, too. The route bends slightly to the right, crosses a low rise, and reaches the twin bridges over the Lyell Fork at 0.6 mile. This is surely one of the most sublime vistas in Yosemite, with the clear turquoise river winding toward you through the green meadow. The color of the water comes from glacial "flour," rock ground so fine by the Lyell Glacier upstream that it remains suspended in the water and reflects this lovely green light. In places, deep bowls have been carved into the granite by the scouring force of the silt carried by spring runoff. The massive gray hulk on the left is Mammoth Peak (not to be confused with Mammoth Mountain, the ski resort, which lies farther south).

Soon after you leave the twin bridges, another path leads back to the Tuolumne Meadows Campground at 0.7 mile. Continue left on the John Muir Trail through

lodgepole forest and over open rock to 1.3 miles, where the Rafferty Creek Trail, the more direct route to Vogelsang, leads uphill to the right (south). You will be returning on this trail. Cross the bridge over the creek on your left and continue through forest and meadows, which, in early season, are a solid mass of pale lavender shooting stars (and mosquitoes). Soon the sound of the river becomes apparent—it's been hidden for a while behind a low ridge—and another glorious view of Lyell Canyon opens up before you.

Follow the path along the river to 5.6 miles, where the Vogelsang Trail leaves the John Muir Trail and angles off to the southwest, leaving the river behind. Near this junction are some good campsites to the right of the trail. This is a notorious bear hangout and the bears here are intelligent and resourceful. Bear canisters are mandatory on this hike anyway, because you will be traveling above 9,600 feet.

Beyond the junction and the camping area, the trail begins to climb, switchbacking through lodgepole pine, sometimes through patches of wild strawberries and alpine prickly currant bushes. As the trail nears the creek on the left, a lovely little meadow appears. Be sure to pause for a moment and look up and ahead for the waterfall flowing from Ireland Lake, just out of sight in the bowl above. Beyond the meadow the trail leaves the stream, first heads southwest, then makes a dogleg to the north and reaches a junction with the Ireland Lake Trail at 8 miles. The trail sign here incorrectly gives the distance to Ireland Lake as 3 miles. It is actually only 1.5 miles (each way) and is well worth a detour if you have the time. The lake lies in a huge open glacial cirque above timberline beneath Parsons and Amelia Earhart Peaks.

Back on the Vogelsang Trail, cross a little creek, then climb a rocky slope that becomes steep toward the top, on tight switchbacks. Stay alert. It's easy to zig when you should have zagged and miss the route. Your goal is obvious, however—it is the low point on the ridge ahead. This is the highest point of your hike at 10,600 feet, and it offers sensational views. The vegetation has changed from upright lodgepole pine to whitebark pine forest that is less than knee-high on this windy ridgetop. Behind you to the northeast is the light-colored Kuna Crest, and beyond that, the Koip Crest, which marks the park boundary. To the south are black Amelia Earhart and Parsons Peaks, and beyond them, the group of tall peaks on the horizon includes Mount Lyell, highest point in Yosemite. To the west, an unnamed lake occupies a broad green bowl with your trail skirting its northwest shore before vanishing over the next ridge.

Descend from the saddle to the outlet of this little lake, noting that the whitebark pines, though still twisted and gnarled, are now growing upright. Hop the outlet stream, cross a low ridge, and enter a larger bowl containing Evelyn Lake. Off to the north beyond Tuolumne Meadows lie the high peaks of Yosemite's north boundary country, crowned by Mount Conness, third highest peak in the park. The trail

◀ *Vogelsang Peak rises high above the High Sierra Camp.*

Vogelsang High Sierra Camp

now crosses the outlet of Evelyn Lake, tops another rise, then descends through a notch that often holds patches of snow well into summer, and as a result is usually filled with flowers. Downhill to the right are glimpses of Boothe Lake and of the Rafferty Creek Trail leading back to Tuolumne Meadows. A little farther along, Fletcher Lake, lying at the base of Fletcher Peak, comes into view on the left. A long meadow dotted with whitebark pine stretches out ahead.

Vogelsang High Sierra Camp (10,100 feet) lies at the far end of Fletcher Lake at 11.5 miles. There are plenty of campsites beneath the trees in the meadow away from the lakeshore. Be sure to camp only on pine duff and not on the fragile green meadow vegetation. There are a few especially fine sites toward the north side of the meadow near the cliff edge with views of Boothe Lake and Mount Conness. There is a distinctive, oddly shaped solar composting toilet for backpackers. Please do not use the toilets at the nearby High Sierra Camp. There is a tap with potable water near the camp that you may use if you don't want to purify lake water. Emergency supplies and snacks are available during posted hours at the camp.

When you are ready to return to Tuolumne Meadows, find the signed junction in front of the High Sierra Camp and descend north, then northeast, gently down the ridge above Boothe Lake to Tuolumne Pass, where you will find another junction at 12.3 miles. You can make a detour of 0.4 mile for a look at Boothe Lake, or continue gently downhill along Rafferty Creek for a long stretch, sometimes through forest, sometimes at the edge of the meadow. Toward the end the descent steepens and at last switchbacks down to the junction of the John Muir Trail at 17.8 miles, closing the loop. From here, return the way you came to Tuolumne Meadows.

Miles and Directions

0.0 John Muir Trailhead.

0.2 Bridge over Dana Fork and junction with Tuolumne Meadows Lodge, keep right.

0.3 Gaylor Lakes Trail, turn right.

0.6 Cross the twin bridges over the Lyell Fork.

0.7 Cutoff to Tuolumne Meadows Campground, turn left.

1.3 Rafferty Creek junction, keep left.

5.6 John Muir Trail/Vogelsang junction, turn right.

8.0 Ireland Lake Trail, continue straight ahead.

11.5 Vogelsang High Sierra Camp.

12.3 Tuolumne Pass/Boothe Lake junction, turn right.

17.8 John Muir Trail/Rafferty Creek junction, turn left.

19.1 Return to Dog Lake parking lot.

Options: Vogelsang Lake and Vogelsang Pass

If you have time, do not pass up the opportunity to see this stunning lake and the wild expanse of alpine country beyond the pass. On the way you can look all the way down to Half Dome at the head of Yosemite Valley, and beyond the pass, southward to the colorful Clark Range. The trail starts behind the office at the High Sierra Camp, winding its way up to Vogelsang Lake through miniature wildflower gardens. It crosses the lake's outlet, then climbs the slope above the western shore along the base of Vogelsang Peak to reach the pass at almost 10,500 feet. You will encounter late-lying patches of snow well into the summer, and you must watch carefully for trail ducks to keep on course. The round-trip distance from the High Sierra Camp is 2.4 miles.

19 May Lake High Sierra Camp

This is the High Sierra Camp most easily reached from the road (not counting Tuolumne Meadows Lodge) so you are bound to have plenty of company on the trail. The lake lies at the base of Mount Hoffman, which marks the geographic center of the park. There are great views back down Tenaya Canyon toward Yosemite Valley along the way.

Start: May Lake Trailhead at Snow Creek.
Distance: 2.4 miles out and back.
Approximate hiking time: 2 to 4 hours.
Difficulty: Easy.
Seasons: All summer; whenever the road is open and free of snow.

Nearest facilities: Food, gas, and phones at Tuolumne Meadows.
Permits: None required for a day hike; available in advance or at the Tuolumne Meadows wilderness center for overnights.
Map: USGS Tenaya Lake quad.

Finding the trailhead: From Tioga Road (Highway 120), drive 27 miles east of Crane Flat, or 20 miles west of Tioga Pass, to the May Lake Road junction. Follow the narrow road north about 2 miles through a meadow known as Snow Flat to the trailhead. Drive carefully here—in many places the road is only wide enough for one vehicle at a time. Leave any food or ice chests in the bear-proof boxes at the trailhead.

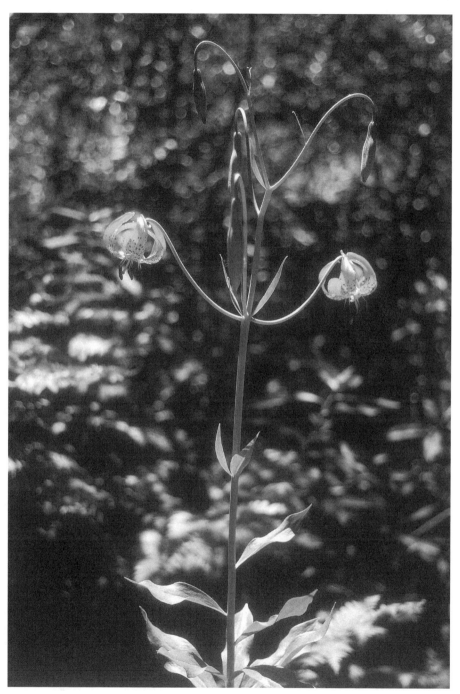

Enjoy leopard lilies near May Lake.

May Lake High Sierra Camp

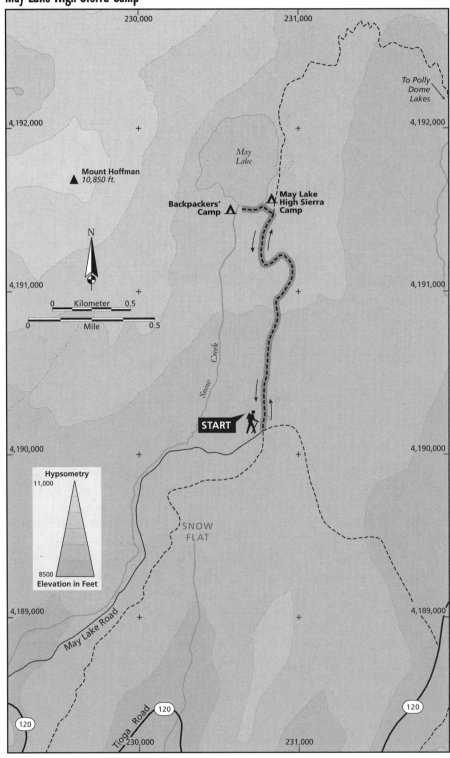

The Hike

Begin your walk in a shady glen with a variety of conifers—lodgepole pine, silver pine, mountain hemlock, and fir—then pass a discolored little pond teeming with fairy shrimp and other interesting creatures. The well-used trail climbs slowly at first, passing through a granite corridor where cracks in the rock bloom with ferns, mountain pride penstemon, shaggy hawkweed, and other wildflowers. Eventually the trail begins a steeper, winding climb, revealing good views now and then down Tenaya Canyon past Clouds Rest and Half Dome. The dramatic pointy peak in the distance is Mount Clark. Back up the canyon you can just barely see Tenaya Lake.

The trail flattens out in forest and in just a few yards reaches a fork. To the left is the backpackers' camping area, to the right is the High Sierra Camp near the lakeshore. Enjoy the lake from camp, but do not jump in. This is the local water supply, and swimming is prohibited. Mount Hoffman, at 10,850 feet, rises dramatically behind the lake. It is well worth a scramble to the top if you have the time because of its central location in the park and 360-degree views. Allow a minimum of two extra hours for the climb. When you're ready, return the way you came.

20 Glen Aulin High Sierra Camp

There are more scenic wonders along the Glen Aulin trail, mile for mile, than on any other route below the high alpine zone anywhere in Yosemite. For most of its length, it follows the course of the Tuolumne River as it wanders through broad meadows beneath the fabulous domes and spires of the Cathedral Range, then rushes and tumbles down in waterfall after waterfall as the canyon steepens and narrows. Your goal, the High Sierra Camp, lies in an idyllic setting beside a pool at the base of an exquisite cascade. Because the route is fairly short and easy, because it is part of the High Sierra Camp loop and the Pacific Crest Trail, and because it is so beautiful, the trail always has plenty of traffic and wilderness permits go quickly. Solitude? Not a chance, but worth the trip anyway.

Start: Glen Aulin Trailhead near Lembert Dome in Tuolumne Meadows.
Distance: 10.4 miles out and back.
Approximate hiking time: 6 to 10 hours.
Difficulty: Easy as a backpack, moderate as a day hike.
Seasons: All summer, whenever the Tioga Road is open.

Nearest facilities: Tuolumne Meadows store, grill, mountain shop, and gas are just west of the Tuolumne Meadows campground.
Permits: None required for a day hike; available in advance or at the Tuolumne Meadows wilderness center for overnight trips.
Maps: USGS Falls Ridge and Tioga Pass quads.

Finding the trailhead: From the west, follow Tioga Road (Highway 120) past the Tuolumne Meadows visitor center, store, cafe, and campground, all on your right. Just after crossing the bridge over the Tuolumne River, turn left (north) into the Lembert Dome parking area. From the east (Tioga Pass) follow Tioga Road past the turnoff to the wilderness center on your left and continue about a hundred yards to the Lembert Dome parking area on your right. You can also ride the Tuolumne Meadows shuttle bus to Lembert Dome. Overnight parking is prohibited in the parking lot so if you are planning to backpack, park along the paved road parallel to Tioga Road. The road turns right at a closed gate where your hike begins.

Special considerations: Because this is such a popular destination, Glen Aulin is notorious for troublesome bears. There are a couple of bear boxes at the backpackers' campground, but there are not enough for everybody. Hanging food is out of the question here. Carry a canister and keep it locked even if it's right beside you.

The Hike

Go through the gate and follow the road (closed to vehicles) westward through the meadow, keeping right and climbing a small rise where the road splits. From the top

The White Cascade drops into a pool in front of Glen Aulin High Sierra Camp.

Glen Aulin High Sierra Camp

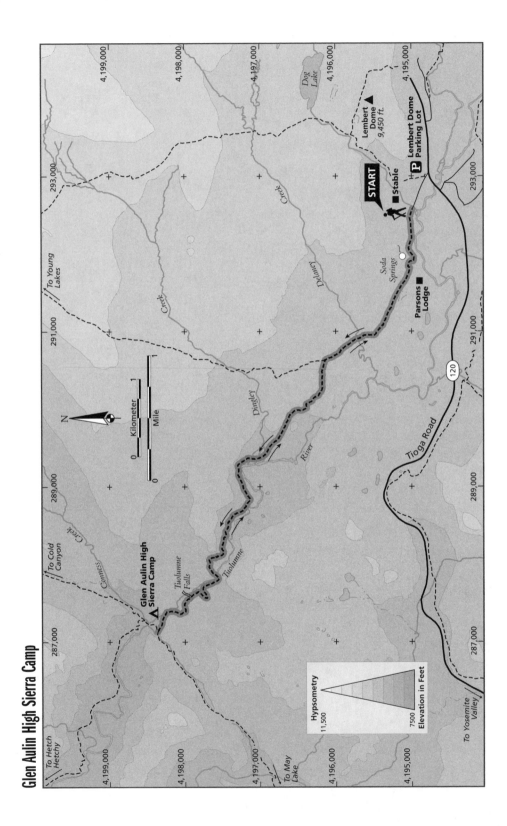

of the rise, head toward the ramshackle log structure partially containing Soda Springs at mile 0.5, a naturally carbonated spring bubbling up rusty water. Just beyond is Parsons Lodge, a stone building with historical exhibits, and beyond that, a log cabin used by park volunteers. There is a public restroom behind the cabin. The path splits in front of the cabin at mile 0.6. Turn right. The left fork goes to the sewage treatment plant. The trail to Glen Aulin, marked by a big sign, meets the road a few yards beyond. Turn left this time. Walk through flowery meadows and lodgepole forest on footing that is heavy and dusty since pack trains going to and from the High Sierra Camp use the path too. Ford Delaney Creek at mile 1.2. It is usually shallow enough to wade, though you can keep your boots dry by crossing on a big log just upstream.

At 1.6 miles, meet a junction with one of the trails that heads north to Young Lakes. Continue northwest, descending very gradually. In less than a mile you emerge from behind a low ridge to behold the spectacular Cathedral Range with the Tuolumne River in the foreground. The next couple of miles along the trail offer one incredible photo-op after another. Sometimes the trail passes over highly polished granite, buffed by glacial ice to a blinding sheen. Follow the ducks across these open spaces to stay on the trail. Climb around a low shoulder of rock and keep watch on your left for the Little Devil's Postpile, an unusual volcanic feature much younger than the surrounding rock.

The trail turns sharply right and drops down a short steep notch and very soon reaches a pair of footbridges across the Tuolumne River at 3.5 miles. From this point on, the river picks up speed and cascades over a series of falls, one after another, all the way to Glen Aulin. One of these, Tuolumne Falls, is close enough to the trail for hikers to feel the spray. Continue descending, enjoying views up Cold Canyon to Matterhorn Peak and Mount Conness on the northern boundary of the park. The trail dives twice into and out of deep forest lined with Labrador tea and corn lily, then emerges again into sunlight on cobblestones or smooth granite marked with ducks. Finally, it meets a junction with the May Lake Trail at 5 miles. A few more steep, slippery switchbacks lead down to a bridge and back to the other side of the river. Few hikers can resist the urge to stop on the bridge and snap a photo, or simply gape at the frothy White Cascade splashing into a pool in front of Glen Aulin High Sierra Camp. You have come 5.2 miles.

To reach the camp, cross a second bridge to the right over Cold Creek. Northward, behind the High Sierra Camp is a backpackers' campground with bear-proof boxes and a solar composting toilet. The campground is much bigger than it looks as it is divided into three separate sections on terraces one on top of another following the ridge above Cold Creek. Each section has a group fire ring to be shared with other campers. Do not build a new one. If you are not going on to Waterwheel Falls, retrace your steps to the trailhead.

Miles and Directions

0.0 Glen Aulin/Soda Springs Trailhead.

0.3 Road splits, keep right, uphill.

0.5 Soda Springs.

0.6 Parsons Lodge, turn right, then left at the trail sign.

1.2 Delaney Creek.

1.6 Junction with Young Lakes Trail; keep left.

3.5 Twin bridges.

5.0 May Lake Trail junction, turn sharp right, downhill.

5.2 Glen Aulin High Sierra Camp, turn right, cross the bridge over the Tuolumne, right again over Cold Creek.

10.4 Return to the trailhead.

Option: Waterwheel Falls

If you plan a hike to Glen Aulin early in the season, at least before the end of July, do not miss the famous Waterwheel Falls, 2.7 miles northwest and 1,400 feet down the river gorge from the High Sierra Camp. Most hikers spend two nights at Glen Aulin and make the steep Waterwheel Falls trip as a day hike.

The roaring Tuolumne River rushes down a smooth slope until it hits a series of grooves in the rocks that sometimes fling the water more than 20 feet into the air in a procession of huge arcs. To get there from the camp, cross the bridge over Cold Creek to the west side, climb over a ridge and wander through a waist-high field of lupines that have flourished since the Glen was burned years ago. Some people still do camp in the Glen to avoid the crowds at the High Sierra Camp, but the only really desirable sites are too near the river and the trail to be strictly kosher. In another mile both trail and river drop over a long series of stair-steps past California Falls and LeConte Falls to the Waterwheels. Watch for a little unmarked spur trail leading toward the bottom of the falls for a better view but *do not* walk out onto the slippery rock beside the water, especially if it is wet. Slimy algae on polished rock is as slick as glass and a slip could be fatal.

21 Sunrise High Sierra Camp

This out-and-back route leads you from Tenaya Lake steadily upward past all three Sunrise Lakes, skirts the north end of Sunrise Mountain, then descends to a terrace above a long and lovely meadow laced with meandering streams. You can do it as a day hike, visit the High Sierra Camp, or spend the night. Backpackers can even buy a shower at this camp. The John Muir and Pacific Crest Trails meet this route in the meadow.

Start: Sunrise Lakes Trailhead at Tenaya Lake.
Distance: 10.4 miles out and back.
Approximate hiking time: 5 to 8 hours.
Difficulty: Moderate.
Seasons: All summer; whenever Tioga Road is open.

Nearest facilities: Food, gas, and phones at Tuolumne Meadows.
Permits: None required for a day hike; available in advance or at the Tuolumne Meadows wilderness center for overnights.
Map: USGS Tenaya Lake quad.

Finding the trailhead: Drive to the southwest end of Tenaya Lake on Tioga Road (Highway 120). The trailhead is across the street from the lake on the south side. You can also ride the Tuolumne Meadows shuttle to Sunrise Lakes Trailhead. Be sure to leave food and ice chests in the bear-proof boxes provided.

The Hike

A paved trail begins behind the parking area on which you turn left (east). Tenaya Lake can be glimpsed back through the trees. Soon the pavement ends and you cross a sandy-bottomed creek draining Tenaya Lake, which you will probably have to wade early in the year. The trail swings right (south) just across the creek at 0.1 mile. A sign incorrectly says SUNRISE: 5 MILES. At 0.2 mile, a trail leading back to Tuolumne Meadows Lodge goes off to the left. Your trail dips and rises now and then as it crosses several little streams, then it begins to climb the east slope above Tenaya Canyon. The switchbacking climb is relieved by views of Mount Hoffman and Tioga Road across the canyon.

At the crest of the ridge you have been climbing (2.5 miles), the trail splits. The right (south) fork leads back to Clouds Rest and Half Dome, the left (east) leads to Sunrise Lakes. For a spectacular view of Half Dome and Clouds Rest, climb the little knoll to the right of the junction just a few dozen feet off the trail.

From the junction, follow a ridgeline for a short time, then drop into the bowl containing the first of the Sunrise Lakes. Its depth makes it a rich, improbable royal blue. Camping is not recommended here (not to mention illegal) because the sides of the bowl slope too steeply and the immediate lakeside is much too fragile for camping. The trail now climbs up out of the bowl and follows its south rim. The second Sunrise Lake, only occasionally visible, lies somewhat below the trail to the north and offers better camping than the first one.

The route crosses a smooth, round lump of classic exfoliating Yosemite granite to reach the uppermost, and largest, of the lakes. There are plenty of camping spaces here along the north shore, but the area is showing signs of overuse. Continue up a moderate hill alongside a wildflower-lined creek to a wide, sandy saddle with scattered mountain hemlock and pine. The jagged Clark Range defines the horizon to the south. The trail eases gently down to the backpackers' camping area above and behind the High Sierra Camp, where there is a toilet, piped water, and bear boxes.

Just beyond and downhill at 5.1 miles, the trail meets a junction with the John Muir/Pacific Crest Trail. Turn left and follow the deeply worn ruts along the edge of the meadow to the High Sierra Camp. From the camp's front door, the view of an emerald green meadow backed by Merced Peak to the southeast and Mount Clark to the southwest invites contemplation and rest. The High Sierra Camp sells snacks and emergency supplies for a limited number of hours during the day. You can even buy a shower there for $3.00, but bring your own towel. Return the way you came.

Miles and Directions

0.0   Sunrise Trailhead.

0.2   Tuolumne Meadows Lodge cutoff.

2.5   Clouds Rest/Half Dome junction.

5.1   John Muir Trail junction.

5.2   Sunrise High Sierra Camp.

10.4   Sunrise Trailhead.

◀ *Sunrise High Sierra Camp overlooks Long Meadow and the Matthes Crest.*

Sunrise High Sierra Camp

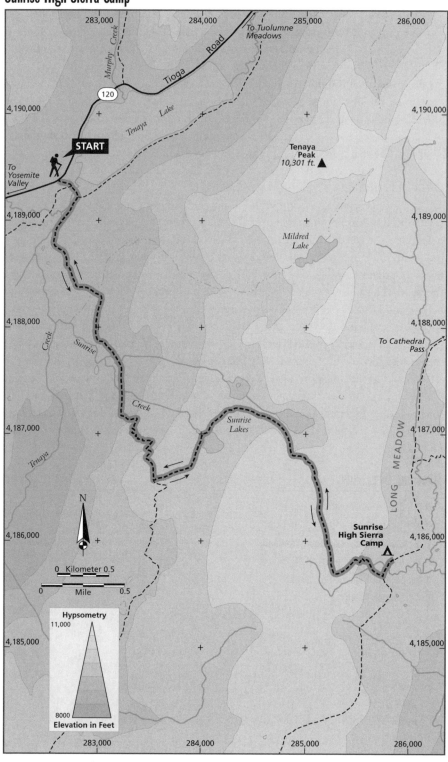

22 The High Sierra Camp Loop

You can visit all of the High Sierra Camps in one multiday backpack on this classic Yosemite route over some of the finest and most varied scenery in the park. Each of the camps has an adjoining camping area for backpackers with bear boxes, pit toilets, and piped water. It is a heavily traveled route; backpackers, guests of the camps, horses, and packers carrying personal gear and supplies, all travel these same trails, campgrounds are usually very busy, and permits are at a premium. You cannot expect a deep wilderness experience, but the camaraderie that comes from sharing the day's adventures with other hikers almost makes up for it. There are always bears hanging out around the camps so you will need a canister. You can begin this loop from any of the trailheads to any of the camps, but beginning at Tuolumne Meadows, making Glen Aulin your first stop, gives you an easy first day on the trail and extra time to adjust to the high elevation.

Start: Glen Aulin Trailhead near Lembert Dome.

Distance: 47.6-mile loop.

Approximate hiking time: 6 days.

Difficulty: Moderate.

Seasons: All summer, whenever Tioga Road is open.

Nearest facilities: Tuolumne Meadows Store, Grill, Mountain Shop, and gas are just west of the Tuolumne Meadows Campground.

Permits: Available in advance or at the Tuolumne Meadows wilderness center.

Maps: USGS Falls Ridge, Tioga Pass, Tenaya Lake, Merced Peak, Vogelsang Peak, and Mount Lyell quads.

Finding the trailhead: From the west, follow Tioga Road (Highway 120) past the Tuolumne Meadows visitor center, store, cafe, and campground, all on your right. Just after crossing the bridge over the Tuolumne River, turn left (north) into the Lembert Dome parking area. From the east (Tioga Pass) follow Tioga Road past the turnoff to the wilderness center on your left and continue about a hundred yards to the Lembert Dome parking area on your right. You can also ride the Tuolumne Meadows shuttle bus to Lembert Dome. Overnight parking is prohibited in the parking lot, so park along the road that runs parallel to Tioga Road toward the stables. Where the road makes a sharp right turn you will find a closed gate with the trailhead sign.

The Hike

Go through the gate and follow the road (closed to vehicles) westward through the meadow, keeping right and climbing a small rise where the road splits. From the top of the rise, head toward the ramshackle log structure partially containing Soda Springs at mile 0.5, a naturally carbonated spring bubbling up rusty water. Just beyond is Parsons Lodge, a stone building with historical exhibits. The path splits at mile 0.6, where you turn right to a big GLEN AULIN TRAIL sign. The trail meets the road a few yards beyond; turn left. Walk through flowery meadows and lodgepole for-

A marmot watches passers-by on the High Sierra Camp Loop.

est on footing that is heavy and dusty from lots of horse and foot traffic. Ford Delaney Creek at mile 1.2. A trail heading north to Young Lakes cuts off to the right at mile 1.6, but your route stays left (northwest). In less than a mile of gradual descent, you emerge from behind a low ridge to behold the spectacular Cathedral Range with the Tuolumne River in the foreground. The next couple of miles along the trail offer one incredible photo-op after another. Sometimes the trail passes over highly polished granite, buffed by glacial ice to a blinding sheen, and you will need to watch for ducks across these open spaces to stay on track. After passing through another short stretch of forest, climb around a low shoulder of rock and keep watch on your left for the Little Devil's Postpile, an unusual volcanic feature much younger than the surrounding rock.

The trail turns sharply right and drops down a short steep notch, and very soon reaches a pair of footbridges across the Tuolumne River at 3.5 miles. From this point on, the river picks up speed and cascades over a series of falls, one after another, all the way to Glen Aulin. One of these, Tuolumne Falls, is close enough to the trail for hikers to feel the spray. Continue descending, enjoying views up Cold Canyon to Matterhorn Peak and Mount Conness on the northern boundary of the park. The trail dives twice into and out of deep forest lined with Labrador tea and corn lily, then emerges again into sunlight on cobblestones or smooth granite marked with ducks. Finally, it meets a junction with the trail to McGee/May Lakes at 5 miles where you turn right. A few more steep, slippery switchbacks lead down to a bridge and back to the other side of the river. Few hikers can resist the urge to stop on the bridge and snap a photo or simply gape at the frothy White Cascade splashing into a pool in front of the High Sierra Camp. You have come 5.2 miles.

To reach the camp, cross a second bridge to the right over Cold Creek. Northward, behind the High Sierra Camp is a backpackers' campground with bear-proof boxes and a solar composting toilet. The campground is much bigger than it looks as it is divided into three separate sections on terraces one above another following the ridge over Cold Creek. Each section has a group fire ring to be shared with other campers. Do not build a new one.

To continue on to May Lake Camp, retrace your steps back across the bridge over Cold Creek, turn left and cross the next bridge to the south side of the Tuolumne River, then climb the short slope to meet the McGee Lake junction at 5.4 miles. McGee Lake is oddly situated at the top of a narrow saddle, each side of which is topped by a dome. Skirt the north shore of the lake, looking straight down the canyon to Tuolumne Peak. There are a few campsites at the lakeside. Now descend mostly through forest to cross Cathedral Creek, then climb again to meet a trail at 9.6 miles that runs down to Tenaya Lake via Murphy Creek. Take the right fork here, and soon meet the May Lake junction at 10 miles. Turn left (south). The trail begins a fairly steep, beautiful climb up an open slope down which little creeks trickle, each watering a miniature garden. Enjoy the views across the canyon to Mount Conness, then drop briefly down the west side of the rocky ridge. When you reenter the forest and swing west, keep an eye out for Raisin Lake through gaps in the rocks. This warm lake is a great place for a swim after your long, hot climb. May Lake is not far away, but swimming there is prohibited. Beyond Raisin Lake, another short set of switchbacks takes you up past a meadow with an ephemeral pond, then meets the northeast end of May Lake and skirts its shore to the High Sierra Camp at 13.3 miles. The backpackers' camping area is beyond the camp at the lake's southern end. Mount Hoffman makes a great day hike if you have time because it is at the center of the park and offers a 360-degree sweep. There is no official trail to the top, but it is so frequently climbed that the way up is obvious.

From May Lake, follow the heavily traveled trail down to the May Lake trailhead at the end of a road at 14.5 miles. Cross the road, then descend through forest to cross Tioga Road at 15.9 miles. There is a complicated set of junctions here, but it's easy to see where to go. Just head north toward Tenaya Lake to the Sunrise trailhead at 16 miles. (The topo shows a campground here, but it was dismantled years ago.)

A paved trail begins behind the Sunrise parking area on which you turn left (east). After the pavement ends you cross a sandy-bottomed creek draining Tenaya Lake, which you'll probably have to wade early in the year. The trail swings right

The High Sierra Camp Loop

Glen Aulin +
High Sierra
Camp

Tuolumne Falls

McGee
Lake

START

Soda
Springs

P

TUOLUMNE

120

MEADOWS

John Muir Trail

Tioga Road

Budd Creek

Elizabeth
Lake

May
Lake

May Lake
High Sierra
Camp

Cathedral
Lakes

Cathedral
Pass

Tenaya
Lake

Sunrise
Lakes

Nelson
Lake

Rafferty
Peak
11,110 ft. ▲

Evelyn
Lake

Sunrise High
Sierra Camp

Echo Creek

Fletcher Creek Trail

Vogelsang
High Sierra
Camp

Vogelsang
Peak
11,516 ft. ▲

Lewis Creek Trail

Bernice
Lake

Merced River

Merced
Lake

Merced Lake
High Sierra
Camp

Hypsometry
12,500

5500
Elevation in Feet

N

0 Kilometers 2

0 Miles 2

282,000 286,000 290,000 294,000

4,199,000

4,194,000

4,189,000

4,184,000

4,179,000

(south) just across the creek at 16 miles. A bit later, a trail leading back to Tuolumne Meadows Lodge goes off to the left. Your trail dips and rises now and then as it crosses several little streams, then it begins to climb the east slope above Tenaya Canyon. The switchbacking climb is relieved by views of Mount Hoffman and Tioga Road across the canyon.

At the crest of the ridge (18.5 miles) the trail splits. The right (south) fork leads back to Clouds Rest and Half Dome, the left (east) leads to Sunrise Lakes. For a spectacular view of Half Dome and Clouds Rest, climb the little knoll to the right of the junction just a few dozen feet off the trail. From the junction, follow the ridgeline for a short time, then drop into the bowl containing the first of the Sunrise Lakes, whose depth gives it a rich royal blue color. Climb out of the bowl and follow along its south rim. The second Sunrise Lake, only occasionally visible, lies below the trail to the north and offers better camping than the first one. The route crosses a smooth, round lump of classic exfoliating Yosemite granite to reach the uppermost, and largest, of the lakes. There are plenty of camping spaces along the north shore, but the area is showing signs of overuse. Continue up a moderate hill alongside a wildflower-lined creek to a wide, sandy saddle with scattered mountain hemlock and pine, where the jagged Clark Range defines the horizon to the south. The trail eases gently down to the backpackers' camp above and behind the High Sierra Camp. There is a toilet, piped water, and bear boxes.

Just downhill at 21.1 miles the trail meets a junction with the John Muir/Pacific Crest Trail. Turn left and follow the deeply worn ruts along the edge of the meadow to Sunrise High Sierra Camp. You can sometimes buy a shower at this camp, but you'll need your own towel. From the High Sierra Camp, head north on the John Muir Trail to a junction at 22 miles. Turn right (east), cross the stream and the meadow, and climb to the Cathedral Fork of Echo Creek. The trail swings south and descends, crossing a couple of tributaries of the Cathedral Fork, to meet the main branch, which you cross on a bridge to the south side, then back to the northeast side again on a second bridge. There are great views up the Merced River canyon from here.

In about a half mile, meet a cutoff back to the John Muir Trail to the west at 28.1 miles. Continue ahead (south) to reach the Merced Lake Trail in Echo Valley, at 28.9 miles. There is space for camping here, but the area has been burned more than once and is not very attractive. Turn left (east). Just past the junction, cross several little branches of Echo Creek yet again and follow the Merced River upstream along its north shore. Pass through a gate to arrive at Merced Lake, whose edge you skirt very closely, pass the marshy meadow at the lake's upper end, then meet the spur to the High Sierra Camp at 31 miles. The backpackers' camp is just beyond.

Now on your way to Vogelsang, walk east through lodgepole and fir forest, crossing several little creeks on footbridges. At 31.3 miles, the Merced Lake Ranger Station and corral appear on the right. Turn left (north) at the junction here, and switchback steeply up above Lewis Creek to meet the Fletcher Creek Trail at 32.3

miles. There are good views up the Fletcher Creek drainage and back down to Merced Lake.

You have two choices of routes to Vogelsang from this point. The Fletcher Creek Trail passes to the west of Vogelsang Peak and is shorter by about a mile. The Lewis Creek Trail passes to the east and is the one described here because though it is longer, it is much more scenic and less frequently used. Following the right fork, you pass the turnoff to the Isberg Pass Trail at 33.3 miles. Continue northeast past the confluence with Florence Creek with its beautiful little waterfall, past the turnoff to Bernice Lake at 36.3 miles, and toil up the open rocky grade to Vogelsang Pass, the highest point on the loop at almost 11,000 feet (37.7 miles). The view back down Lewis Creek is spectacular, with the entire Clark Range spread out to the south. Across the drainage, lonely Gallison and Bernice Lakes nestle in their barren cirques. Round a corner at the top of the pass, skirt some tiny ponds, then descend the bouldery slope to Vogelsang Lake at the base of Vogelsang Peak, where fat marmot sentries watch and whistle alarm calls from nearby rocks. Cross the lake's outlet on logs and wind down the partly rocky, partly muddy slope toward the huddle of white tents of the High Sierra Camp below. The outlet stream just behind the camp comes from unseen Fletcher Lake around the corner; cross it on a log and make your way around to the front of the camp at a junction at 39 miles. The backpackers' camping area with toilets and bear boxes is on the north side of Fletcher Lake, east of the High Sierra Camp.

When you are ready to return to Tuolumne Meadows, find the signed junction in front of the High Sierra Camp and descend north, then northeast, gently down the ridge above Boothe Lake to Tuolumne Pass, where you will find another junction at 39.8 miles. Turn right and continue gently downhill along Rafferty Creek for a long stretch, sometimes through forest, sometimes along the edge of the meadow. Toward the end, the descent steepens and at last switchbacks down to a junction with the John Muir Trail at 45.3 miles. Keep left to mile 45.9 where your trail turns right. The other fork goes into the back of the Tuolumne Meadows Campground. In a few dozen yards, cross the twin bridges over Lyell Fork of the Tuolumne River and enjoy one of the most sublime vistas in all of Yosemite southward up the canyon. Now just follow the signs through the forest to the Tuolumne

Meadows Lodge/High Sierra Camp at mile 46.6. From here you can walk the spur road back to Tioga Road and follow that westward back to your car near Lembert Dome.

Miles and Directions

0.0 Glen Aulin Trailhead.

0.5 Soda Springs.

0.6 Parsons Lodge, turn right, then left.

1.2 Ford Delaney Creek.

1.6 Young Lakes cutoff, keep left.

3.5 Cross bridges over the Tuolumne River.

5.0 May Lake and McGee Lake Trail junction, turn right.

5.2 Glen Aulin High Sierra Camp.

5.4 Return to May Lake/McGee Lake junction, turn right.

9.6 Murphy Creek Trail, keep right.

10.0 May Lake junction; turn left (south).

13.3 May Lake High Sierra Camp.

14.5 Cross May Lake trailhead road.

15.9 Cross Tioga Road, turn left.

16.0 Sunrise Trailhead.

18.5 Clouds Rest/Sunrise Lakes junction, turn left.

21.1 Sunrise High Sierra Camp and John Muir Trail junction. Turn left.

22.0 Cathedral Pass Trail junction. Turn right, leaving John Muir Trail.

28.1 Cutoff back to the John Muir Trail.

28.9 Echo Valley, turn left (east).

31.0 Merced Lake High Sierra Camp.

31.3 Merced Lake Ranger Station, turn left.

32.3 Fletcher Creek Trail junction, turn right.

33.3 Isberg Pass Trail cutoff.

36.3 Bernice Lake cutoff.

37.7 Vogelsang Pass.

39.0 Vogelsang High Sierra Camp.

39.8 Boothe Lake junction, turn right.

45.3 Rejoin John Muir Trail, keep left.

45.9 Tuolumne Meadows High Sierra Camp cutoff, turn right.

46.6 Tuolumne Meadows High Sierra Camp.

47.6 Glen Aulin Trailhead.

The Southern Park

The trails into the southern park begin from Wawona, Glacier Point Road, or the short spur road off Highway 41 to the Mariposa Grove of Big Trees. Most trailheads start at around 4,000 feet, and offer hiking opportunities earlier in the season than in other parts of Yosemite. You'll find more solitude in this part of the park, too, because there is less water in high summer, the time when most people come to Yosemite. The crown of the southern park is Mount Clark, whose distinctive, narrow summit can be seen from many miles away.

Many of the southern trails begin near Wawona, the site of a historical overnight stage stop on the way to Yosemite Valley. The beautiful old Wawona Hotel, built in the 1870s, is still in operation. You can visit the Pioneer Yosemite History Center to learn about the early days of Yosemite, or even play a round of golf. There is a campground, gas station, gift shop, grocery store, and stables. Wawona is about 4 miles inside the park from the Highway 41 entrance to Yosemite. Just past "town," a new bridge crosses the Merced River, and just past that is Chilnualna Fall Road on the right. Many of the trailheads out of Wawona are off this road, all are clearly marked, and all have parking areas and bear boxes. The road ends just past North Wawona, a little settlement with a store and a few cottages for rent. It is part of an inholding (private property surrounded by a national park). You can get information and wilderness permits at the wilderness center located in Hill's Studio, right next door to the Wawona Hotel.

Another approach to the southern park is by way of Chiquito Pass in the Ansel Adams Wilderness, part of the Sierra National Forest, at the southeast corner of Yosemite. The drive to the trailhead is a long one, but the rewards are great. This is some of the finest hiking in Yosemite, classic glacial scenery, abundant water well into fall, and fewer people. You can get into this area from Wawona on a pleasant, but unspectacular two- or three-day trip, but the Chiquito Pass trailhead puts you into prime high country in only 2 miles.

Since the trailhead is outside of Yosemite, wilderness permits are issued by the Sierra National Forest. You can reserve a permit by mail or pick one up on a first-come, first-served basis from the wilderness office in Oakhurst. You can also get information about road conditions. Call the office at (559) 877–2218. Gas and supplies, restaurants and accommodations are available at the resort town of Bass Lake, 20 miles from the trailhead. There is camping nearby at both Upper and Lower Chiquito Campgrounds.

23 Mariposa Grove of Big Trees

The giant sequoias are the largest living things on earth and are among the oldest, living up to 3,000 years. The bristlecone pines in the White Mountains to the east are older, and the coast redwoods are taller, but these are certainly the most massive and arguably the most awe-inspiring. The Mariposa Grove, the largest of three in Yosemite, is divided into upper and lower groves. A veritable maze of trails, all well marked, runs through both, so you can easily design your own hike to be longer or shorter than the one described here. This hike takes you past all the highlights of both groves with a minimum amount of backtracking. Trails are marked by a series of interpretive panels with fascinating bits of information about the trees and their habitat.

Start: Trailhead at the northeast corner of the parking lot.
Distance: 5.9-mile double loop.
Approximate hiking time: 2 hours to all day.
Difficulty: Moderate, but only because there are some relatively steep ups and downs.
Seasons: Spring, summer, and fall, whenever the road is open.

Nearest facilities: Restrooms, water, snacks, and a gift shop at the parking lot where the tram tours begin; pit toilets are at the museum and along trails.
Permits: None.
Maps: USGS Mariposa Grove quad; "Mariposa Grove of Giant Sequoias Guide and Map" by Jon Kinney, at the trailhead, 50 cents.

Finding the trailhead: From the entrance station to Yosemite on Wawona Road (Highway 41), head right (east) for 2 miles to the Mariposa Grove. There is limited parking at the trailhead, so it is suggested that you park at the lot across the street from the entrance station or in front of the store at Wawona and take the free shuttle bus to the grove. The buses run every twenty minutes. Open-air tram tours are available too. They take about an hour and cost $11.50. The trailhead is marked by a sign at the northeast end of the parking lot.
Special considerations: Do not expect a wilderness experience here. The gift shop at the parking lot and the row of tour buses will tell you that. Years ago, visitors could drive their cars through the grove, but now only tram tours use the paved roads and snatches of the drivers' patter sometimes intrude. Still, the sense of reverence you get in the presence of these giants is an experience not to be missed just because it must be shared with others. Besides, if you get to the grove by 8:00 A.M., you can have the place to yourself.

The Hike

From the busy parking lot, follow the signed trail eastward across the tram road to the Fallen Monarch at mile 0.1, a sequoia made famous by old photos of a group of U.S. Cavalry—on their horses—lined up on top of it. Follow the trail past a beautiful grouping of trees called The Bachelor and the Three Graces at 0.3 mile, then climb to the massive, beheaded Grizzly Giant at 0.8 mile, said to be the largest tree in the grove. Walk around to the far side of the Grizzly Giant and follow the path 0.1 mile downhill to the California Tunnel Tree. The tunnel was cut in 1895 for

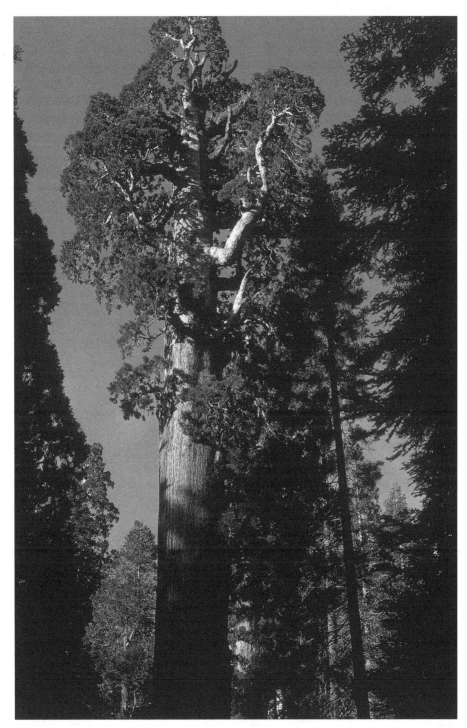

The Grizzly Giant is the largest of the sequoias in the Mariposa Grove.

Mariposa Grove of Big Trees

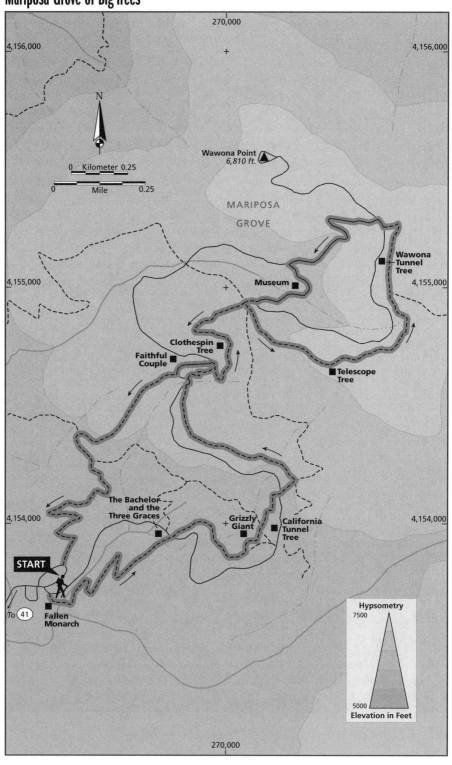

4,156,000 · 270,000 · 4,156,000

N

0 Kilometer 0.25

0 Mile 0.25

Wawona Point
6,810 ft.

MARIPOSA

GROVE

Wawona
Tunnel
Tree

Museum

4,155,000 · 4,155,000

Clothespin
Tree

Faithful
Couple

Telescope
Tree

The Bachelor
and the
Three Graces

Grizzly
Giant

California
Tunnel
Tree

4,154,000 · 4,154,000

START

To 41

Fallen
Monarch

Hypsometry
7500

5000
Elevation in Feet

270,000

stagecoaches full of tourists to pass through. Some things never change. Go through the Tunnel Tree and continue uphill northwest to the Faithful Couple at 1.6 miles, two trees that have grown so closely together that they appear to be one at the base. Cross the tram road to reach the aptly named Clothespin Tree and, at 2 miles, reach a confusing four-way trail junction near the tour bus road. Just follow the signs there to the museum at 2.2 miles, in a lovely little meadow with a nature trail through it. The museum has exhibits and books about the trees, a knowledgeable volunteer to answer questions, a water fountain, and restrooms nearby.

From the museum, head south, following the signs again to the Telescope Tree at 2.7 miles. It's off the trail a few yards to the right. Don't miss the experience of standing inside and gazing up and out the top of a still living tree.

In the upper grove the crowds will have thinned, and the still, solemn dignity of the forest begins to settle over you . . . unless you are joined by a chattering, scolding chickaree or Douglas squirrel (not to be confused with the chickadee, a small bird that also resides here). Chickarees are among the most entertaining creatures of sequoia and fir forests, lively, quick, and very vocal. Their backs are gray-brown, their undersides buffy white. A black racing stripe running horizontally along the body separates top from bottom. They play an important role in giant sequoia reproduction.

At 3.1 miles look downhill to the left to spot the fallen Wawona Tunnel Tree. This is the highest point on the hike at 6,600 feet. There's not much to see now, but from 1881 when the tunnel was cut through the standing Big Tree, this was one of the most popular tourist attractions in California. In 1969 a heavy snowfall finally toppled it. Continue downhill and counterclockwise back to the museum at 3.6 miles, then follow the signs back to the parking lot.

Options: Wawona Point Vista

From the museum or the fallen Wawona Tunnel Tree, it's only 1 mile more (round-trip) and 200 feet of climbing to the ridgetop at 6,800 feet for a bird's-eye view of the whole Wawona area, with the Merced River snaking through the middle.

Wawona–Mariposa Grove Trail

This one takes you to (or from) the Mariposa Grove on foot. From the Grizzly Giant to the Wawona Hotel is 6.5 miles with an elevation change of 1,700 feet. It can be a long, hot, dusty, and smelly hike because the elevation is low and the lower section of the trail is used regularly by horses, but many hikers take the shuttle bus from Wawona up to the Mariposa Grove and walk this route back down.

In Addition

Making Baby Sequoias

You don't have to know anything at all about giant sequoia ecology to enjoy the sense of wonder derived from a stroll through one of these enchanted groves. Still, even a superficial study of the trees reveals one surprise after another, each one deepening your respect and admiration.

Despite their immense size and great age, they are dependent for their very existence on the unlikely aid of a beetle, a squirrel, and fire.

The average big tree might have 11,000 cones on it at any one time, with an average of 200 seeds per cone, adding up to 2.2 million seeds per tree. That ought to be enough to produce dozens of seedlings, but getting these seeds planted and germinated isn't easy and the trees can't do it without help. The cones and the seeds within them are very small. Unlike many other conifers, sequoias do not drop their cones from the tree when they are ripe, nor do the cones open while still on the tree, dropping their seeds to the ground. The seeds must get planted some other way.

Fortunately, Douglas squirrels, also called chickarees, love to eat the young green scales of big tree cones. They are territorial creatures whose loud, scolding chatter warns neighboring chickarees to stay away. They sometimes begin gnawing into the cone scales right on the branch where they are found, opening the cones and allowing the seeds to fall. (Sequoia seeds are so tiny that most animals do not seek them for food.) At other times, the chickarees cut down enormous numbers of cones, gather the pile from beneath the tree, and cache them away to eat later. They usually pick dark, damp storage places to keep the cones moist and fresh, but some do dry out and release the seeds into the soil.

A much less conspicuous animal, a small wood-boring beetle, does her bit for the giant sequoia by depositing her eggs in the seams where the bracts or scales of the cone fit together. When the babies hatch, they chew their way inside, frequently cutting the vessels that supply the cones with water and minerals. The scales dry out, shrink, and separate, and the seeds fall out.

Fire plays several roles in sequoia health and reproduction. Intense heat helps to dry the cones so that the seeds can be released, clears the ground beneath the trees of litter, and keeps the soil soft and light so the tiny seeds can germinate. The groves have obviously coexisted with fire for millennia. Almost every mature tree in the grove shows the scars of repeated burns. Their bark is extremely thick, lacks much flammable pitch, and is impregnated with fire-resistant tannins. Our misdirected efforts to protect the groves from fires over the past few decades have almost been their undoing. Until recently, when more information about the ecology of the giant sequoias became available, we had been carrying out an unintended program of big tree birth control.

24 Chilnualna Fall

Chilnualna Creek seldom flows slowly, but instead tumbles in cascades and waterfalls almost constantly for most of its length. The most spectacular sections and highest waterfalls are found at the beginning and end of the hike, and the trail has been built so that it comes closest to the river at the beginning and end. It's a steady uphill pull, but the grade is comfortable. This route would be much more heavily used if it were not tucked away in a little corner of Yosemite. The waterfall is as exciting as any in Yosemite Valley, but few tourists know about it.

Start: Chilnualna Fall Trailhead off Chilnualna Fall Road.
Distance: 8.2 miles out and back.
Approximate hiking time: 6 to 8 hours.
Difficulty: Moderate; it's short, but all uphill.
Seasons: Spring, early summer, and fall. Midsummer is hot. Fall is pleasant, but the waterfalls are disappointing.

Nearest facilities: Food, gas, and phones in North Wawona.
Permits: None required for a day hike; available in advance or at Wawona for overnights.
Maps: USGS Wawona and Mariposa Grove quads.

Finding the trailhead: Follow Chilnualna Fall Road from Wawona, through the little village of North Wawona for 2 miles to a signed parking lot on the right.
Special considerations: Watch for rattlesnakes in this low-elevation area, especially in the morning and evening hours. They are not aggressive, but they do not like to be handled or stepped on.

The Hike

Follow the trail signs from the parking lot and cross the paved road. Another sign there routes horse traffic to the left and foot traffic to the right. The footpath, much too rugged for horses, heads steeply up, sometimes on big granite stair-steps right beside the roaring water, then cuts away from the stream where the horse and foot trails rejoin in 0.2 mile at a big trail sign. Long, wide switchbacks make the northward climb almost painless. The forest floor is covered with a solid carpet of the white shrub called kit-kit-dizze under oak, pine, and incense cedar. At about a mile, the trail switchbacks to a point near the creek, then climbs out of reach of water until very near the end of the hike, except for little tributary streams that are reliable only in early season. Views of the sensuous rounded curve of Wawona Dome come and go. As you gain height, more of Chilnualna's upper fall comes into view behind clouds of rising mist. When the trail approaches the elevation of the falls, it rounds a ridge blasted out of the rock by dynamite and deposits the hiker right beside the thundering cataract. Brilliant magenta mountain pride penstemons line

Chilnualna Fall

cracks in the streamside rocks. From here you can see all the way back down to Wawona Meadow.

Climb a few more hot and brushy switchbacks until the trail emerges onto slabs of classic, scoured, exfoliating Yosemite granite and an even more dramatic section of the falls. The smooth rock near the water invites exploration, but move carefully—the rocks are slippery and it's a long way down. A sign at a trail junction tells you it is 5.6 miles back to Wawona, but that is the distance to the ranger station where the trailhead used to be, not to the one where you began. This is the end point of your day hike. Return the way you came.

Miles and Directions

0.0 Chilnualna Fall Trailhead. Keep right at horse/foot trail split.

0.2 Horse and foot trail rejoin, continue uphill.

1.0 Trail is nearest the creek.

4.1 Chilnualna Fall.

8.2 Return to trailhead.

Options: You can make Chilnualna Fall the first leg of a multiday, early season outing. From the signed fork of the trail at the falls, you can go left for another 8.9 miles to Bridalveil Creek Campground on Glacier Point Road, or turn right, following Chilnualna Creek for 7 miles, to Chilnualna Lakes on the Buena Vista Crest Loop. There are campsites in the forest above Chilnualna Fall within a half mile of the trail junction along both routes.

25 Buena Vista Crest

This area returns lots of rewards for little effort. Elevations are low so it is accessible when the higher country is still under snow, yet there is plenty of glacially sculpted scenery and lots of lakes, including Royal Arch Lake, one of the prettiest in the park. You can hike this lollipop-shaped loop in either direction, but the elevation gain is more gradual if you travel clockwise.

Start: Bridalveil Creek Campground Trailhead.
Distance: 28.2-mile lollipop loop.
Approximate hiking time: 3 to 6 days.
Difficulty: Easy.
Seasons: Early summer through fall, though many streams are dry by August.

Nearest facilities: North Wawona; snacks and phones at Glacier Point.
Permits: Required; available at the wilderness center in Wawona.
Maps: USGS Half Dome and Mariposa Grove quads.

Finding the trailhead: Drive up Glacier Point Road 9 miles to the Bridalveil Creek Campground turnoff on the right. Turn in and drive straight through the campground to its south end. Just as the road begins to curve left, signs on the right say CAMPFIRE CIRCLE and HORSE CAMP 0.2 MILE. The trailhead is just beyond the signs. Because parking space is somewhat cramped, the trailhead sign will probably be hidden behind parked cars.

Special considerations: This low-elevation country is at its finest before mid-July, when water sources become fewer and farther apart, and wildflowers are past their prime. To experience this region of Yosemite at its best, you need to be prepared for swampy meadows and dicey stream crossings. The trail is sometimes flooded in the Chilnualna Lakes basin, making route-finding tricky. Carry a map, extra dry socks, and insect repellent. The scenery is worth the wet feet.

The Hike

Begin walking in a southeasterly direction along Bridalveil Creek. Yellow metal signs high up in the lodgepole pines mark cross-country ski trails. The trail rambles through forests and meadows filled with wildflowers. At 1.4 miles, a side trail cuts back toward Glacier Point Road to connect with the Ostrander Lake Trail. This junction lies in a ghost forest of lodgepole pines that was burned in 1987, leaving ideal conditions for a spectacular wildflower display. Pass a packer campsite (arguably illegal; too near the stream and the trail), hop a branch of the creek, and at 2.2 miles, meet a second trail that angles back to the northwest to meet the Ostrander Lake Trail again. Your path crosses a couple of small streams that may be dry by midsummer, then climbs moderately up a slope under both white and red fir glowing with chartreuse lichens.

The way becomes steeper and warmer as the forest cover thins to brush, then opens up in a sunny ridgetop clearing carpeted in pastels: yellow sulfur-flower buckwheat, pink pussypaws, and blue Brewer lupine. Drop back down into forest, then slosh through a boggy meadow to reach another trail junction at 4.7 miles, where

Graceful arches of granite crown Royal Arch Lake.

the Deer Camp Trail takes off to the right (west). Continue south past Turner Meadow, waist-deep in corn lilies, to yet another trail junction at 6 miles, beyond which there is a good campsite. Continue along the left (southeast) fork until, at 6.7 miles, you reach the junction that marks the beginning of the loop part of the hike. Follow the trail sign left (east) toward Chilnualna and Buena Vista Lakes and climb along Chilnualna Creek until you reach the first of the lakes at 10.2 miles. There is plenty of good camping here. The lake is shallow, small, tranquil, and lovely in early season, but is rapidly silting in on its way to becoming a meadow. It loses much of its appeal by August, though by that time the blueberry bushes surrounding the lake are loaded with fruit.

Leaving the first lake, pass over a low rise, hop over the outlet of the second Chilnualna Lake, about a half mile off the trail to the east, then skirt the third lake, which offers some camping that may be swampy and mosquito-ridden early in the year. Sometimes sections of the trail become completely inundated, so you will have to consult your map and watch for tree blazes to stay on course. Climb up out of the lake basin along a rubbly granite slope where the foliage parts at the top to unveil a fabulous vista all the way to the Cathedral Range to the north. To the east, dramatic Mount Clark pulls the colorful Clark Range—Red Peak, Gray Peak, Merced Peak—behind it on a collision course with Half Dome and Mount Starr King. Here, at 11.9 miles, a trail heads northward toward Mono Meadow on Glacier Point Road, but your route continues straight ahead to Buena Vista Lake, sparkling in its glacial cirque at 12.2 miles. The highest point on the ridge above the lake is Buena Vista Peak (9,709 feet), an easy scramble. There is plenty of good camping here.

Buena Vista Crest

To Glacier Point

269,000 272,000 275,000 278,000

4,174,000

N

To Yosemite Valley

START

Glacier Point Road

YOSEMITE NATIONAL PARK

0   Kilometers   2

0   Miles   2

Bridalveil Creek Campground

Bridalveil Creek

4,170,000

4,174,000

4,170,000

Ostrander Lake

HORSE RIDGE

Buena Vista Creek

4,166,000

To Deer Camp

4,166,000

Buena Vista Lake

Turner Meadow

Chilnualna Creek

Chilnualna Lakes

Buena Vista Peak 9,709 ft.

4,162,000

4,162,000

Royal Arch Lake

Grouse Lake

Johnson Lake

Crescent Lake

To Buck Camp

To Chilnualna Fall

Hypsometry
10,000

4500
Elevation in Feet

4,158,000

SIERRA NATIONAL FOREST

4,158,000

269,000 272,000 275,000 278,000

Climb out of this lake basin, then to Buena Vista Pass—the highest point on this loop at 9,300 feet—then descend, first through flowery meadows, then over exfoliating granite slabs, and finally through forest. You'll emerge at the small but stunning Royal Arch Lake at 15 miles. Huge granite slabs have popped free and peeled away from the underlying rock like layers of onion, leaving graceful arches that frame the lake. There is limited camping at the south end of the lake. Be sure to camp at least 100 feet from the fragile lakeshore.

Proceeding downhill, the Buck Creek Trail cuts off to the left (east) at 15.7 miles. Your route turns right (west) and descends past grassy Johnson Lake. Crescent Lake, about a half mile farther, has better campsites—and blueberries! Rock-hop your way across Crescent Lake's outlet stream, cross a moraine dotted with red fir, pass Grouse Lake (hidden in the trees to your left), and continue down, down, down to a junction at 20.7 miles, where you turn right (north). The left fork leads back to Wawona via Chilnualna Fall. Very soon, at 21.5 miles, you rock-hop Chilnualna Creek to meet the junction closing the loop section of your hike. From here, retrace the "stick" portion of the lollipop back to the trailhead at Bridalveil Creek Campground.

Miles and Directions

0.0 Trailhead at Bridalveil Creek Campground.

1.4 Connector trail to Ostrander Lake Trail, continue straight ahead.

2.2 Second connector trail to Ostrander Lake Trail, continue straight ahead (south).

4.7 Deer Camp Trail junction, go straight.

6.0 Chilnualna Fall Trail junction, keep left.

6.7 Chilnualna Lakes junction, keep left. The loop part of the hike begins here.

10.2 First Chilnualna Lake.

11.9 Mono Meadow Trail junction, continue straight ahead.

12.2 Buena Vista Lake.

15.0 Royal Arch Lake.

15.7 Buck Creek Trail junction, keep right.

20.7 Wawona via Chilnualna Fall junction, turn right.

21.5 Chilnualna Lakes Trail junction, keep left. This closes the loop part of the hike.

28.2 Trailhead at Bridalveil Creek Campground.

26 Wawona Meadow

This is one of Yosemite's often-overlooked gems, especially for wildflower lovers, who will find some rare and unusual species blooming in early season. Except for an occasional group of equestrians, you'll have this little piece of the park mostly to yourself. The going is easy along a dirt road no longer used by vehicles, with almost no elevation change. The route is a loop, described in a counterclockwise direction, but you can go either way.

Start: Wawona Meadow Trailhead at a big signboard with photos and information about the area.
Distance: 3.5-mile loop.
Approximate hiking time: 1 hour if you jog, most of a day if you botanize.

Difficulty: Easy.
Seasons: May and June for wildflowers, though the trail is open all year.
Nearest facilities: Wawona.
Permits: None.
Map: USGS Wawona quad.

Finding the trailhead: Drive to the little village of Wawona on the Wawona Road (Highway 41). The Wawona Hotel is on the north side of the road, the golf course is on the south. Just across from the hotel, a road cuts through the middle of the golf course to a parking area and trailhead marked with a big sign.

The Hike

Begin by skirting the south side of the golf course under a cover of incense cedar and ponderosa pine. Very soon the manicured lawn of the golf course is left behind and the real meadow begins. The road runs between forest and meadow for most of the way, and this border zone, known as the ecotone, is usually the richest in living organisms. You are almost guaranteed a cluster of mule deer. They are very tame, but do not attempt to pet or feed them. Deer account for more serious injuries in Yosemite than bears.

Now and then a little spur trail leads out into the meadow. It can be boggy and muddy toward the center and the vegetation is fragile, so step with care. Down among the grasses and sedges, look for little three-petaled white star tulips in May. The tall cabbagelike stalks growing in clumps are poisonous corn lily, sometimes confused with skunk cabbage. There are islands of willow and chokecherry, usually broadcasting birdsong selections from warblers and blackbirds.

On the shady forest floor watch for saprophytes (leafless, fleshy plants that live on decaying material in the soil) like the scarlet snow plant, the knobby brown spikes of pinedrops, and the odd little orchids, like coral root. You can even find

Damp and shady forest floor is home to this lady's slipper orchid.

Wawona Meadow

N

0 Kilometer 0.25   0.25

0   Mile   0.25

4,157,000

To
Fresno

Road

+

267,000

41

—

267,000

To
North
Wawona

266,000

Wawona

Wawona
Hotel

To Yosemite Valley

265,000

START

Chowchilla

Mountain   Road

Meadow

Circle

Road

Golf
Course

+

+

266,000

+

Hypsometry

8000

3500

Elevation in Feet

265,000

4,157,000

lady's slipper orchids in damp patches. In June great fragrant clumps of western azalea burst into bloom along with several kinds of lilies.

At 1.7 miles another trail coming down from the Mariposa Grove joins the road from the right alongside a little creek. Stay on the road and step across another little chokecherry-lined rivulet flowing around rock islands crowded with monkey-flowers. The road becomes partly eroded asphalt and runs through a section of forest in which the bases of the trees are slightly blackened from a management fire.

At 3.2 miles reach a closed gate, and just beyond it cross Wawona Road. The trail continues on to the Wawona Hotel where, at 3.4 miles, it crosses the road to the south side again and cuts back through the golf course to the trailhead.

Miles and Directions

0.0 Wawona Meadow Trailhead.

1.7 Creek crossing and trail junction, stay on the road.

3.2 Wawona Road, cross to the north side.

3.4 Wawona Road, cross back to the south side.

3.5 Wawona Meadow Trailhead.

27 Ostrander Lake

The stone hut at Ostrander Lake is a favorite winter destination for skiers. In summer there is good camping near the lakeside and lots of flowers along the way. The out-and-back trail is relatively flat at the beginning, undulates a bit in the middle, and leaves most of the serious elevation gain for the end.

Start: Ostrander Lake Trailhead off Glacier Point Road.
Distance: 12.4 miles out and back.
Approximate hiking time: 5 to 10 hours.
Difficulty: Strenuous as a day hike, moderate as a backpack.
Seasons: All summer, whenever the Glacier Point Road is open.

Nearest facilities: Wawona; snacks and phones at Glacier Point.
Permits: None for a day hike. Required for an overnight stay, available at Wawona or Yosemite Valley.
Maps: USGS Half Dome and Mariposa Grove quads.

Finding the trailhead: Drive up the Glacier Point Road about 9 miles from the Chinquapin turnoff on the Wawona Road (Highway 41) to a marked parking area on the right. It's about a mile past (east of) the turnoff to the Bridalveil Creek Campground.

The stone ski hut sits next to Ostrander Lake.

The Hike

The trail begins in a ghost forest of lodgepole pine, a good place to watch for brown creepers, mountain chickadees, and northern flickers (a kind of woodpecker) harvesting insects in the decaying wood. The forest was burned in 1987, opening the ground to sunshine and flowers. In the drier places grow yarrow, paintbrush, lupine, goldenrod, and tall purple fireweed in a riot of color; in the marshier areas are willow, lilies, yampah, and Bigelow sneezeweed—nature renewing itself in a flamboyant explosion of new life.

At 1.7 miles is a junction with a trail that cuts back to the right to join the Bridalveil Creek Campground Trail. Keep left and continue on through alternating sun and shade to a second fork, where in a little clearing another connector trail turns right again to join Bridalveil Creek in another place.

You'll probably notice that the mileage figures on the trail signs at this junction do not agree. Don't let it confuse you. The difference is slight and the route is the same. Past this point there is only an occasional burned snag among the flourishing white fir and ponderosa pine. This is fortunate for the hiker, because now the trail begins to climb. Traces of old asphalt appear underfoot, evidence that this used to be

Ostrander Lake

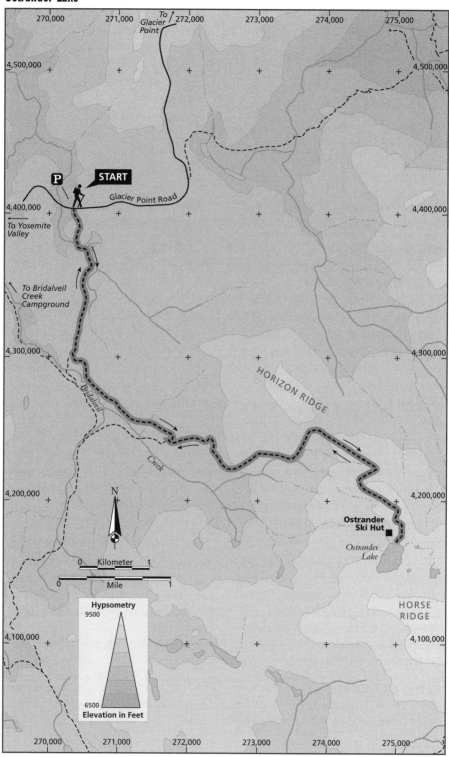

Hypsometry
9500

6500
Elevation in Feet

a road. The trail leaves the forest and passes over open rock slabs skirting the base of domelike Horizon Ridge among patches of low-growing manzanita and silvery sagebrush. Now it swings northward to a saddle, abruptly turns southeast to climb straight up a smooth, rounded hill, then makes one broad switchback before reaching the summit. A worn path on the left leads to a view of Half Dome and Mount Starr King, and behind the trees to the right, the Clark Range.

The main trail now descends through a pure stand of red fir and drops into the rocky basin containing Ostrander Lake at 6.2 miles. Horse Ridge, a wonderful example of exfoliating granite, bounds the lake on the south. Its overhanging brow makes it distinguishable from many miles away, even though it is not very high. The ski hut overlooks the lake on the north; campsites are found to the west. A sign on the hut warns winter visitors not to attempt to cross Horse Ridge due to avalanche danger. Enjoy lunch or set up camp, then return the way you came.

Miles and Directions

0.0 Ostrander Lake Trailhead.

1.7 First connector trail to Bridalveil Creek Campground; keep left.

2.3 Second connector trail to Bridalveil Creek Trail; keep left.

6.2 Ostrander ski hut.

12.4 Return to Ostrander Lake Trailhead.

28 Ottoway Lakes

This is the shortest route into the rugged and remote Clark Range. The first part of the hike is through a recent burn, but the dramatic setting of the colorful Ottoway Lakes basin more than makes up for the less interesting beginning. There's a good deal of climbing involved, but nothing extremely steep, unless you decide to make the optional side trip to Red Peak Pass.

Start: Mono Meadow Trailhead off the Glacier Point Road.
Distance: 30.4 miles out and back.
Approximate hiking time: 2 to 4 days.
Difficulty: Strenuous if you do it in 2 days, moderate if you take more time.
Seasons: July through September.

Nearest facilities: Wawona for most needs; snacks and phones at Glacier Point.
Permits: Required. Available in advance or from the wilderness centers in Wawona or Yosemite Valley.
Maps: USGS Half Dome and Merced Peak quads.

Finding the trailhead: From Wawona Road (Highway 41) drive 10 miles up the Glacier Point Road from Chinquapin. The trailhead, with ample parking, is on the right. (The trailhead sign is behind the parking area. It is not visible from the road.)

Explore the irregular shoreline of Lower Ottoway Lake.

The Hike

From the trailhead sign, drop down from the Glacier Point Road on a much-trampled soft dirt path into soggy Mono Meadow at 0.6 mile. The numerous creeklets through the meadow support a dense growth of tall wildflowers of all kinds and colors, sometimes thick enough to obscure the trail. Back in dense lodgepole forest, the trail crosses a tributary of Illilouette Creek. A log, slightly hidden in willows to the left, is the easiest way to the other side. A little later, after negotiating some fairly steep downhill switchbacks, arrive at a junction at 2.9 miles. The placement of the signs is confusing because there are two sets of them. Go straight past the first sign (toward Nevada Fall), and in just a few yards you'll see the second where you turn right (east) toward Ottoway Lakes and Merced Pass.

Plod through heavy sand over open ground beneath a series of bare rounded domes, the largest of which is Mount Starr King. Reenter what used to be Jeffrey pine forest, bleak and fire-blackened now. The trail draws nearer and nearer to the south bank of Illilouette Creek. When you are near enough to the stream to spot the trampled barren dirt below the trail where people have camped too near the water,

Ottoway Lakes; The Clark Range and Red Peak Pass

stay alert for a line of small boulders/big rocks across the trail that indicate the ford. Pause to pick out the place where the trail resumes on the other side, between cut logs, before you start across. It's hard to find if you cross at a different place. The creek is wide and deep enough to go over your boot tops for most of the year, though sometimes you can find a log or rock crossing upstream by late summer. On the north side of the creek is a sandy flat and another junction at 3.1 miles. Turn right (east) toward Merced Pass. Head gradually upward passing yet a third cutoff to the left back toward Nevada Fall at mile 4.5.

The grade through the charred remains of forest is gradual and a bit tedious until you reach the Clark Fork of Illilouette Creek at mile 5.5, above what used to be a pretty waterfall. Nearby there are a couple of campsites among trees that escaped the fire. It may not be apparent from the ground, but a glance at your map shows how many streams draining the Clark Range flow together to swell the main branch of Illilouette Creek. One of these feeder streams is Red Creek, which you cross just a few hundred yards beyond the Clark Fork. Now climb steadily alongside the northern bank of Illilouette Creek, hopping or wading several more tributary streams. None are deep enough to pose any problem in crossing, but they do inundate the trail in early season.

At 12.1 miles reach the Merced Pass junction. The right fork leads to timbered Merced Pass and on to Fernandez Pass on the eastern boundary of the park. Follow the left fork toward Ottoway Lakes. This junction lies between Upper and Lower Merced Pass Lakes, neither of which is visible from the trail. The lower lake is down in a bowl to the west of the junction. The upper one is more scenic and has some camping. Follow an unmarked trail to the east about midway between the Merced Pass and Ottoway Lake trails for a few hundred yards to find it.

As you draw nearer to Ottoway Lakes, more of the red metamorphic rock of parts of the Clark Range comes into view. Finally, at 15.2 miles, Lower Ottoway Lake appears right at the contact between the younger gray granite and the ancient red slate. The setting of this lake is stunning with the sharp point of Merced Peak behind the cascading creek connecting the upper and lower lakes. The irregular rocky shoreline of the lake has dozens of little bays and inlets trimmed with white Labrador tea and red mountain heather that invite many hours of exploration. There are several small campsites among the rocks and whitebark pines at the west side of the lake near the outlet.

If you plan to continue on up to or over Red Peak Pass, Lower Ottoway Lake is the last timber for many miles. If a thunderstorm is brewing, wait it out here. If this is your final destination, return the way you came.

Miles and Directions

0.0 Mono Meadow Trailhead.

0.6 Mono Meadow.

2.9 Double junction; at the first sign go straight toward Nevada Fall, at the second sign turn right toward Ottoway Lakes.

3.1 Junction north of Illilouette Creek, turn right.

4.5 Another Nevada Fall junction, keep right.

5.5 Clark Fork crossing.

12.1 Merced Pass Trail junction, turn left.

15.2 Lower Ottoway Lake.

30.4 Return to Mono Meadow Trailhead.

Option: Red Peak Pass

For an additional 2.9 miles (one way) and 1,600 feet elevation gain, you earn one of the most superb sights in Yosemite. From Red Peak Pass at 11,200 feet, you can look out over a vast bowl of multicolored rock dotted with lakes in blues ranging from turquoise to lapis lazuli, beyond which lie the park's biggest mountains, including 13,114-foot Mount Lyell. To get there from Lower Ottoway Lake, follow the path that skirts the northwestern shore, then works its way up the north side of the cirque to a point above bleak and beautiful Upper Ottoway Lake and another unnamed tarn. The route then swings left and heads up a notch on switchbacks that become shorter and steeper as you reach the top. The pass is tucked into a narrow slot in the ridgeline that limits what you can see, so hike down the far side for just a few minutes more for the best views. The worn spot on the left at the top of the pass is the place where climbers leave the trail to bag Red Peak.

29 The Clark Range and Red Peak Pass

The distinctive, finlike shape of Mount Clark dominates southern Yosemite and is recognizable from high points all over the park. This multiday backpack circumnavigates the mountain, crossing the Clark Range at Red Peak Pass. The scenery is unrivaled in beauty and variety, a treat for the eye and the mind: colorful metamorphic rocks, dozens of lakes and waterfalls, broad vistas of neighboring ranges, and wildflowers galore. It's also less crowded, at least after the first day of hiking, than most other parts of Yosemite. The route described here begins and ends at Happy Isles in Yosemite Valley, but you can begin and end at any one of several points, including Glacier Point and Mono Meadow. If wilderness permits are not available for one trailhead, you can try another.

See map on page 136

Start: The John Muir Trailhead at Happy Isles.
Distance: 50.6-mile loop.
Approximate hiking time: 4 to 8 days.
Difficulty: Strenuous.
Seasons: July through September.
Nearest facilities: Almost anything you need in Yosemite Valley, but remember there is no gas in the valley.
Permits: Required. Available in advance or from the wilderness center in Yosemite Valley.
Maps: USGS Half Dome, Merced Peak, and Mount Lyell quads.

Finding the trailhead: Park in the backpackers' parking lot next to Curry Village and follow the well-marked path to Happy Isles, or ride the Yosemite Valley shuttle bus from anyplace in the valley and get off at Stop 16/Happy Isles.
Special considerations: Check with the park service about trail conditions before starting out since Red Peak Pass is frequently buried under snow until late in the season, and stream crossings are dangerous at high runoff times.

The Hike

From the big sign marking the beginning of the John Muir Trail, join the throngs of tourists ascending the eroded asphalt path through black oak and ponderosa pine forest among enormous lichen-draped boulders. In about a half mile, across the thundering Merced to your right, watch for 370-foot Illilouette Fall tucked back into a deep cut in the Panorama Cliff. The trail steepens briefly, then suddenly descends to the Vernal Fall Bridge at mile 0.8. Upstream, Vernal Fall drops 317 feet over the lowest step of the Giant Staircase.

Cross the bridge to the south side of the river and turn left (upstream) passing a lateral trail on the right that leads back to the stables. Just beyond, at mile 0.9, meet the Mist Trail, an alternate route to the top of Nevada Fall, not recommended for backpackers since it is steep, slippery, and wet. Stay on the John Muir Trail, which switchbacks relentlessly uphill. There are plenty of excuses to stop and rest on the

View Upper Ottoway Lake from Red Peak Pass.

way. Across the valley to the northwest is Upper Yosemite Fall. To the northeast across the river gorge, the rounded backside of Half Dome comes into view, along with Mount Broderick, Liberty Cap, and finally, 594-foot Nevada Fall. This heart-stopping view is finest at Clark Point (2.3 miles), where a lateral trail cuts over to the Mist Trail nearer to the river. Continue climbing, passing beneath a dripping rock overhang decorated with delicate hanging gardens of ferns, columbines, and monkeyflowers. At 3.3 miles the Panorama Trail leading back to Glacier Point joins this one from the right (south). The trail drops a bit, hops a couple of little rivulets, then emerges into a wide, sunny expanse of smooth granite at the top of Nevada Fall. Here, at 3.5 miles, a footbridge crosses the river. Stay behind the protective railings; hikers ignore the warning signs and are washed over the falls with depressing regularity. This is a perfect place for lunch or a snack, but please do not share your food with the panhandling squirrels and jays.

Cross the footbridge back over the river and follow its north shore to a junction at 3.8 miles with the upper end of the Mist Trail, just beyond an outhouse. Continue upstream, climbing the heavily used trail over inlaid cobbles. The path soon levels out and passes from sunlight into shade, and the Merced changes from a rushing, raging torrent to become quiet, dark, and deep.

At 4.3 miles your trail parts company with the John Muir Trail, which heads off to the left (east) toward Half Dome. After slogging through heavy sand for a half mile, another lateral trail at 4.8 miles takes off to the left to join the John Muir and Half Dome Trails. Just ahead is Little Yosemite Valley, your first camping opportunity (and your last for the next 2 miles, where camping is prohibited.) It's a busy and popular place, especially for bears. You should be carrying a bear canister, but there are also lots of bear-proof boxes at the campground, along with an elegant, two-story solar composting toilet. The park service has constructed two communal fire rings for campers to share. Do not scar this already overused area by building another one.

Beyond Little Yosemite Valley the trail continues through level forest. In a little more than a mile, beneath Moraine Dome, the steep granite walls close in, pinching the valley shut, forcing the river to pick up speed and vigor. It cascades noisily for a short time before slowing and widening out once again through Lost Valley, blackened by a recent fire. Climb out of the valley, passing under the enormous dome of Bunnell Point on the right, where the river pours down the long slippery slide of Bunnell Cascade and is finally crossed on a bridge to the south side. Climb switchbacks blasted out of the granite, then pause to wipe away the sweat and enjoy the view of the river roaring through the spectacular gorge ahead.

Descend again to recross the river where you enter Echo Valley, another frequently burned area through which several creeks flow to join the Merced. At 11.4 miles, where Echo Creek comes in, a trail to Sunrise High Sierra Camp cuts off to the north. Soon the Merced begins to race beside the trail again as you climb the final mile to Merced Lake. There is a stock gate at the west end of the lake at 12.6 miles. Be sure to close it behind you. Skirt the lakeshore to reach the High Sierra Camp at the far end of the lake at 13.3 miles. The backpackers' camp is beyond the High Sierra Camp, where you can buy emergency items and snacks during posted hours. There are bear boxes and toilets at the campground. Campers may use the water tap at the High Sierra Camp to avoid purifying water, but are asked to use the toilets at the backpackers' campground.

The route continues east through lodgepole and fir forest, crossing several little creeks on footbridges. At 14.1 miles the Merced Lake Ranger Station, manned all summer, appears on the right. There is also a junction with the Lewis Creek Trail here. You keep right (southeast), climbing gradually at first, then more steeply, until you reach the west end of pretty Washburn Lake at 15.8 miles. Wade three tributary streams flowing into the lake from the north; the third of these is deep enough to go over your boot tops in early season. Past the lake, the trail rambles along the ever-changing river, now cascading from one pool to another, now sliding slowly through sensuous curves. Just beyond a packer campsite, complete with stump table and chairs, cross the river again on a pair of footbridges. The trail begins to climb in earnest now, passing perfect viewpoints for watching first the Lyell Fork, and later the Triple Peak Fork, tumble over the cliffs in spectacular waterfalls. Cross the Merced Peak Fork on yet another footbridge and climb over steep, open rock to join the Triple Peak Fork above the falls. The climb tops out at about 8,800 feet before leveling off to wander through flowery meadows for several miles. Camping is marginal on your side of the river; there is not much level ground and it's often marshy. If the river is low enough to wade, however, there are plenty of good dry sites on the other side.

At 24.2 miles, meet the Isberg/Red Peak Pass junction. Turn right (west), climbing at first moderately, then more steeply as you cross a ridge coming down from Triple Divide Peak. The timber becomes more scattered and stunted, and the trail becomes less distinct as you ascend. After a mile or so, you lose 200 feet of hard-won elevation gain as you drop into a lakelet-dotted bowl where it is possible to find a few small, sheltered campsites. As you climb out of the basin, you can see Red Devil Lake off the trail to the north. It's more heavily timbered than the topo indicates, and is the last place to camp before the pass. The skyline to the east becomes more spectacular with every step. In the center are the fairly regular twin peaks of Mount Maclure (left) and Mount Lyell (right), highest peak in the park. To the left of these, beyond Mounts Florence and Rogers, are Mounts Ritter and Banner and the Minarets. On a different scale, dozens of snowmelt rivulets at your feet nourish miniature gardens of alpine flowers.

At last, at mile 28.5, the trail makes a dogleg to the left, the switchbacks shorten and steepen, and you top Red Peak Pass, tucked between two blocky rock towers at 11,200 feet. Pause long enough to catch your breath and to marvel at the panorama of red and white rock, splattered with blue lakes, backed by the high peaks.

Descend steeply down the far side of the pass on sandy switchbacks, heading straight for Upper Ottoway Lake and its neighboring tarns, then swing right (west) on rougher, rockier footing, to reach the north shore of Lower Ottoway Lake. There is little opportunity for camping until you reach the western edge of the lake near its outlet at mile 31.4. The elevation here is 9,700 feet, so fires are not allowed. Campsites are small and bouldery, but the setting is stunning. Merced Peak presides over the lake at the head of its sheltering cirque. The shoreline is dotted with graceful mountain hemlocks and whitebark pines, white Labrador tea, and carpets of red mountain heather, and has lots of interesting bays and inlets that invite exploration and swimming.

From the lake, the trail descends along the north side of the outlet stream, crossing it at mile 32. The route drops through mostly mixed forest, but at times crosses slabs of granite, crisscrossed with white dikes and blotched with chunks of darker material. The forest floor between the rocks is often soggy since snow lingers late in the year in this shady notch. At mile 34.5, meet the Merced Pass Trail junction. The left fork leads to timbered Merced Pass and on to Fernandez Pass on the eastern boundary of the park. The junction lies between Upper and Lower Merced Pass Lakes, though neither is visible from the trail. The lower lake is down in a bowl to the west of the junction. The upper one is more scenic and has some camping. To find it, follow an unmarked trail located about midway between the Merced Pass and Ottoway Lake trails to the east for a few hundred yards.

From the junction descend to the right (northwest). The trail drops to pick up Illilouette Creek at mile 35.5 where the first of a number of tributaries join the main stream. None are deep enough to pose any problem in crossing but they do inundate the trail in early season. Keep an eye on tree blazes to stay on track. Soon the trail crosses to the north side of Illilouette Creek and descends through forest that changes from lodgepole pine, silver pine, and red fir, to Jeffrey pine, white fir, and incense cedar. The open rocky spots host gnarled junipers.

Illilouette Creek continues to splash down through a flower-lined gulch to your left, but in a couple of miles the hillside loses most of its former charm. A recent fire has denuded the valley for several miles, leaving nothing but black stumps. At mile 40.1, the trail crosses Red Creek, then the Clark Fork of Illilouette Creek, where there is a campsite sheltered by unburned trees just before the crossing. The trail then climbs a rise toward the base of Mount Starr King to meet a signed junction at mile 42 with the Nevada Falls Trail. Turn right here, continue around the ridge above Illilouette Creek, through brush, over open rock, and through burned forest, to meet the Panorama Trail at 45.6 miles. Keep right and follow switchbacks down to meet the John Muir Trail at mile 46.7. Turn left and retrace your steps back to Happy Isles at 50.6 miles.

Miles and Directions

0.0 Happy Isles.

0.8 Vernal Fall Bridge, turn left, upstream.

0.9 Mist Trail.

2.3 Clark Point.

3.3 Panorama Trail junction.

3.5 Footbridge at Nevada Fall, turn left and cross bridge.

3.8 Upper end Mist Trail, keep right.

4.3	John Muir/Half Dome Trail junction, keep right, leaving the John Muir Trail.
4.8	Second John Muir Trail junction at Little Yosemite Valley.
11.4	Echo Valley, keep right at the Sunrise Trail junction.
13.3	Merced Lake High Sierra Camp.
14.1	Merced Lake Ranger Station/Lewis Creek Trail junction, keep right.
15.8	Washburn Lake.
24.2	Isberg/Red Peak Pass junction, turn right.
28.5	Red Peak Pass.
31.4	Lower Ottoway Lake outlet.
34.5	Merced Pass Trail junction, keep right.
35.5	Meet Illilouette Creek.
40.1	Cross Clark Fork.
42.0	Nevada Fall Trail, turn right.
45.6	Panorama Trail, turn right.
46.7	John Muir Trail, turn left.
50.6	Happy Isles Trailhead.

30 Merced River High Trail

This extended backpack route is one of Yosemite's best-kept secrets. There is lots of trail traffic between Yosemite Valley and Merced Lake, but not much beyond. A few hikers go on to Red Peak Fork, then head south over Red Peak Pass, but very few turn north. Those who do are rewarded with mountain scenery of indescribable beauty, as well as an experience of the Merced River from a perspective you can't get anywhere else. You can trace the river's course from the snowfields of the Clark Range and the lake-dotted country at its base, where countless tributary streams originate, then watch the smaller streams merge to become bigger ones that fling themselves over the cliffs of the Merced River gorge in dozens of waterfalls. From here, the river rushes toward the Giant Staircase where it plunges over Vernal and Nevada Falls into Yosemite Valley. Another advantage to this loop is that because it is lower in elevation than the route south over Red Peak Pass, you can get into the backcountry earlier in the season while the higher passes are still under snow.

Start: Happy Isles Trailhead.
Distance: 51.5-mile lollipop loop.
Approximate hiking time: 4 to 8 days.
Difficulty: Moderate if you take your time, strenuous if you hurry.
Seasons: July through September.

Nearest facilities: Everything you need (except gas) in Yosemite Valley.
Permits: Available in advance or from the wilderness center in Yosemite Valley.
Maps: USGS Half Dome, Merced Peak, Mount Lyell quads.

The Merced River rushes through its dramatic gorge of polished granite above Little Yosemite Valley.

Finding the trailhead: Park in the backpackers' parking lot next to Curry Village and follow the well-marked path to Happy Isles, or ride the Yosemite Valley shuttle bus from anyplace in the valley and get off at Stop 16/Happy Isles.

The Hike

From the big sign marking the beginning of the John Muir Trail, join the throngs of tourists ascending the eroded asphalt path through black oak and ponderosa pine forest among enormous lichen-draped boulders. In about a half mile, across the thundering Merced to your right, watch for 370-foot Illilouette Fall tucked back into a deep cut in the Panorama Cliff. The trail steepens briefly, then suddenly descends to the Vernal Fall Bridge at mile 0.8. Upstream, Vernal Fall drops 317 feet over the lowest step of the Giant Staircase.

Cross the bridge to the south side of the river and turn left (upstream) passing a lateral trail on the right that leads back to the stables. Just beyond at mile 0.9, meet the Mist Trail, an alternate route to the top of Nevada Fall, not recommended for backpackers since it is steep, slippery, and wet. Stay on the John Muir Trail, which

Merced River High Trail

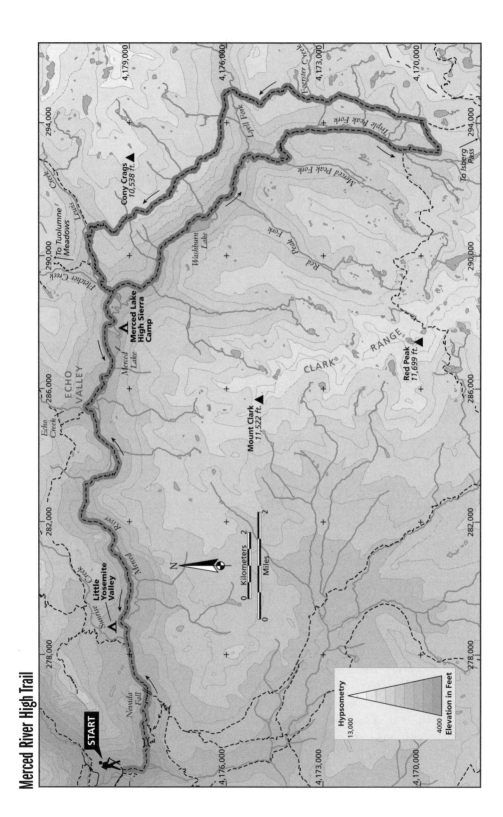

switchbacks relentlessly uphill. There are plenty of excuses to stop and rest on the way. Across the valley to the northwest is Upper Yosemite Fall. To the northeast across the river gorge, the rounded backside of Half Dome comes into view along with Mount Broderick, Liberty Cap, and finally, 594-foot Nevada Fall. This heart-stopping view is finest at Clark Point (2.3 miles), where a lateral trail cuts over to the Mist Trail nearer to the river. Continue climbing, passing beneath a dripping rock overhang decorated with delicate hanging gardens of ferns, columbines, and monkeyflowers. At 3.3 miles the Panorama Trail leading back to Glacier Point joins this one from the right (south). The trail drops a bit, hops a couple of little rivulets, then emerges into a wide, sunny expanse of smooth granite at the top of Nevada Fall. Here, at 3.5 miles, a footbridge crosses the river. Stay behind the protective railings; hikers ignore the warning signs and are washed over the falls with depressing regularity. This is a perfect place for lunch or a snack, but please do not share your food with the panhandling squirrels and jays.

Cross the footbridge back over the river and follow its north shore to a junction at 3.8 miles with the upper end of the Mist Trail, just beyond an outhouse. Continue upstream, climbing the heavily used trail over inlaid cobbles. The path soon levels out and passes from sunlight into shade, and the Merced changes from a rushing, raging torrent to become quiet, dark, and deep.

At 4.3 miles your trail parts company with the John Muir Trail, which heads off to the left (east) toward Half Dome. After slogging through heavy sand for a half mile, another lateral trail at 4.8 miles takes off to the left to join the John Muir and Half Dome Trails. Just ahead is Little Yosemite Valley, your first camping opportunity (and your last for the next 2 miles, where camping is prohibited). It's a busy and popular place, especially for bears. You should be carrying a bear canister, but there are also lots of bear-proof boxes at the campground, along with an elegant, two-story solar composting toilet. The park service has constructed two communal fire rings for campers to share. Do not scar this already overused area by building another one.

Beyond Little Yosemite Valley the trail continues through level forest. In a little more than a mile, beneath Moraine Dome, the steep granite walls close in, pinching the valley shut, forcing the river to pick up speed and vigor. It cascades noisily for a short time before slowing and widening out once again through Lost Valley, blackened by a recent fire. Climb out of the valley, passing under the enormous dome of Bunnell Point on the right, where the river pours down the long slippery slide of Bunnell Cascade and is finally crossed on a bridge to the south side. Climb switchbacks blasted out of the granite, then pause to wipe away the sweat and enjoy the view of the river roaring through the spectacular gorge ahead.

Descend again to recross the river where you enter Echo Valley, another frequently burned area through which several creeks flow to join the Merced. At 11.4 miles, where Echo Creek comes in, a trail to Sunrise High Sierra Camp cuts off to the north. Soon the Merced begins to race beside the trail again as you climb the final mile to Merced Lake. There is a stock gate at the west end of the lake at 12.6

miles. Be sure to close it behind you. Skirt the lakeshore to reach the High Sierra Camp at the far end of the lake at 13.3 miles. The backpackers' camp is beyond the High Sierra Camp, where you can buy emergency items and snacks during posted hours. There are bear boxes and toilets at the campground. Campers may use the water tap at the High Sierra Camp to avoid purifying water, but are asked to use the toilets at the backpackers' campground.

The route continues east through lodgepole and fir forest, crossing several little creeks on footbridges. At 14.1 miles the Merced Lake Ranger Station, manned all summer, appears on the right. There is also a junction with the Lewis Creek Trail here. You keep right (southeast), climbing gradually at first, then more steeply, until you reach the west end of pretty Washburn Lake at 15.8 miles. Wade three tributary streams flowing into the lake from the north; the third of these is deep enough to go over your boot tops in early season. Past the lake, the trail rambles along the ever-changing river, now cascading from one pool to another, now sliding slowly through sensuous curves. Just beyond a packer campsite, complete with stump table and chairs, cross the river again on a pair of footbridges. The trail begins to climb in earnest now, passing perfect viewpoints for watching first the Lyell Fork, and later the Triple Peak Fork, tumble over the cliffs in spectacular waterfalls. Cross the Merced Peak Fork on yet another footbridge and climb over steep, open rock to join the Triple Peak Fork above the falls. The climb tops out at about 8,800 feet before leveling off to wander through flowery meadows for several miles. Camping is marginal on your side of the river; there is not much level ground and it's often marshy. If the river is low enough to wade, however, there are plenty of good dry sites on the other side. At 24.2 miles, meet the Isberg/Red Peak Pass junction. The right fork takes you into the Clark Range.

Your route follows the left fork. Immediately rock-hop or wade the river, then plod steadily upward, first toward the south, then northeast, following a giant switchback. At 25.4 miles, reach another trail junction where you turn left (north). The right fork leads to Isberg Pass at the border of the park. You are now on the High Trail. At first it dips and climbs along the east side of the ridge with only a few frustrating glimpses of the open, lake-filled country to the east, but hold on to your hat! In about a mile, the vegetation thins and you cross to the west side of the crest where a stupendous panorama of the multicolored Clark Range unfolds, stretching from

Triple Divide Peak to Mount Clark. Far below the Merced River flows through the canyon, fed by dozens of cascades and waterfalls rushing down the slickrock on the opposite side. Your trail drops about 400 feet to cross Foerster Creek, climbs again, then passes a small pond and proceeds over fairly level ground. There are many excellent campsites between Foerster Creek and the pond, with flat sitting-rocks for comfortable sunset viewing. Shortly thereafter the trail tops out at 10,000 feet. Just beyond the crest another stunning view of the Merced River canyon and Washburn Lake opens out. Beyond lie the highest peaks in Yosemite, including Mount Lyell, highest in the park at 13,114 feet.

Now the trail plunges downward for almost 1,000 feet on steep switchbacks to meet and cross the Lyell Fork. This crossing can be dangerous in early season. The safest way across is on a big fallen log about 200 yards downstream. The climb back out of this canyon is fortunately more gradual than the trail into it.

The trail continues to follow the ridge, at one point passing through a broad crack in the cliff, occasionally affording more stunning views of the Clark Range. It dips to ford two forks of the stream that feeds Washburn Lake, climbs, then contours around the base of Cony Crags, a distinctively rugged rock outcrop, and at last drops steeply into the gorge cut by Lewis Creek. At 35.4 miles, a trail heads back northeast to Vogelsang; continue to descend to a second Vogelsang junction at 36.4 miles. Here your solitude ends. Just ahead lies Merced Lake High Sierra Camp. If you want one more night away from the crowds, detour about a quarter mile up the Fletcher Creek Trail to a well-developed campsite. Upon returning to the main trail, continue to descend on steep switchbacks until you reach the Merced Lake Ranger Station at a junction with the Merced Lake Trail at 37.4 miles, closing the lollipop loop. Return to Merced Lake and back to Happy Isles the same way you came.

Miles and Directions

- **0.0** Happy Isles.
- **0.8** Vernal Fall Bridge, turn left, upstream.
- **0.9** Mist Trail.
- **2.3** Clark Point.
- **3.3** Panorama Trail junction.
- **3.5** Footbridge at Nevada Fall, turn left and cross the bridge.
- **3.8** Upper end of Mist Trail, keep right.
- **4.3** John Muir/Half Dome Trail junction, keep right, leaving John Muir Trail.
- **4.8** High Trail junction at Little Yosemite Valley.
- **11.4** Echo Valley, keep right at the Sunrise Trail junction.
- **13.3** Merced Lake High Sierra Camp.
- **14.1** Merced Lake Ranger Station/Lewis Creek Trail junction, keep right.
- **15.8** Washburn Lake.
- **24.2** Isberg/Red Peak Pass junction, turn left, crossing the river.

25.4 High Trail junction, turn left.

35.4 Lewis Creek Trail to Vogelsang, keep left.

36.4 Second Vogelsang junction, keep left.

37.4 Merced Lake Trail at the ranger station, closing the loop. Turn right.

51.5 Happy Isles Trailhead.

Option: If you have a lot of time, you can take the High Trail back to the valley. That heads up, north out of Echo Valley to the Sunrise Trail, then west to meet the John Muir Trail. Follow it back to the valley. You are only retracing your steps for a short distance between the Merced Lake ranger station and Echo Valley, and again from Little Yosemite Valley to Happy Isles.

31 Chain Lakes

This is a perfect weekend hike into the classic glacial scenery that is the hallmark of Yosemite. The route takes you up a glacial moraine, then along a series of lakes gouged out by the flow of ice, over rock that displays fine examples of glacial polish and striations. There are wildflowers in profusion and trout in the lakes. This corner of the park is less well known because it's off the beaten path, and the drive to the trailhead is longer than most, but it's well worth your time. A possible bonus is that you might have better luck getting a permit to enter the park here than at some of the more familiar trailheads.

Start: Chiquito Pass Trailhead in the Sierra National Forest south of the park boundary.
Distance: 16 miles out and back.
Approximate hiking time: 8 to 12 hours.
Difficulty: Strenuous as a day hike, moderate as an overnight.
Seasons: Mid-June through September, whenever Beasore Road is open.
Nearest facilities: Bass Lake.
Permits: None required for a day hike; avail-able in person from the visitor information center on Highway 41 in Oakhurst or in advance by mail from the North Fork Ranger Station. Permits are free, but reservations cost $5.00 per person. There are quotas in place and reservations are recommended.
Map: USGS Sing Peak.
Trail contacts: Bass Lake Ranger District, Attn: Wilderness Permits, USFS 57003, Road 225, North Fork, CA 93643; (559) 877-2218.

Finding the trailhead: From Highway 41 just north of Oakhurst, turn right (southeast) on Road 222 toward Bass Lake. In 4 miles the road forks. Take the left (southeast) fork, Road 274, and drive 2 miles to another fork where you make a sharp turn to the left (north) on Forest Service Road 7, Beasore Road. Continue on Beasore Road for 20 miles up and over Cold Springs Saddle and back down again to FS Road 5S04, where you turn left (north). It's hard to miss this junction. Globe Rock, an enormous granite orb balancing on an alarmingly puny pedestal, perches just above the road on the right. Road 5S04 is unpaved, but well maintained. Follow it for 2.5 miles to a clearing at the top of a ridge to the signed Chiquito Pass Trailhead. There is no water at the trailhead.

Chain Lakes

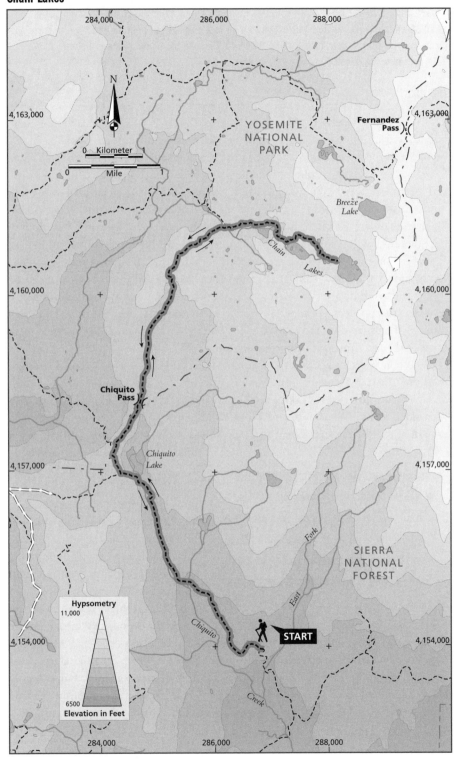

Special considerations: Since you are entering the park from forest service territory, get your permit from the forest service in Oakhurst, not in Yosemite. This is bear country, too, so carry a canister. There are no bear boxes at the trailhead. Dispose of all your garbage before you get there and hide ice chests.

The Hike

The sign at the trailhead tells you Chiquito Pass is 2 miles ahead, the Yosemite boundary 3 miles. (The USDA Forest Service rounds off mileage to whole numbers.) From the sign, head northeast through Jeffrey and lodgepole pines and white firs, climbing easily. At about 1 mile, the path crosses a tributary of Chiquito Creek and becomes steeper and rockier as it follows the main branch of the creek upstream. At mile 2.1 the way levels out and officially enters the Ansel Adams Wilderness, then resumes its ascent and levels out again through a section of boggy—and buggy—forest. Cross Chiquito Creek just below the outlet of the lake at a wide and muddy ford (or cross on big boulders upstream) and soon reach the south end of Chiquito Lake at mile 2.6. The lake is shallow and surrounded by sedges and reeds and is obviously on its way to becoming a meadow. Camping is possible nearby, but is not especially attractive because the lakeside is hard to reach through the vegetation and mud. Besides, you're not in Yosemite yet and may have to share the lakeshore with some smelly cattle.

The trail veers away from the lakeside and at mile 2.7 meets a signed junction with the Quartz Mountain Trail heading off to the left. This leads to another trailhead that cuts off a mile of hiking to the pass, but the road to reach it is hard to find, very slow, rocky, and rutted, and often blocked by boulders or snow. Continue straight ahead on the Chiquito Pass Trail through dense wildflower gardens, and at mile 3.1 top the pass, enter Yosemite, and ignore another cutoff to the Quartz Mountain trailhead. Pass through a gate, making sure to close it behind you to keep the cows out of Yosemite. On the other side of the fence is another junction with a trail whose left fork connects with trails to the Wawona area. Turn right (northeast) here toward Chain

▶ Chain Lakes are good examples of what geologists call glacial chain lakes, glacial step lakes, or most colorfully, paternoster lakes, because from above, they look like a string of rosary beads. Paternoster lakes are fairly common features of mountain valleys that have been cut into stair-steps by glaciers.

Lakes. Pass a little pond on your left and plod upward on deep heavy footing to the top of a glacial moraine, a ridge of unsorted dirt and boulders deposited by a glacier long since melted. Both red firs and silver pines join the white firs and lodgepoles as you gain elevation. The trail winds its way through a series of soupy but riotously blooming open bits of forest and wades a tributary of the south fork of the Merced River at mile 4.5. The grade you ascend now is moderate, but the sandy trail makes it seem steeper. At mile 6, you reach a high point of 8,700 feet before rounding the shoulder of a ridge and dipping to cross a creek fed by Chain Lakes at mile 6.5. This creek is deep and swift and potentially dangerous to cross early in the season.

On the far side of the creek is another trail junction. The left fork heads downhill toward Moraine Meadow and Fernandez Pass. The trail sign says you will find the Chain Lakes 0.9 mile away to the right (east), but you reach the shore of the first lake in a shorter distance than this at mile 7. A sign gives the lake's elevation as 9,050 feet. The lake's setting is charming and there are campsites nearby, but check out the higher lakes first before pitching your tent. The trail arcs around the upper, eastern end of this first lake, now almost completely silted in, then follows the creek connecting the first lake with the next one. Notice the beautifully ice-polished and incised granite on the way.

The second lake at mile 7.4 has an irregular, aesthetically pleasing shoreline and several little islands in the middle decorated with groupings of mountain hemlock that seem too perfectly arranged to be accidental. As you draw near the shore, however, you'll note that the lakeside is rather trampled. There are some good campsites on the opposite side of the trail from the lake that you should use if you plan to stay here.

To reach the highest lakes, climb the rocky ridge north of the second lake, taking care not to lose the trail in the jumble of boulders. The terrace above the ridge is enchanting, dotted with lovely little tarns connected by tinkling creeks that drop over mossy rocks in miniature waterfalls. Their shorelines bloom with red mountain heather and azalea-like bushes of Labrador tea, and the cracks in every rock outcropping are bursting with hot pink mountain pride penstemon. Unfortunately, the hordes of voracious mosquitoes that breed in the pools can spoil your appreciation of this little paradise early in the season, but most are gone by August. The last, and largest of the Chain Lakes at mile 8 is snuggled deep into a cirque at the base of Gale Peak at about 9,300 feet. It's definitely worth a visit, but camping nearby is difficult because there is so much water and so few flat, dry sites. The second lake is the most popular camping spot. Return the way you came.

Miles and Directions

0.0   Chiquito Pass Trailhead.

2.1   Ansel Adams Wilderness entrance.

2.6   Chiquito Lake.

2.7   Quartz Mountain Trail junction, keep right.

3.1   Chiquito Pass, go through a gate, keep right at junction.

4.5   South Fork Merced River crossing.

6.0   High point of the hike.

6.5   Fernandez Pass Trail junction, turn right.

7.0   Lowest Chain Lake.

7.4 Middle Chain Lake.

8.0 Upper Chain Lake.

16.0 Chiquito Pass Trailhead.

Options: Fernandez Pass and Breeze Lakes

Fernandez Pass (10,175 feet) is an alternate, though longer (24 miles round-trip), destination for a backpack from the Chiquito Pass Trailhead. If you are planning a trip to Chain Lakes and have more than just one night to spend, this is a great, if fairly vigorous (11 miles round-trip), day hike to make on a layover day. From the Chain Lakes/Fernandez Pass junction head north to Moraine Meadows, then southeast through flowery forest, and finally climb steeply northeastward up a rocky notch to meet the Ansel Adams/Yosemite border again at the pass. The views to the south are thrilling, with Mounts Ritter and Banner and the Minarets on the skyline and the peaks of the Clark Range marching away toward the north. About 0.7 mile before you reach the pass, a short spur trail heads south to Breeze Lake, lying in a deep cirque beneath Gale Peak. There are campsites not far from the shore.

South of Tuolumne Meadows

Highway 120, the Tioga Road, is the only automobile route that runs all the way across Yosemite. It leaves the park on its northeastern border at Tioga Pass at 9,945 feet, the highest automobile pass in California. Tuolumne Meadows is the only developed area on this side of Yosemite with a visitor center, store, cafe, mountaineering shop, campground, lodge, and gas. This is the largest high-elevation meadow in the Sierra Nevada, and its beauty is stunning. The land to the south contains some of the most sensational peaks and passes in the park, especially the Cathedral Range, with its crowning glory, Cathedral Peak, and Mount Lyell with its associated glacier. Dozens of day hikes and backpacks begin from Tioga Road between Tenaya Lake and Tioga Pass, as well as a number of trails connecting Tuolumne Meadows with Yosemite Valley, including the John Muir and Pacific Crest Trails.

A free shuttle bus runs between Tuolumne Lodge and Olmstead Point every hour, and from Tuolumne Lodge to Tioga Pass four times each day. The Tuolumne Meadows Hikers' Bus leaves Yosemite Valley and stops at Crane Flat and White Wolf on the way to Tuolumne Meadows Lodge every day. There is a charge for this one, the amount depending upon where you want to be dropped off. A schedule and map of shuttle stops are available at the visitor center.

The only camping is at the Tuolumne Meadows Campground (part reservation, part first-come, first-served), and there is a walk-in camping area for backpackers limited to a one-night stay. Tuolumne Lodge has tent cabins and meals, available by reservation far in advance, or sometimes by last-minute good luck.

You can get wilderness permits for overnight stays in the backcountry at the Tuolumne Meadows Wilderness Center if you have not applied in advance. The wilderness center is just off Tioga Road on the way to the Tuolumne Lodge east of the campground. This region is very popular with backpackers, so get there early and be flexible in your trip planning.

32 Tenaya Lake

By Yosemite standards, Tenaya is a very big lake, and a very popular one, too, because of its wide sandy beach and its proximity to the Tioga Road. You can stroll along the shore for as long as you like on a relatively flat trail, then return the way you came, or begin at one end and hike to the other, using the free shuttle bus to return to the start.

Start: Picnic area at the northeast end of the lake.
Distance: 3 miles out and back.
Approximate hiking time: From half an hour to half a day.
Difficulty: Easy.

Seasons: All summer, whenever the Tioga Road is open.
Nearest facilities: Gas, food, and lodging at Tuolumne Meadows.
Permits: None.
Maps: USGS Tenaya Lake quad.

Walk the shores of Tenaya Lake, just a few steps from Tioga Road.

Tenaya Lake

Hypsometry
9600

8000
Elevation in Feet

283,000
284,000
4,191,000
4,191,000

To
Tuolumne Meadows

120

START

P

Murphy Creek

Tioga Road

Tenaya Creek

4,190,000
4,190,000

Tenaya Lake

120

To
Yosemite
Valley

Tenaya Creek

4,189,000
4,189,000

Sunrise Trail

N

0   Kilometer   0.25

0   Mile   0.25

283,000
284,000

Finding the trailhead: Ride the free shuttle bus from Tuolumne Meadows to Stop 9 at the northeast end of Tenaya Lake, or drive to the same spot on Tioga Road (Highway 120). Turn into the picnic area parking lot where you will find toilets, bear boxes, and a sign directing you to the trail.

The Hike

Follow the trail sign to the picnic tables on the beach and head south along the shore. Unless it is quite late in the summer, you will probably have to wade the inlet creek. The beach is a good vantage point from which to watch climbers clinging to the bare rock faces of the surrounding domes, polished to a sheen by the glacier that gouged out the lake. Pick up the obvious trail that runs alongside the lake's south shore and stroll through garden after garden of wildflowers beside several trickling brooks, wandering as far as you wish along the lakeside before returning to the trailhead. If you don't want to retrace your steps, when you meet the Sunrise Trail at the east end of the lake, turn right and follow it a short distance to the Tioga Road, at Stop 10, then ride the shuttle back to Stop 9. The topo map shows a campground here, but this has been dismantled. It is possible to circumnavigate the entire lake, but once you reach its north side, you must walk along the shoulder of busy Tioga Road for the whole length of the lake to get back to the parking lot.

▶ Tenaya Lake was named for Chief Tenaya, who, with all his people, was driven from his home in Yosemite by the U.S. Cavalry in 1852.

33 Clouds Rest

The narrow summit of Clouds Rest is the best seat in the house for enjoying the drama of Yosemite Valley and the country around it. From this vantage point, the star of the show, Half Dome, appears impossibly enormous as it thrusts its way up from the flat valley floor. The Sunrise Lakes Trailhead at Tenaya Lake is the nearest and most direct route to Clouds Rest, but it is still a hard workout as a day hike. Fortunately, you can spend the night near a tributary of Tenaya Creek about 4.5 miles from the start.

Start: Sunrise Lakes Trailhead at Tenaya Lake.
Distance: 14.4 miles out and back.
Approximate hiking time: 8 to 10 hours.
Difficulty: Strenuous.
Seasons: All summer; whenever Tioga Road is open.
Nearest facilities: Food and gas at Crane Flat

and Tuolumne Meadows. Toilets only at trailhead; no potable water.
Permits: None for a day hike. Available in advance or from the wilderness center in Tuolumne Meadows or Yosemite Valley for an overnighter.
Map: USGS Tenaya Lake quad.

Finding the trailhead: Drive to the southwest end of Tenaya Lake on Tioga Road (Highway 120). The trailhead is across the street from the lake on the south side. You can also ride the Tuolumne Meadows shuttle to Stop 10, Sunrise Lakes Trailhead. Be sure to leave food and ice chests in the bear-proof boxes provided.

Special considerations: The actual summit is not advised for those who have no head for heights. It's a long and narrow knife-edged ridge, not at all dangerous if you watch your step, but very high and exposed. Fortunately, it is possible to bypass the scary part on a parallel horse trail near the top where you can still get good views. Don't even think about this hike if there is the slightest chance of a thunderstorm.

The Hike

A paved trail begins behind the parking area. Turn left (east). Soon the pavement ends. Cross a sandy-bottomed creek draining Tenaya Lake that you'll probably have to wade early in the year. The trail swings right (south) just across the creek at 0.1 mile. A sign, slightly inaccurate, says SUNRISE: 5 MILES. At 0.2 mile, a trail leading back to Tuolumne Meadows Lodge goes off to the left. The trail dips and rises as it crosses several little streams, then begins to climb the east slope above Tenaya Canyon. The switchbacking ascent is relieved by views of Mount Hoffman and Tioga Road across the canyon.

At the crest of the ridge (2.5 miles) the trail splits. The left (east) fork leads to Sunrise Lakes. Continue due south, following the sign to Clouds Rest, and descend to the base of Sunrise Peak, whose slickrock slabs swoop gracefully down to a little meadow. The trail skirts the meadow, then climbs a ridge of boulders shed from the peak on which some scraggly aspens are fighting for a foothold. As you drop into deeper forest, you get one teasing glimpse partway down into Yosemite Valley before

Grab a view of Half Dome from Clouds Rest.

the trail levels out. Pass a small pond, then cross several little tributaries of Tenaya Creek. There are some small campsites nearby; these are your last sources of water. Now climb easily to the Merced Lake junction at 4.7 miles and continue straight ahead (southwest), climbing more steeply through an open forest of western white pine. The thin slice of granite that is the summit gradually appears as you gain elevation. Follow the ridgetop as it swings around toward the peak and watch for Mount Clark protruding from the crest across Merced Canyon like a giant shark tooth. As the trail climbs, it crosses to the west side of the ridge and gives you a taste of the view up Tenaya Canyon from the top.

At 7 miles you reach the base of the summit itself. To the right, slightly above you, watch for the sign that says FOOTPATH TO CLOUDS REST. It isn't conspicuous, but if you should miss it, you can continue around the eastern flank of the peak on a horse trail to meet a more obvious signed junction, then double back up to the summit. On the footpath, scramble steeply over rocks weathered to the shapes of gigantic stacks of pancakes, with little bunches of purple rockfringe and pale buckwheat lining their edges. From here it becomes clear why the Sierra Nevada has been called the "Range of Light." The dazzling white granite rises in wave after wave of ridges to the horizon, with Tenaya Lake glowing like a jewel in the center, and

Clouds Rest

Matterhorn Peak and the Sawtooth Ridge crowning it all. Down-canyon, you can look over the bulbous tops of North Dome and Basket Dome, and beyond them the long arm of Yosemite Valley stretching all the way to El Capitan. Directly ahead of you is Half Dome, seen from its most dramatic angle. If you have binoculars or very sharp eyes, you may be able to spot climbers struggling up the steel cables to the summit. To the east the Merced River canyon winds off into the distance below the park's highest peaks—Mounts Lyell, Maclure, and Florence. When you can tear yourself away, retrace your steps to your camp or the trailhead.

Miles and Directions

0.0 Sunrise Lakes Trailhead.
0.2 Cutoff to Tuolumne Meadows Lodge.
2.5 Sunrise Lakes junction.
4.7 Merced Lake junction.
7.0 Clouds Rest footpath.
7.2 Clouds Rest summit.
14.4 Return to Sunrise Lakes Trailhead.

Option: Half Dome
The route up Half Dome from Yosemite Valley is more direct, but this is a great way to bag two of Yosemite's premier peaks on one trip. It's an exhilarating hike, though strenuous and somewhat exposed, with lots of ups and downs. It's too long for a day hike; the distance from the trailhead at Tenaya Lake and back is 25 miles with more than 6,000 feet elevation gain, but there are campsites and water between Clouds Rest and Half Dome. You could also do this as a 20-mile shuttle, beginning at Tenaya Lake, going over Clouds Rest and Half Dome, ending in Yosemite Valley, and riding the bus back up to Tenaya Lake. Bear canisters are *mandatory* in this area for back-packers.

From Clouds Rest, the trail drops steeply down along the west side of the ridge over big boulders and giant stair-steps toward the pointed teeth called the Pinnacles, then crosses back to the east side and switchbacks down to a junction where the horse trail rejoins the summit footpath. It then swings west beneath the pinnacles and drops on more steep switchbacks to meet the John Muir Trail. A short detour to the left (east) down the John Muir Trail leads to a few campsites and the only water between Half Dome and Clouds Rest. Return to the Half Dome Trail and begin climbing easily through forest, then laboring up the huge, sparsely timbered shoulder of Half Dome to the base of the summit. Steel cables help you negotiate the final 400 feet to the top. Do not proceed beyond the forest if bad weather threatens.

34 Cathedral Lakes

The hike to the two Cathedral Lakes is probably the most popular of any in the Tuolumne area (not counting the High Sierra Camp Loop) so wilderness permits are hard to come by, and the trail and lakesides show signs of overuse. Still, the setting of the lakes in the heart of the Cathedral Range is almost too picturesque to be real, and the distance from the Tioga Road is short. Cathedral Pass, above the upper lake, is a convenient route between Yosemite Valley and Tuolumne Meadows, and is part of the John Muir Trail. The bears consider these lakes their local supermarket, and there are no bear-proof boxes, so you must carry a bear canister.

Start: Cathedral Lakes Trailhead.
Distance: 8 miles out and back to visit both lakes.
Approximate hiking time: 4 to 8 hours.
Difficulty: Moderate as a day hike, easy as a backpack.
Seasons: July through September.

Nearest facilities: Food, gas, and supplies at Tuolumne Meadows; nothing at the trailhead.
Permits: None for a day hike. Available in advance or from the Tuolumne Meadows wilderness center for overnighters.
Maps: USGS Tenaya Lake quad.

Finding the trailhead: Just west of the Tuolumne Meadows visitor center is the signed trailhead on the south side of the street. Parking is along both sides of the Tioga Road. You can also ride the Tuolumne Meadows shuttle to Stop 7. Be sure to leave all food and ice chests in the bear-proof boxes.

The Hike

Start hiking southwest on a wide, flat path for 0.1 mile to a junction marked by a big sign with maps and trail information. Your route lies straight ahead, climbing easily through lodgepole pine forest and gaining about 500 feet in elevation before it levels out, skirting the base of the rounded backside of what appears to be another standard-issue Yosemite dome. The trail passes alongside a flowery meadow, crosses several branches of Cathedral Creek, and resumes its climb, steeper now than it was in the beginning. When it levels out again, you can see that the rocky bulge on your left narrows toward the top, culminating in the graceful profile of Cathedral Peak. The wide, sandy trail descends a little, presenting a view to the south of another striking formation, the square, raggedy ridge of

Tresidder Peak. Continue trending left through a lovely but often buggy dell to find the junction to Lower Cathedral Lake at 3 miles. To visit this one first, turn right (southwest) and descend through more exquisite flower gardens to the lower lake at 3.5 miles. The lake lies at the end of a meadow enclosed by a classic glacial cirque. Cathedral Peak seen head-on from here looks like a single, needlelike spire piercing the heavens. The lake is surrounded by warm, flat rock slabs that invite sunbathing. There is plenty of overused camping toward the northwest shore. Wood fires are prohibited.

To reach the higher lake, return to the trail junction at 4 miles, then turn right and ascend a rocky path to the beautiful subalpine bowl containing Upper Cathedral Lake, surrounded by Cathedral, Echo, and Tresidder Peaks. The low saddle to the south is Cathedral Pass. It takes only minutes to reach the pass for the best view of the lake basin. There are plenty of campsites in the area.

A short climb to the top of the pass before returning to the trailhead is worth the effort. The view of the upper lake flanked by Cathedral Peak in craggy profile is stunning.

Miles and Directions

0.0 Cathedral Lakes Trailhead.

0.1 Tuolumne Meadows High Sierra Camp/Tenaya Lake junction.

3.0 Cutoff to Lower Cathedral Lake, turn right.

3.5 Lower Cathedral Lake.

4.0 Return to cutoff, turn right.

4.5 Upper Cathedral Lake.

8.0 Cathedral Lakes Trailhead.

◀ *It's easy to pick out the needlelike spire of Cathedral Peak.*

Cathedral Lakes

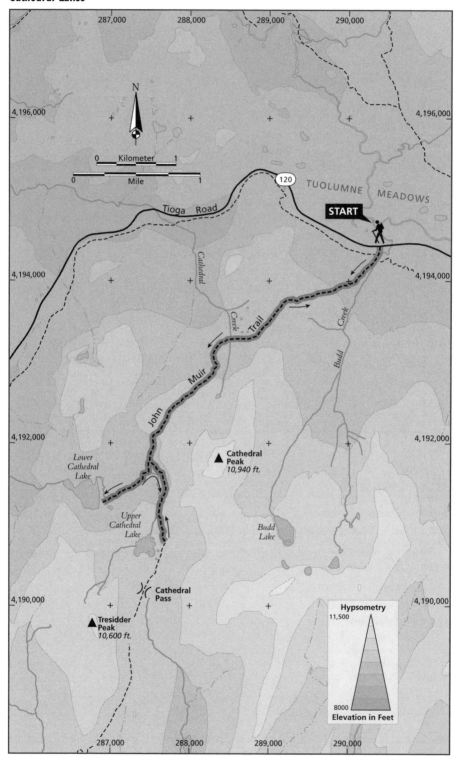

35 Elizabeth Lake

Elizabeth Lake lies in a picture postcard setting at the foot of Unicorn Peak, a walk of only an hour or two from the Tuolumne Meadows Campground, so it is very popular; start early in the morning to avoid the crowds. If you have less than a full day to spend in the high country, but would like a true taste of subalpine backcountry travel in a small dose, this hike is a good choice. It's also a perfect warm-up hike if you have just arrived in Tuolumne Meadows and need to acclimatize before tackling a longer or more demanding trip.

Start: Elizabeth Lake Trailhead in the Tuolumne Meadows Campground.
Distance: 4.6 miles out and back.
Approximate hiking time: 2 to 4 hours.
Difficulty: Moderate, only because of steady climbing.

Seasons: All summer, whenever Tioga Road is open.
Nearest facilities: Food, phones, gas at Tuolumne Meadows. Toilets and water at the trailhead.
Permits: None.
Map: USGS Vogelsang Peak quad.

Finding the trailhead: Drive to the Tuolumne Meadows Campground, about 9 miles west of the Tioga Pass Entrance Station on Tioga Road (Highway 120). At the kiosk at the campground entrance, pick up a map of the campground and a parking permit. Follow the map through the campground, turning left between Loops B and C, and pass the group campsites to where the road is barred by a locked gate. Park here and look for the clearly marked trailhead. Store all food and ice chests in the bear-proof boxes.

The Hike

The trail climbs steadily uphill through forest, going straight ahead (south) at a junction with the John Muir Trail at 0.1 mile. As the path ascends, it draws nearer and nearer to Unicorn Creek, which drains Elizabeth Lake. A little beyond the halfway point, the slope becomes gentler and finally levels out at the end of a meadow dotted with young lodgepole pines that have been forced into contorted shapes by the weight of winter snows. The trail curves to the right and crosses Unicorn Creek, and soon Elizabeth Lake appears, sparkling at the foot of Unicorn Peak. A number of

Elizabeth Lake

trails have been worn around the lake, so you can wander its shores as long as you like before retracing your steps to the trailhead. Do try to stick to the main trails as you do so to avoid further damage to the meadow. Because of the fragility of the vegetation and the lake's proximity to the campground and the road, overnight camping is prohibited. Return to the trailhead the way you came.

Miles and Directions

0.0 Elizabeth Lake Trailhead.

0.1 Trail junction.

2.3 Elizabeth Lake.

4.6 Elizabeth Lake Trailhead.

LODGEPOLE PINES Lodgepole pines are by far the most common conifers in the Tuolumne region, and indeed throughout the entire Sierra Nevada at elevations between 7,000 and 10,000 feet. They're easy to identify: Their trunks and branches have small irregular scales that look like gray cornflakes and they have small cones, less than 2 inches long. The surest way to know a lodgepole, however, is to examine the needles. The needles of all pine trees are attached to their twigs in bundles of one to five, held together at the base by a papery sheath. The number of needles in a bundle are a clue to the species. Several kinds of pines have three needles per bundle, several others have five, but only lodgepoles have two. To make it even easier, pluck a bundle of lodgepole needles and separate the two so that they are at right angles to one another. Now you have "L" for lodgepole.

These are a pioneering species, the first to move in around the edges of a meadow since they don't mind wet feet as much as other pines do, and may gradually transform the meadow to forest. They grow quickly, reproduce at an early age, and are adapted to periodic fires. (In fact, the subspecies that grows in the Rockies requires fire for reproduction, but ours do not.) They are also subject to periodic infestations of needle miners, moths whose larvae can destroy great swathes of forest in a season or two. You can see several of these "ghost forests" in the Tuolumne area, big patches of dead trees surrounded by healthy ones. It's part of the normal cycle of life and death; the forest will recover.

Their scientific name, *Pinus contorta,* reflects their growth habit when young. Young trees become twisted and bent into grotesque and interesting shapes by heavy winter snows and may retain their gnarled bumps and bends into maturity. Lodgepole pines in the Rockies reflect their common name better, growing straight, slender, and much closer together. Lodgepoles are sometimes erroneously called tamaracks, trees that do not grow in California.

36 Lyell Fork and Donohue Pass

The first part of this hike is a beautiful, easy ramble along the Lyell Fork of the Tuolumne River as far as the Vogelsang Pass junction. It's an 11.2-mile round-trip journey from Tuolumne Meadows and back, and a favorite weekend family backpack. Hardier hikers can continue all the way to the headwaters of the Lyell Fork at Donohue Pass just below the Lyell Glacier, tucked beneath the shaded crest of Mount Lyell, the highest peak in Yosemite at 13,114 feet. Mount Maclure, only slightly lower and farther west along the same ridge, shelters its own glacier that also feeds the Tuolumne River. Since this route follows both the John Muir Trail and the Pacific Crest Trail, you're bound to encounter lots of through-hikers along the way at the height of the summer season.

Start: John Muir Trailhead across the road from the Dog Lake parking lot.
Distance: 24.8 miles out and back.
Approximate hiking time: 4 to 8 hours to the Lyell Fork junction and back, 4 to 6 days round-trip to the pass.
Difficulty: Easy to the Vogelsang junction, moderate to strenuous to Donohue Pass, depending on how fast you take it.

Seasons: July through September.
Nearest facilities: Groceries, cafe, gas, and phones at Tuolumne Meadows.
Permits: None for a day hike; required for overnight stay—available in advance or from the Tuolumne Meadows wilderness center.
Maps: USGS Tioga Pass, Vogelsang Peak, and Koip Peak quads.

Finding the trailhead: From the west, drive Tioga Road (Highway 120) eastward past the Tuolumne Meadows visitor center, store, and campground, all on the right. Cross the bridge over the Tuolumne River. In about a mile, turn right at the entrance to the wilderness center. Follow the road as it curves round to the left for about a half-mile to the Dog Lake parking lot on the left. The trailhead is on the right (south) side of the road.
Special considerations: This is a notorious bear hangout, and the bears here are intelligent and resourceful. Carry a canister and remember to keep it locked.

The Hike

Cross the road south of the parking lot to the trailhead sign. Follow the trail southeast to a footbridge over the Dana Fork at 0.2 mile. Ignore the cutoff back to the Tuolumne Meadows Lodge and cross the bridge, then turn left and follow the river upstream, pausing to enjoy the wildflower gardens along the shore, where dozens of different species vie for attention. At 0.3 mile is another cutoff to the left toward Gaylor Lakes. Keep right here, too. (You might have noticed that although the trailhead sign was marked VOGELSANG 6.7 and the sign in front of you says VOGELSANG 6.8 you haven't been walking backward. The trail signs have been erected at different times and are not always consistent.) The route now bends slightly to the right, crosses a low rise alongside a marshy area, and reaches the twin bridges over the Lyell Fork at

A portion of the John Muir Trail runs along the Lyell Fork of the Tuolumne River.

0.6 mile. This is surely one of the most sublime vistas in Yosemite, with the clear turquoise river winding toward you through the green meadow. At your feet deep bowls have been worn into the granite by the scouring force of silt carried from the mountains by spring runoff, and the water swirls in beautiful patterns from one bowl to the next. The massive gray hulk on your left is Mammoth Peak (not to be confused with Mammoth Mountain, the ski resort, which lies farther south).

Soon after you leave the twin bridges, at 0.7 mile, another path leads back (right) to the Tuolumne Meadows Campground. Continue left on the John Muir Trail through lodgepole pine forest and over open rock to 1.3 miles, where the Rafferty Creek Trail heads uphill to the right, the more direct of two routes to Vogelsang. Cross the bridge over the creek on your left and continue through forest and meadows that, in early season, are a solid mass of pale lavender shooting stars (and mosquitoes). Soon the sound of the river becomes apparent—it's been hidden for a while behind a low ridge—and a glorious view of Lyell Canyon opens up before you. Sometimes the river flows deep and clear, sometimes it slides over slickrock into perfect bathing pools. Any one of a thousand spots along the bank invites lunch, a snack, a sunbath, or a nap.

At 5.6 miles the John Muir Trail and the Vogelsang/Ireland Lake Trails split. Good campsites are just uphill to the right of the trail sign. If you do not plan to continue on to Donohue Pass, this is the spot to turn around and make your way back to Tuolumne Meadows.

To continue on to Donohue Pass, keep left at the trail split and accompany the meandering river upstream through the riotously blooming meadow. Just beyond the point where Kuna Creek drops down from the Kuna Crest to join the Lyell Fork

Lyell Fork and Donohue Pass

from the east, the trail begins to climb, winding among avalanche debris. Views of the river snaking away to the north down the canyon get better and better as you gain elevation. Cross the river on a bridge to arrive at Lyell Base Camp. It's a busy place, used by climbers preparing to tackle the mountain. There are plenty of good campsites here, and plenty of bears.

The trees begin to disappear as you climb beyond the camp, and from here on you get superb views up the canyon to the high peaks and glaciers. One of the finest of these is from the outlet of a little lake at the end of a meadow. This outlet can be tricky to cross at high water. It's safer to wade than to hop across on the slippery rocks, but the water is extremely cold. Just past this crossing is a low rocky rise sheltered by whitebark pines that could be used as a last, simply exquisite, campsite before the pass. Climb another little rise, turn left (east), and cross the outlet of another tarn, not as difficult as the last one. Now work your way up over open granite, negotiating snow patches that often remain until mid-summer, to Donohue Pass and the Yosemite park boundary at 11,000 feet. Beyond, the John Muir and Pacific Crest Trails descend through an open rocky basin toward Rush Creek in the Ansel Adams Wilderness.

▶ The turquoise color of the water in the Lyell Fork comes from glacial "flour," rock ground so finely by the Lyell Glacier upstream that it remains suspended in the current and reflects green light.

Miles and Directions

0.0 John Muir Trailhead at Dog Lake lot.

0.2 Footbridge over Dana Fork, cross bridge and turn left.

0.3 Cutoff to Gaylor Lakes, keep right.

0.6 Twin bridges.

0.7 Tuolumne Meadows Campground cutoff, turn left.

1.3 Rafferty Creek junction, turn left, crossing the bridge.

5.6 Vogelsang Trail junction, keep left.

9.9 Lyell Base Camp, cross bridge.

12.4 Donohue Pass.

24.8 Return to trailhead.

37 Mono Pass and Parker Pass

Mono Pass was a major trade route across the Sierra between the Miwok people on the west side and the Piutes on the east. It was also the site of the Golden Crown Mine, active in the early 1880s. Some of the structures built during that time are still standing. The setting is incomparable: a beautiful meadow at the eastern crest of the Sierra containing lakes of the most vivid blue ringed by the warm red rocks of Mount Lewis and Mount Gibbs. Parker Pass is very different from Mono Pass, wide and dry and windswept, flanked by weirdly shaped peaks, a landscape so like the Tibetan Plateau that a herd of yaks would not look out of place here.

Start: Mono Pass Trailhead 1 mile south of the Tioga Pass Entrance Station on Tioga Road.
Distance: 10.2 miles out and back.
Approximate hiking time: 4 to 6 hours.
Difficulty: Moderate as a day hike, easy as a backpack.
Seasons: Summer and fall, whenever Tioga Road is open.

Nearest facilities: Tuolumne Meadows store, grill, mountain shop, gas just west of Tuolumne Meadows Campground.
Permits: None for a day hike; available in advance or at the Tuolumne Meadows wilderness center for overnighters.
Maps: USGS Koip Peak, Mount Dana, and Tioga Pass quads.

Finding the trailhead: On Tioga Road (Highway 120) drive about 6 miles east of Tuolumne Meadows, or a little more than a mile south of the Tioga Pass Entrance Station. The marked trailhead and parking lot are on the southeast side of the road.
Special considerations: The entire watershed of the Dana Fork of the Tuolumne River is closed to camping, so you must go just a bit beyond Mono Pass itself to camp. Even the park service is a bit hazy about the precise location of the boundary line, but as long as you pitch your tent to the east of the old miners' cabins, you're legal.

The Hike

From the parking area the trail winds its way generally southwestward through lodgepole pine forest alternating with little fingers of Dana Meadow. The Dana Fork of the Tuolumne River flows through one of these deeply enough to require wading early in the summer. Just beyond this creek the trail swings left (east), climbing through more forest and meadow. The bulky granite mass to the right is Mammoth Peak, the northern culmination of the Kuna Crest. (Don't confuse this with Mammoth Mountain, the ski area south of Yosemite.)

At mile 1.3 the remains of an old pioneer cabin slouch beside the trail, and at about the same time you pick up the gurgling of Parker Pass Creek on the right. Following the creek upstream, you cross a tributary stream feeding the main creek amid a dense exhalation of swamp onions, and just beyond, at mile 2.3, meet a junction with the Spillway Lake Trail that angles off to the south, taking Parker Pass Creek

Parker Pass straddles the boundary between Yosemite and the Ansel Adams Wilderness.

with it. The Mono Pass Trail continues southeast and the grade steepens. As it climbs you get glimpses across the valley of the light gray Kuna Crest to the right with a colorful strip of red metamorphic rock at its base, a foretaste of things to come.

At 3 miles pass a rockslide where you're sure to see pikas scurrying around if you're willing to sit quietly for a few minutes. Another tributary of Parker Pass Creek burbles along on the other side of the trail. Pass a second tumbledown cabin. Just beyond it the forest opens to reveal red Mount Lewis at the head of the broad meadow. At mile 3.4 the signed Parker Pass Trail cuts off to the right (south) across the marshy meadow.

From here, an almost level stroll takes you to Mono Pass at mile 3.7 at the border between Yosemite and the Ansel Adams Wilderness. On the far side of Summit Lake, the larger of the two in the meadow, on a sandy bench among whitebark pines, are four more miners' cabins lined up in a neat row. An unmarked use trail cutting across the meadow takes you directly there. From Mono Pass you can explore the old mining prospects, climb Mount Gibbs just to the north, or continue down the main trail that drops steeply into Bloody Canyon to visit Sardine Lakes, notable for

Mono Pass and Parker Pass

their startling turquoise color. When you're ready, return the way you came then turn left toward Parker Pass.

Parker Pass, at 11,000 feet, is the next gap south of Mono Pass on the Sierra Crest. It, too, marks the boundary of Yosemite and the Ansel Adams Wilderness, and camping is prohibited on the Yosemite side. The trail crosses the meadow and climbs over a sandy ridge studded with whitebark pines, where you get a good view of Spillway Lake at the base of the Kuna Crest. The pass itself is marked by a veritable forest of signs. If you have the time and energy, the trail over the pass continues on down a beautiful valley past dozens of little ponds, then climbs again toward Koip Pass. Along the way, through gaps in the mountains, you can see all the way down to Mono Lake. Retrace your steps to Tioga Road.

Miles and Directions

0.0 Trailhead.

1.3 Pioneer cabin.

2.3 Spillway Lake junction.

3.0 Rockslide.

3.4 Parker Pass Trail junction.

3.7 Mono Pass. Backtrack to Parker Pass Trail.

4.0 Turn left (south) toward Park Pass.

5.1 Parker Pass.

10.2 Return to Mono Pass Trailhead.

North of Tuolumne Meadows

The Grand Canyon of the Tuolumne River dominates this region and defines its northern boundary. The Lyell Fork of the Tuolumne originates at the Lyell Glacier, and the Dana Fork rises from the snowfields of Mount Dana, both to the south. The forks meet in Tuolumne Meadows and wander languorously northwest for a few miles, then begin their headlong rush toward the Pacific Ocean in an almost continuous series of cascades and waterfalls. The canyon they have carved was gouged even deeper by glaciers, which produced a narrow slot in the granite with vertical walls that are in some places higher than those of Yosemite Valley.

For general information about the Tuolumne Meadows area, including a discussion of facilities, services, permits, camping, and shuttle buses, see the South of Tuolumne Meadows section.

All the hikes described here explore the country between Tuolumne Meadows and this Grand Canyon. Since every trailhead in this section originates from or near Tioga Road, there will be other hikers in the backcountry, and there will be some competition for wilderness permits. Still, the trails in this region are not as heavily used as are those south of the road. There are high peaks, passes, waterfalls, and sensationally beautiful scenery, but overall the terrain is slightly less rugged and the average elevation is a little lower than the country to the south. Furthermore, there are no trails heading directly into Yosemite Valley.

38 Waterwheel Falls and the Grand Canyon of the Tuolumne

This is a rugged multiday shuttle hike following the course of the Tuolumne River downstream from Tuolumne Meadows as it tumbles over waterfalls and cascades, including the famous Waterwheels, through the Grand Canyon of the Tuolumne almost as far as Hetch Hetchy Reservoir. The trail drops all the way to 4,200 feet before laboring back up 3,600 feet to White Wolf at the very end. It's a wild, exhilarating hike for those in good condition. You will need two cars, leaving one at White Wolf, the other at the Glen Aulin Trailhead, or take advantage of the Tuolumne Meadows Shuttle.

Start: Glen Aulin Trailhead at Tuolumne Meadows.

Distance: 28.1 miles one way.

Approximate hiking time: 3 to 5 days.

Difficulty: Strenuous.

Seasons: Early July is best for cooler temperatures and full-flowing waterfalls.

Nearest facilities: Tuolumne Meadows; snacks and phones at White Wolf.

Permits: Available in advance or from the Tuolumne Meadows wilderness center.

Maps: USGS Falls Ridge, Hetch Hetchy Reservoir, Tamarack Flat, Ten Lakes, and Tioga Pass quads.

Finding the trailhead: From the west, follow Tioga Road (Highway 120) past the Tuolumne Meadows visitor center, store, cafe, and campground, all on the right. Just after crossing the bridge over the Tuolumne River, turn left (north) into the Lembert Dome parking area. From the east (Tioga Pass), follow Tioga Road past the turnoff to the wilderness center on the left and continue about a hundred yards to the Lembert Dome parking area on the right. You can also ride the Tuolumne Meadows shuttle to Lembert Dome. Overnight parking is prohibited in the parking lot, so park along the paved road parallel to Tioga Road. At a closed gate, this road turns sharply right and heads toward the stables. The trail begins at the gate.

The Hike

Go through the gate and follow the road (closed to vehicles) westward through the meadow, keeping right and climbing a small rise where the road splits. From the top of the rise at mile 0.5, head toward the ramshackle log structure partially containing Soda Springs, a naturally carbonated spring bubbling up rusty water. Just beyond is Parsons Lodge, a stone building with historical exhibits. The path splits at mile 0.6, where you turn right to a big GLEN AULIN TRAIL sign. The trail meets the road a few yards beyond. Turn left and walk through flowery meadows and lodgepole pine forest on footing that is heavy and dusty from lots of horse and foot traffic. Ford Delaney Creek at mile 1.2. A trail heading north to Young Lakes cuts off to the right at mile 1.6, but your route stays left (northwest). In less than a mile of gradual

Grooves in the rocks fling water into high arcs, giving these falls their name—Waterwheels.

descent you emerge from behind a low ridge to behold the spectacular Cathedral Range with the Tuolumne River in the foreground. The next couple of miles along the trail offer one incredible photo-op after another. Sometimes the trail passes over highly polished granite, buffed by glacial ice to a blinding sheen, and you will need to watch for ducks across these open spaces to stay on track. After passing through another short stretch of forest, climb around a low shoulder of rock and keep watch on your left for the Little Devil's Postpile, an unusual volcanic feature much younger than the surrounding rock.

The trail turns sharply right and drops down a short, steep notch, and very soon reaches a pair of footbridges across the Tuolumne River at 3.5 miles. From this point on, the river picks up speed and cascades over a series of falls, one after another, mile after mile. As you descend, you can enjoy views up Cold Canyon to Matterhorn Peak and Mount Conness on the northern boundary of the park. The trail dives twice into and out of deep forest lined with Labrador tea and corn lily, then emerges again into sunlight on cobblestones or smooth granite marked with ducks. Finally, it meets the May Lake/McGee Lake Trail at 5 miles. A few more steep, slippery switchbacks lead down to a bridge and back to the other side of the river. Few hikers can

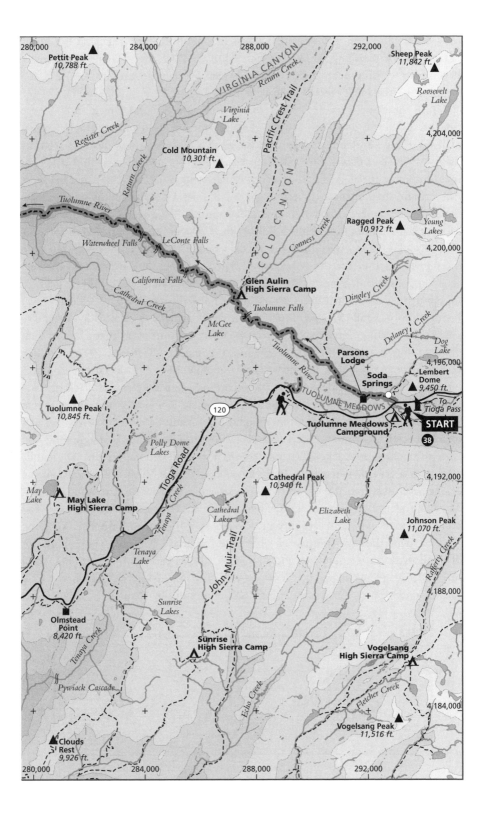

resist the urge to stop on the bridge and snap a photo or simply gape at the frothy White Cascade splashing into a pool in front of the High Sierra Camp at 5.2 miles. If you plan to camp here, cross a second bridge over Cold Creek to the right and walk behind the High Sierra Camp to find the backpackers' campground.

From the camp, cross back over to the west side of Cold Creek, cross over a ridge, and descend into the burned-over glen. Wander for a mile through a waist-high sea of lupines that have taken advantage of the open ground newly created by the fire. The river flows quiet and deep beside you for awhile, then both trail and river drop over the first of a long series of stair-steps past California Falls, LeConte Falls, and finally the famous Waterwheels at 7.8 miles. Here in early season the roaring Tuolumne rushes down a smooth slope until it hits a series of grooves in the rocks that sometimes fling the water more than 20 feet into the air. Watch for a little spur trail leading toward the riverside for a better view, but do not walk out onto the slippery rock beside the water, especially if it is wet. The combination of slimy algae on polished rock creates a surface as slick as glass, and a slip could be fatal.

Return to the main trail and continue to switchback down to a bridge over Return Creek at mile 9.6. Soon the canyon walls narrow and eventually become so precipitous at Muir Gorge that the trail must make a detour over the top of a smooth polished shoulder. It then drops steeply into the drainage of Register Creek, which you cross on rocks below a pretty cascade at mile 14.7. A little farther on, cross Rodgers Creek on a bridge. Now that you are well into the zone of black oak and chaparral, the canyon can be hot and the flies voracious. Stay alert for rattlesnakes as well. Fortunately, there are lots of inviting little pools alternating with lovely cascades for cooling off. As you approach Pate Valley, the ground becomes soggier and you wade through dense bracken fern and leopard lilies until you meet a junction at mile 19.5 with a trail that heads up Piute Creek to Pleasant Valley. Cross a couple of bridges over two branches of the river to its south side and enter Pate Valley proper. There are plenty of good campsites here along the river beneath shady oaks and ponderosa pines where masses of white azaleas scent the air in June. This is a good place to spend the night no matter what time you arrive, because the climb up out of the canyon can be very hot and should be tackled early in the morning. Make sure you have plenty of water if it is past mid-July since Morrison Creek, the only stream you will meet on your way up, is sometimes dry by then.

Leave the river and begin the trudge up the switchbacks, eventually getting high enough to look back upon Hetch Hetchy Reservoir down the canyon. After the first set of switchbacks, cross Morrison Creek in a cool aspen grove, then climb another set of switchbacks alongside the creek. At 25.7 miles, pass the first junction with a shortcut trail to Harden Lake and continue straight ahead (west), climbing less steeply at first, then mounting a last set of switchbacks to Harden Lake (no camping allowed) at 27.2 miles. From the lake, follow the fire road back up to White Wolf at 28.1 miles.

Miles and Directions

0.0   Glen Aulin Trailhead.

0.5   Soda Springs.

0.6   Parsons Lodge, turn right, then left at the sign.

1.2   Ford Delaney Creek.

1.6   Young Lakes Trail junction, keep left.

3.5   Cross twin bridges over the Tuolumne River.

5.0   May Lake/McGee Lake junction, turn right.

5.2   Glen Aulin High Sierra Camp.

7.8   Waterwheel Falls.

9.6   Cross Return Creek.

14.7 Cross Register Creek, then Rodgers Creek.

19.5 Piute Creek junction, go straight into Pate Valley.

25.7 First Harden Lake junction.

27.2 Harden Lake.

28.1 White Wolf.

39 Lukens Lake

This easy and popular out-and-back day hike through forest and meadow to a quiet lake is a favorite with wildflower lovers.

Start: Lukens Lake Trailhead.
Distance: 1.6 miles out and back.
Approximate hiking time: 1 to 3 hours.
Difficulty: Easy.
Seasons: All summer, whenever Tioga Road is open.

Nearest facilities: Food and phones at White Wolf, gas at Crane Flat and Tuolumne Meadows.
Permits: None.
Map: USGS Yosemite Falls quad.

Lukens Lake is a favorite destination for wildflower lovers.

Lukens Lake

Finding the trailhead: On Tioga Road (Highway 120) drive about 2 miles east of the White Wolf junction. The signed parking area is on the south side of the road, but the trail begins on the north side.

The Hike

Cross Tioga Road carefully and head uphill through an almost pure red fir forest. The cones underfoot come from the occasional western white pine or mountain hemlock. Fir cones do not fall but decompose and release their seeds while still on the tree. Watch for odd leafless plants like pinedrops, brilliant red snow plant, and little saprophytic orchids on the forest floor. The sunny spots scattered here and there among the trees are dense with chinquapin, green and gold shrubs with spiny but delicious nuts ready for eating in midsummer.

▶ **Theodore Lukens, for whom the lake is named, was at one time mayor of Pasadena, California.**

The trail tops a rise, drops again to pick up a creek lined with dozens of species of waist-high wildflowers, and turns left to follow the stream to Lukens Lake. The lake is shallow and grassy and warmer than most lakes in the Sierra, and is reputed to be a good fishing spot. The moisture that nourishes the lush display of wildflowers means lots of mosquitoes, too, so take repellent. Camping is prohibited near the lake since it is much too close to the road, so when you have botanized to your heart's content, retrace your steps to Tioga Road.

40 Ten Lakes

The Ten Lakes Basin contains only seven bodies of water large enough to be called lakes, along with an indeterminate number of smaller ponds. The trail climbs Ten Lakes Pass, drops into the basin, and skirts two of the ten lakes before climbing back out of the basin again. You can scramble to several other lakes on a layover day if you're not in a hurry. After leaving the basin you make another descent into the isolated valley of the South Fork of Cathedral Creek, climb again to round a shoulder of Tuolumne Peak, then swing south to return to the Tioga Road via May Lake. Many people start at the Ten Lakes Trailhead, visit the lakes, then return the same way, but if you can arrange a car shuttle, this horseshoe-shaped loop makes an especially rewarding backpack through varied and beautiful country.

Start: Ten Lakes Trailhead.
Distance: 22.4 miles one-way shuttle.
Approximate hiking time: 2 to 6 days.
Difficulty: Moderate.
Seasons: All summer, whenever Tioga Road is open.

Nearest facilities: Food, phones, and gas at Crane Flat and Tuolumne Meadows.
Permits: Required. Available in advance or at the wilderness center in Tuolumne Meadows.
Maps: USGS Falls Ridge, Ten Lakes, Tenaya Lake, and Yosemite Falls quads.

Finding the trailhead: On Tioga Road (Highway 120) drive about 20 miles east of Crane Flat or 26 miles west from Tuolumne Meadows. There is parking on both sides of the highway. The Ten Lakes Trail departs from the north side. You will need to leave another car or arrange to be picked up at the May Lake Trailhead, at the end of the spur road that heads north of Tioga Road along Snow Creek.

Special considerations: This area holds snow later than most, so check with rangers to make sure the trail is passable in early summer.

The Hike

From the parking area, follow the trail that parallels the road west to the junction with the Yosemite Creek Trail at 0.1 mile. The trail heads northward through the forest over level ground, then emerges into sunshine. You soon begin to climb along the western slope above Yosemite Creek amid ceanothus and manzanita, hopping little mossy (and slippery) rivulets. A foaming white cascade tumbles down a shallow notch across the canyon to the east below Mount Hoffman. The trail reenters the forest and crosses several creeks, then meets the White Wolf Trail at 2.1 miles. Continue straight ahead (north) and, amid a patch of some truly gigantic lupines, cross a branch of Yosemite Creek that can present a challenge early in the year. The trail climbs relentlessly, working its way northeast to reach Half Moon Meadow at the base of an open granite ridge. There are a few marginal campsites at the northern end. Leaving the meadow, the path climbs very steeply between two little

Hike to the Ten Lakes basin for classic glacial scenery.

creeks and wonderful wildflower gardens. The grade lessens as the trail passes through a moist patch of sedges, then reaches the top of the ridge above Half Moon Meadow at the Grant Lakes junction at 5.9 miles. The Grant Lakes lie at the bottom of a flowery bowl and offer more solitude than you will find at Ten Lakes.

Cross over the open ridge called Ten Lakes Pass and pause to gasp at a stupendous panorama that extends from Mount Conness past the great red Tioga Crest, across to Matterhorn Peak and the Sawtooth Ridge, all the way to Tower Peak. The Grand Canyon of the Tuolumne River cuts a deep gash between the ridge just in front of you and the peaks behind. Now the trail drops down off the pass to the west, but don't put away your camera yet, for another grand vista soon appears. Here, four of the (approximately) Ten Lakes descend from bowl to bowl, north to south down toward the Grand Canyon of the Tuolumne against a backdrop of more dramatic high peaks. You now drop steeply through willows, then slosh through a marshy spot to a stream connecting two of the lakes that can be tricky to cross early in the year. The southern shore of one of the larger Ten Lakes lies just beyond at 6.3 miles. There is plenty of camping here, but you will have lots of neighbors and a bear or two. This is a popular spot for a layover, where you can drop your pack and visit several of the other lakes above and below this one.

The route between this lake and the next one along the main trail is obscure. Watch for tree blazes and keep an eye on the topo to find the spot where the trail makes a steep rocky climb to a ridge high above the east side of the lake you just left. Now the trail swings southeast and passes fairly close to the shoreline of another lake at mile 8.2. This one also has good camping and is not usually as crowded as the first. Now descend through a forested gully, round a corner, and begin a steep drop down spectacular granite slabs decorated with some picturesque old junipers into the beautiful basin of the south fork of Cathedral Creek. There are a few campsites back off the trail where you can rest your aching knees and cool your feet after the long descent. The South Fork can be challenging to cross in early season because the water is deep and you can't see the bottom. A walking stick is handy here. Once on the east side, at mile 10.4, the trail follows the creek for almost 2 miles before it switchbacks up the hillside, then climbs northward to round a shoulder of Tuolumne Peak, rising and falling over lots of little pockets where snow patches linger late into the summer. It drops through a narrow slot and turns a corner where it follows a narrow ridge alongside a couple of tiny tarns on the south and an open panorama of the Cathedral Range to the north. Now the trail makes a long descent down the forested mountainside until it levels out in a boggy hollow filled with avalanche debris. There it meets a junction with the trail to Glen Aulin at 17.5 miles.

Turn right (south), cross a wide saddle, then begin a steep but stunning climb up a mostly open slope down which little creeks trickle through tiny gardens. Across the Murphy Creek drainage to the east are Polly Dome, Mount Conness, and the northern Sierra crest on the skyline. The path then drops briefly down the west side of the rocky ridge. When it enters the forest again, watch to the left for a glimpse of Raisin Lake, almost hidden behind rocks. This is a welcome stop for a swim after your long, hot climb. May Lake is not too much farther, but it is closed to swimming. Beyond Raisin Lake another short steep set of switchbacks takes you up a slope, past a meadow with an ephemeral pond, then meets the northeast end of May Lake and skirts its shore to the High Sierra Camp at 21.2 miles. From here, drop down a rocky slope onto the flat forest floor where, after a few more minutes, you reach the trailhead at the end of Snow Flat Road.

Ten Lakes

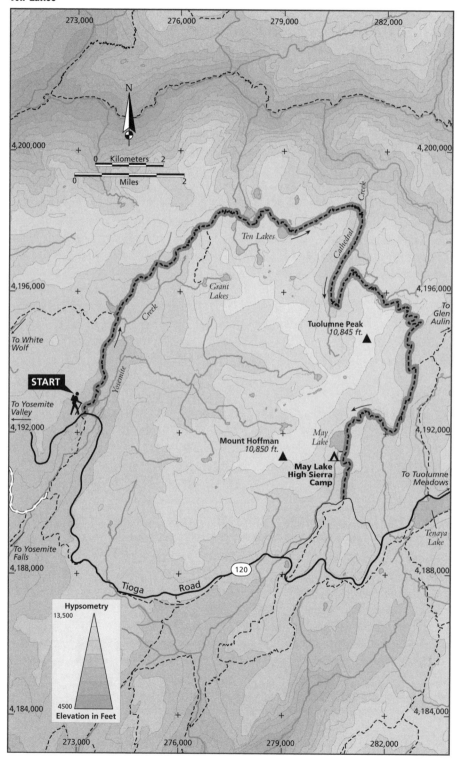

Miles and Directions

0.0 Ten Lakes Trailhead parking lot.

0.1 Yosemite Creek Trail.

2.1 White Wolf junction.

5.9 Grant Lakes junction.

6.3 First of Ten Lakes.

8.2 Second of Ten Lakes.

10.4 Cathedral Creek crossing.

17.5 Glen Aulin junction.

21.1 May Lake.

22.4 May Lake Trailhead.

Options: You can make a grand tour of almost the whole southern drainage of the Grand Canyon of the Tuolumne by turning north toward Glen Aulin at the junction at mile 17.5. From Glen Aulin, you can follow the Tuolumne River down past Waterwheel Falls, through the Grand Canyon of the Tuolumne to Pate Valley, then climb out of the gorge to White Wolf. From there, turn southeast to close the loop at the Ten Lakes Trailhead. You could also begin this big loop from White Wolf, or from the Glen Aulin Trailhead. There is lots of elevation change involved and it can be hot in the bottom of the canyon while the Ten Lakes Basin still has patches of snow, so check trail conditions before you go. You should allow a full week for this one since the distance is a bit over 50 miles and the terrain is rugged.

41 Soda Springs and Parsons Lodge

This is an easy exploration of the largest subalpine meadow in the Sierra with wildflowers galore, a good chance of seeing wildlife, and a taste of Yosemite history.

Start: Soda Springs Trailhead east of the visitor center in Tuolumne Meadows.
Distance: 1.2 miles out and back, or as long as you want to make it.
Approximate hiking time: 1 hour to all day.
Difficulty: Easy.

Seasons: All summer, whenever Tioga Road is open, though the going can be sloppy in June.
Nearest facilities: Food, phones, and gas at Tuolumne Meadows.
Permits: None.
Map: USGS Tioga Pass and Vogelsang Peak quads.

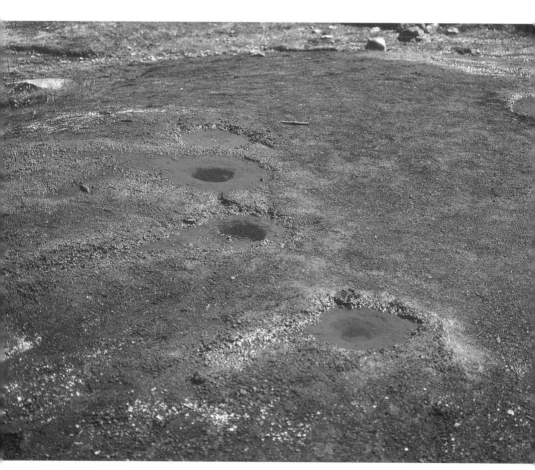

The ground bubbles with naturally carbonated soda springs.

Soda Springs and Parsons Lodge

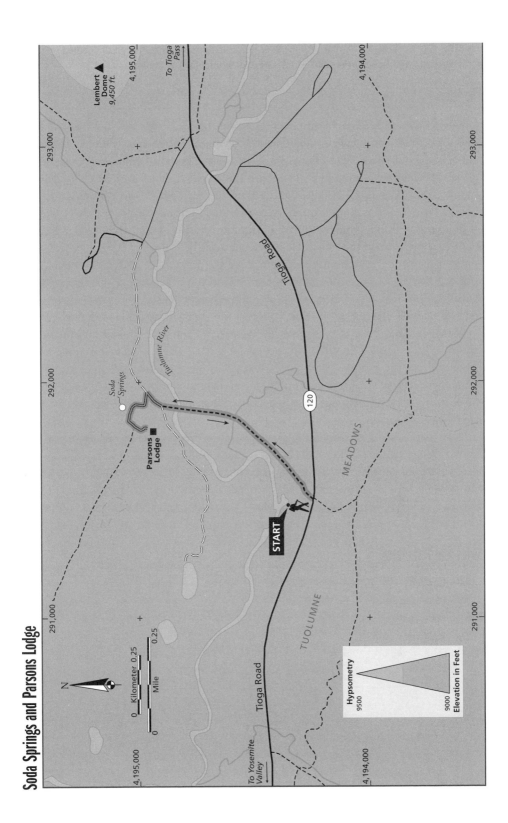

Finding the trailhead: From the visitor center in Tuolumne Meadows, drive a few hundred yards east on Tioga Road to the signed trailhead on the north side of the road.

The Hike

A wide, sandy trail heads right into the heart of enormous Tuolumne Meadows amid a riot of wildflowers: purple meadow penstemon and shooting stars, white pussytoes and yellow goldenrod. Off to the right (east) is long, sloping Lembert Dome, and farther beyond, the two red hulks of Mount Dana and Mount Gibbs. To their right is gray granite Mammoth Peak (not to be confused with Mammoth Mountain, the ski area farther to the south). Ahead, across the main channel of the river winding its sinuous way through the meadow, the path crosses a wood-and-stone footbridge. Pause here and turn around for a panoramic view of the Cathedral Range, with the spires of Cathedral Peak itself, then Echo Peak and the Cockscomb rising behind rounded Fairview Dome. To continue, just beyond the bridge the trail intersects a gravel road on which you turn left (west) and proceed a few yards to a sign directing you to Soda Springs and Parsons Lodge to the right (north) up a little slope.

Parsons Lodge, built of local stone by the Sierra Club in 1915 and sold to the National Park Service in 1973, is open daily during the summer and contains exhibits about the history of the area. Next door, the log-built McCauley Cabin houses park service volunteers who are eager to share local lore. Rest for a while on the rocks in front of the lodge to watch the activities of the marmot families who live in burrows nearby.

Now head toward the roofless log structure clearly visible to the east. Here, naturally carbonated soda springs bubble out of the ground in dozens of places, staining the soil red-brown. This is a good place to see mule deer, especially mornings and evenings as they come to lick the minerals deposited by the springs. You can spend a whole day wandering these meadows, using the well-marked trails to create your own loop, or you can return the way you came to Tioga Road.

Miles and Directions

0.0 Trailhead.
0.5 Parsons Lodge.
0.6 Soda Springs.
1.2 Trailhead.

42 Dog Lake

This is an easy and popular out-and-back day hike through lodgepole pine forest to a lovely lake, tucked out of sight of Tuolumne Meadows behind Lembert Dome.

Start: Dog Lake Trailhead.
Distance: 3.2 miles out and back.
Approximate hiking time: 1 to 3 hours.
Difficulty: Easy.

Seasons: All summer, whenever Tioga Road is open.
Nearest facilities: Tuolumne Meadows.
Permits: None.
Map: USGS Tioga Pass quad.

Finding the trailhead: From the west, drive Tioga Road (Highway 120) eastward past the Tuolumne Meadows visitor center, store, and campground, all on the right. Just after crossing the bridge over the Tuolumne River, turn left into the Lembert Dome parking area. From the east (Tioga Pass) on Tioga Road, pass the turnoff to the wilderness center and Tuolumne Meadows Lodge on the left, then turn right into the Lembert Dome parking lot a few hundred yards beyond.

The Hike

Set out northward from the signed trailhead through lodgepole pines, cross an open rocky slab polished to a high sheen in places by glacial ice, then reenter the forest. The trail forks at 0.1 mile. (This split is not shown on the topo.) Take the left fork. At 0.2 mile another trail comes in from the stables to the left. This time, take the right fork. Just a few yards after that, another trail comes in from the same place. Keep right again. Climb steeply alongside the sheer face of Lembert Dome, then cross a little creek. The grade now becomes gentler. At 1.2 miles a trail cuts off to the right around the back side of Lembert Dome; continue straight ahead toward Dog Lake. At 1.5 miles, turn right onto the Dog Lake Trail and at 1.6 miles, reach an opening in the forest that perfectly frames the lake. The sign in front of you says the water level of the lake is 9,240 feet, while it is marked 9,170 feet on the topo map. Take your pick. Dog Lake is surrounded on three sides by lodgepole pine, but at the far east end, a green meadow provides the foreground for the huge red bulks of Mount Dana and Mount Gibbs. The official mapped trail continues for about a half mile along the south shore of the lake, but it is possible to circumnavigate the whole thing, adding about 1.5 miles to your hike. The meadow around the lakeshore, especially at the east and north ends, can be boggy, and it is very fragile, so travel with care. From the northeast end of the lake, there's a good view of Cathedral Peak poking up through the forest. Camping is not permitted here because the area is too delicate and too close to the road. Return the way you came.

Dog Lake; Lembert Dome

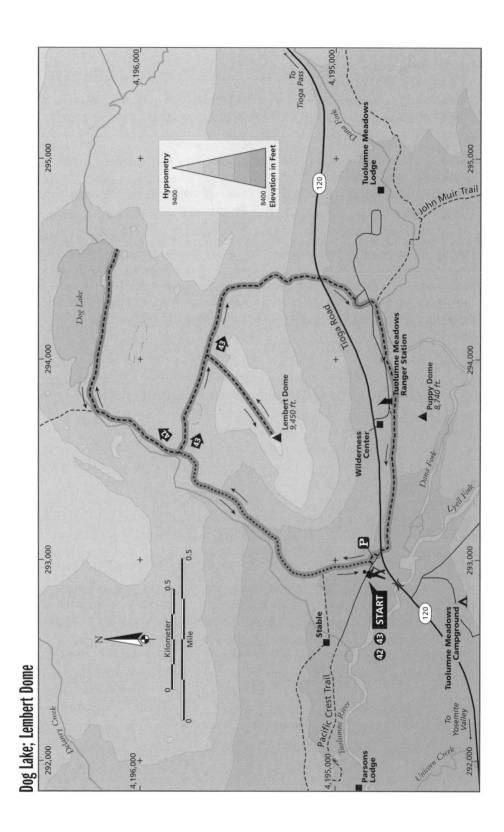

Miles and Directions

0.0 Lembert Dome/Dog Lake Trailhead.

0.1 Dog Lake/Lembert Dome split, keep left.

0.2 Trail to stables, keep right.

1.2 Trail to Lembert Dome, keep left.

1.5 Dog Lake cutoff, turn right.

1.6 Dog Lake.

3.2 Return to trailhead.

43 Lembert Dome

Lembert Dome, among the premier features of Tuolumne Meadows, is the huge, lop-sided, smoothly polished mound of granite just north of Tioga Road. This hike takes you to the top of the dome, approaching from the west and returning to the east to make a loop. The views from the top are marvelous.

See map on page 198

Start: Lembert Dome Trailhead.
Distance: 3.2-mile loop.
Approximate hiking time: 2 to 3 hours.
Difficulty: Moderate.
Seasons: All summer; whenever Tioga

Road is open.
Nearest facilities: Everything you need in Tuolumne Meadows.
Permits: None.
Map: USGS Tioga Pass quad.

Finding the trailhead: From the west, follow Tioga Road (Highway 120) past the Tuolumne Meadows visitor center, store, cafe, and campground, all on the right. Just after crossing the bridge over the Tuolumne River, turn left into the Lembert Dome parking area. From the east (Tioga Pass) on Tioga Road, pass the turnoff to the wilderness center on the left, continue about a hundred yards, then turn right into the Lembert Dome parking area.

Special considerations: Near the top of the dome, the going is steep and the rock is slick and smooth. You'll need good boots with lug soles, and if you're bothered by heights, don't try it. If you have doubts, remember that coming down a steep slope is more difficult than going up.

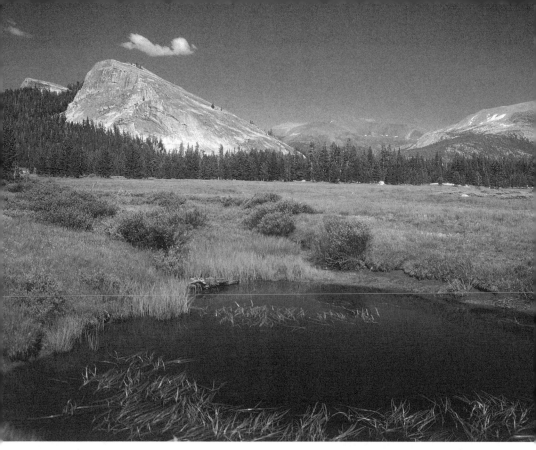

When you tire of the view, examine Lembert Dome for glacial features like scratches and polished rock.

The Hike

Set out northward, past the picnic tables and restrooms, from the Dog Lake/Lembert Dome Trailhead sign beneath the lodgepoles, then cross an open rocky slab where the route is marked by big boulders. The granite has patches polished to a high sheen by glaciers. If you look carefully, you can see the striations or scratches in the rock showing the direction in which the rivers of ice flowed.

The trail forks at 0.1 mile. Continue straight ahead toward Dog Lake. At 0.2 mile, another trail comes in from the stables to the left (west). This time, take the right fork. Just a few yards after that, yet another trail comes in from the same place. Keep right again. Climb fairly steeply alongside the sheer face of Lembert Dome, then cross a little creek. The grade becomes more gradual now. At 1.2 miles, turn right (east) at another signed junction. The left fork goes on uphill to Dog Lake. Saunter along an almost flat path, passing a little pond at the base of the dome. At 1.7 miles is a junction not shown on the topo. You'll return to this point after visiting the summit. Turn right here and climb westward up a wooded ridge to a rocky saddle between Lembert Dome itself and a smaller bump known as Dog Dome. Follow the layered exfoliating granite slabs that form a natural stairway straight up the slope, then pick the easiest way to the top, at 2 miles. The slope is a little less steep toward the left (south) side of the dome.

When you have caught your breath, stroll around on top, where the footing is more level, to take in the view. You can see the high peaks of the north boundary country, the warm red rocks of Mount Dana and Mount Gibbs on the eastern crest, and the Lyell Fork of the Tuolumne River flowing down from the Lyell Glacier to meet the Dana Fork in the broad green meadow. To the south, the spires of the Cathedral Range pierce the sky, and to the west, a series of rounded domes extend into the distance toward Yosemite Valley.

When you are ready, return to the last trail junction (2.3 miles), turn right (east), and follow the fairly steep switchbacks downhill to Tioga Road. Cross the road at 2.6 miles and continue down to a parking lot on a small side road (the one that leads to Tuolumne Meadows High Sierra Camp). Cross this road (south) and find a sign marking the John Muir Trail at 2.7 miles. Turn right and follow this alongside the road, then recross Tioga Road to the Lembert Dome parking area.

Miles and Directions

0.0 Lembert Dome Trailhead.

0.1 Keep left at trail fork.

0.2 Trail from stables, keep right.

1.2 Junction with trail to Dog Lake, turn right.

1.7 Trail to top of Lembert Dome.

2.0 Summit of Lembert Dome.

2.3 Return to trail junction.

2.6 Cross Tioga Road.

2.7 John Muir Trail sign, turn right.

3.2 Lembert Dome parking area.

44 Young Lakes

The three Young Lakes lie in a subalpine lake basin with superb panoramic views of the Cathedral Range along the way. The hike starts out steeply, but becomes more gradual as you climb. It's a good weekend backpack, but if you can, take an extra day to explore the high country beyond. You can make a semiloop of the hike since there is an alternate, though less scenic, trail to the west on which you can return.

Start: Young Lakes Trailhead at Lembert Dome picnic area.
Distance: 13.4 miles out and back.
Approximate hiking time: 1 day if you hurry, 2 days are better.
Difficulty: Strenuous as a day hike, moderate as a backpack.

Seasons: All summer, whenever Tioga Road is open.
Nearest facilities: Food, phones, and gas in Tuolumne Meadows.
Permits: None required for a day hike; available in advance or at the Tuolumne Meadows wilderness center for overnight.
Map: USGS Tioga Pass quad.

Finding the trailhead: From the west, drive Tioga Road (Highway 120) eastward past the Tuolumne Meadows visitor center, store, and campground, all on the right (south). Just after crossing the bridge over the Tuolumne River, turn left into the Lembert Dome parking area. From the east (Tioga Pass) on Tioga Road, pass the turnoff to the wilderness center and Tuolumne Lodge on the left. A few hundred yards beyond, turn right into the Lembert Dome parking lot and picnic area. You can also ride the Tuolumne Meadows shuttle to Lembert Dome. If you plan to spend the night at Young Lakes, park along the road that roughly parallels the highway. Overnight parking is prohibited in the Lembert Dome lot. Be sure to stow all food and food containers in the bear-proof boxes along the road.
Special considerations: A bear canister is required by law at Young Lakes.

The Hike

Set out northward from the Lembert Dome/Dog Lake Trailhead sign through lodgepole pines, crossing an open rocky slab polished to a high sheen in spots by glaciers. When you reenter the forest at 0.1 mile the trail forks. Take the left fork toward Dog Lake. At 0.2 mile a second, then a third trail comes in from the stables to the left (west). Keep right at both junctions. Continue climbing steeply alongside the sheer face of Lembert Dome. When you reach a little creek the grade becomes less extreme, and at 1.5 miles, you meet the Dog Lake Trail heading off to the right. Your trail continues straight ahead, crossing the outlet stream from the lake and ascending a moderate slope for about a half mile to a pretty meadow where you hop or wade Delaney Creek. From the middle of the meadow you can see the great red peaks of Mount Gibbs and Mount Dana on the skyline, so different from the surrounding gray granite. Climb easily up a forested little ridge beyond the meadow around the west side of an unnamed granite dome, then

Young Lakes

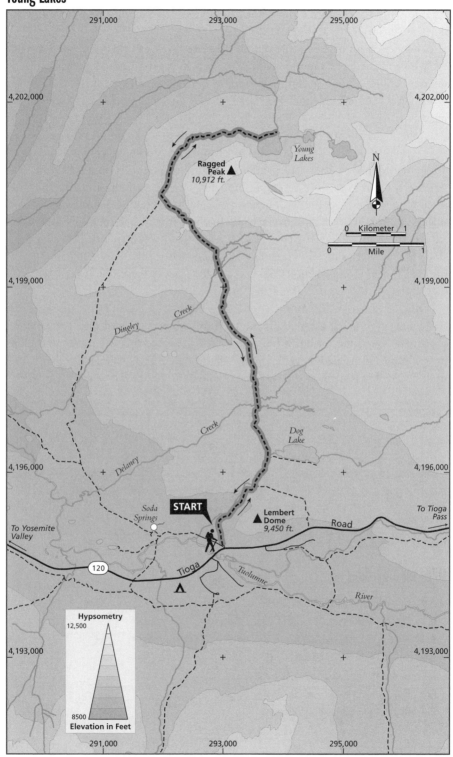

emerge onto a meadowy terrace with twisted whitebark pines and little flower-lined streams trickling through.

The view from here must be one of the finest in the entire Sierra Nevada with the whole Cathedral Range, including Unicorn, Echo, and Cathedral Peaks, spreading out before you. To the right is Mount Hoffman, geographic center of Yosemite; to the left is Mount Lyell, highest peak in the park sheltering the Lyell Glacier. Leaving this perfect spot, the trail climbs a short distance over a sandy shoulder of Ragged Peak, the highest point on this hike, then descends to a junction on the other side at 5.2 miles. The trail joining yours is an alternate route to Young Lakes from Tuolumne Meadows. Your trail continues northward, gradually curving to the east, skirting Ragged Peak, finally dipping into the basin containing the lowest of the three Young Lakes at 6.7 miles. There is plenty of good camping along the western side of this first lake, and most backpackers pitch their tents here, but the higher lakes are equally beautiful and less crowded. To reach them, follow the use trail that runs along the northern shore and scramble up alongside the little waterfall that connects the lakes. From the uppermost lake you can look down upon the lower ones, with snaggle-toothed Ragged Peak jutting up behind them.

On your return to Tuolumne Meadows, you can vary your hike by keeping right (west) instead of left at the trail junction 1.5 miles below Young Lakes. You will end up not far from Soda Springs where you turn left (east) to follow a dirt road back to the trailhead. This route is heavily forested all the way, so you will miss the great views of the Cathedral Range on the way down unless you return the way you came.

Miles and Directions

0.0 Young Lakes Trailhead.

0.1 Dog Lake/Lembert Dome split, keep left.

0.2 Trails to stables, keep right.

1.5 Trail to Dog Lake, keep left.

5.2 Soda Springs Trail junction, turn right.

6.7 First Young Lake.

13.4 Return to Young Lakes Trailhead.

45 Gaylor Lakes

This is a steep but short day hike into a truly alpine environment where permanent snowfields lie in the shady folds of the mountains, and even in July you might have to skirt snow patches or wade through slush. Your reward is a grand open basin filled with masses of miniature belly flowers and the chirps and whistles of pikas and marmots among a scattering of pristine lakes and ponds.

Start: Gaylor Lakes Trailhead.
Distance: 5 miles out and back.
Approximate hiking time: 2 to 4 hours.
Difficulty: Moderate.
Seasons: All summer, whenever Tioga Road is open.

Nearest facilities: Food, phones, and gas in Tuolumne Meadows.
Permits: None.
Map: USGS Tioga Pass quad.

Finding the trailhead: The trailhead is on Tioga Road (Highway 120) immediately inside the eastern park entrance, on the west side of the road.

The Hike

Follow the well-used path uphill through subalpine forest. The trail tops out on a broad, open saddle on broken metamorphic rock. Behind you, massive red Mount Dana thrusts upward above Dana Meadows. Beyond a few clumps of windblown whitebark pine, the trail drops as steeply as it rose to the first of the Gaylor Lakes. It skirts the north edge of the lake, which seems to reach to the very lip of the shallow dish in which it sits. Beyond it, the spiky tops of the Cathedral Range appear to be emerging from the surface of the lake itself.

Climb gradually north past Gaylor Peak, skirt the west end of another lake, swing around a ridge to the left, then climb to another ridgetop at the border of the park. There you'll find the old Great Sierra Mine, a failed silver-mining operation that commands another grand view. You can explore this lake basin for hours, or you can cross the low rise immediately west of Gaylor Peak to discover the Granite Lakes in another shallow bowl at the base of a classic glacial cirque.

Gaylor Lakes

301,000

To 395

Great
Sierra
Mine

N

0   Kilometer 0.25
0   Mile   0.25

4,200,000   4,200,000

Gaylor
Lakes

YOSEMITE
NATIONAL
PARK

INYO
NATIONAL
FOREST

120

Gaylor
Peak
11,004 ft.

4,199,000   4,199,000

Tioga

Road

START

4,198,000   4,198,000

Tioga
Pass

Hypsometry
8000

DANA MEADOWS

3500
Elevation in Feet

To Tuolumne
Meadows

301,000

There is a second route leading to the lakes that begins a few miles farther west on Tioga Road, but the trailhead is not obvious and the distance to the first lake is longer. The two trails do not meet in the lake basin, so if you want to make a longer shuttle hike, you will have to travel about a mile cross-country between the trails, or return the way you came.

Miles and Directions

0.0 Gaylor Lakes Trailhead.

1.5 First Gaylor Lake.

2.5 Great Sierra Mine.

5.0 Gaylor Lakes Trailhead.

Hetch Hetchy

etch Hetchy Reservoir, begun in 1914, completed in 1923, then expanded in 1938, provides water and power for the city of San Francisco. For this reason, since September 11, 2001, park rangers at the entrance kiosk record license numbers of all vehicles entering and leaving the area. Before the dam captured and tamed the Tuolumne River, the Hetch Hetchy Valley was said to rival Yosemite itself in scenic beauty. John Muir's famous, if fruitless, battle against the dam brought the need to preserve such wilderness treasures to the attention of the public and gave impetus to the growth of the National Park Service and to the conservation movement as a whole. Even now, a campaign is under way to convince legislators to raze the dam, drain the reservoir, and allow Hetch Hetchy to return to its original state. The area around the lake has the best display of springtime wildflowers in the park. It's a great place to hike in early season when the higher country is still under snow, and is pleasant in October when the black oaks change color. In midsummer, it's dry and hot. No swimming or boating is allowed in the reservoir.

There are no overnight accommodations at Hetch Hetchy, except for a walk-in backpackers' campground. You must have a wilderness permit to use it, and you are limited to a one-night stay. The Hodgden Meadow Campground near the Big Oak Flat entrance is the closest park campground and requires reservations. There is also a concessionaire-operated forest service campground on Evergreen Road open on a first-come, first-served basis, and other accommodations in nearby Groveland.

To reach the main Hetch Hetchy trailhead at O'Shaughnessy Dam, you must leave Yosemite Park at the Big Oak Flat entrance station (if you are coming from the east), then reenter it at the Hetch Hetchy entrance station about 8 miles up Evergreen Road. From the west, turn off the highway before you reach the main (Big Oak Flat) entrance station. (See directions at the beginning of each hike.) Wilderness permits are available at the Hetch Hetchy entrance station and the Big Oak Flat entrance station. It's a good idea to ask about the condition of the road before you start out because it washes out regularly and may be closed for repairs.

46 Wapama Falls

This is an out-and-back day hike along the controversial Hetch Hetchy Reservoir through a riotous show of springtime wildflowers and past the base of one gentle waterfall to the crash and spray of a mighty one—at least in springtime when high country snows are melting.

Start: Trailhead at O'Shaughnessy Dam.
Distance: 5 miles out and back.
Approximate hiking time: 4 to 6 hours.
Difficulty: Easy.
Seasons: Mid-April through June.

Nearest facilities: Food and accommodations at Evergreen Lodge near Camp Mather. Phones, toilets, water near the trailhead, gas at Crane Flat.
Permits: None.
Map: USGS Lake Eleanor quad.

Finding the trailhead: Drive 1 mile west of the Big Oak Flat entrance station to Yosemite on Highway 120. Turn right (north) on Evergreen Road and drive about 7 miles. At Camp Mather, turn right (northeast) on Hetch Hetchy Road. Pass through the park entrance station in about a mile, then continue on for 8 miles more to where the road ends in a one-way loop. Partway around is the dam, and just beyond it, a parking area.

The Hike

Walk across the dam past some historical markers. On the far side at 0.1 mile, enjoy the troupe of acrobatic swallows swooping and diving before the entrance to a dark and dripping tunnel. Pass through the tunnel and continue along the level road skirting the lake; it's lined with live oak, bay trees, and poison oak, along with dozens of species of wildflowers, among them the unusual pink-and-yellow harlequin lupine. Little trickles of water seep from cracks in the rocks to nourish buttercups, monkeyflowers, and columbines. In May, if you're lucky, you'll catch the spring migration of the little brown-and-orange California newts crossing the trail in such numbers that you must step carefully to avoid squashing them. The low elevation

The O'Shaughnessy Dam, completed in 1924, flooded Hetch Hetchy Valley, said to have rivaled Yosemite Valley in beauty.

here also makes this a likely spot for snakes of several kinds, including rattlers. They are not aggressive, but they do not like to be handled or stepped on.

The road climbs fairly gently for a while, then, at 0.9 mile, it continues on to the left, while the trail to the falls cuts to the right toward the lake. The route rises and falls and curves back and forth past more delicate little gardens, waterfalls, and pools while Kolana Rock broods darkly over the reservoir on the other side.

Farther along, Tueeulala Falls tumbles down over the trail. Early in the season you'll probably get your feet wet as you pass, but by mid-June the creek that feeds it is usually dry. The trail continues along the cliff above the lake, climbing and descending for a short distance more until at last, at 2.5 miles, the spray and thunder of Wapama Falls make themselves felt. Toward the bottom, the fall splits into several sections, each of which is crossed on a separate footbridge. Sometimes the bridges are shin-deep underwater, though safe to wade; at other times the force of the falling torrent is so great that it is risky to cross. You can enjoy the falls from either side, or from the middle—if you crave a refreshing shower. Return the way you came.

Wapama Falls; Rancheria Falls; Lake Vernon and Tiltill Valley

Miles and Directions

0.0 O'Shaughnessy Dam Trailhead.

0.1 Tunnel.

0.9 Trail/road junction, turn right onto the trail.

2.5 Wapama Falls.

5.0 Return to trailhead.

THE CALIFORNIA NEWT A newt is a particular kind of salamander. Most of the year they live on land, hiding under leaves and rocks. They have rough skin, not at all slimy, but they need water to breed, and in springtime the males develop smooth skin and their tails become flattened vertically to make swimming more efficient. California newts (also known as "water dogs") are not as wary of sunlight as other salamanders are, especially when it's mating time, which makes them easier to spot than other species. They are poisonous to eat, so are avoided by most predators, and are themselves carnivorous, snapping up snails, worms, and insects. They are not dangerous to handle so long as you rinse your hands afterward. When startled, they throw back their heads and raise their tails to flash their bright orange undersides in a defense posture.

47 Rancheria Falls

Lots of flowers, birds, bears, and reptiles are likely company on this popular spring-time backpack. The route runs along the north shore of Hetch Hetchy Reservoir, past Tueeulala and Wapama Falls where you can expect to be thoroughly drenched by spray, to campsites beside the spot where Rancheria Creek tumbles down a series of cascades into the lake. You can do it as a strenuous day hike, but there are lots of moderate ups and downs that make it more demanding than it looks. Rancheria Falls has always been a notorious hangout for "problem" bears, so a canister is required for an overnight stay.

See map on page 212

Start: Trailhead at O'Shaughnessy Dam.
Distance: 13.8 miles out and back.
Approximate hiking time: 6 hours to 2 days.
Difficulty: Moderate.
Seasons: Mid-April to June.
Nearest facilities: Food and accommodations at Evergreen Lodge near Camp Mather;

phones, toilets, and water near the trailhead; gas at Crane Flat.
Permits: None for a day hike. Available in advance or at the Hetch Hetchy entrance station for backpackers.
Maps: USGS Hetch Hetchy Reservoir and Lake Eleanor quads.

Finding the trailhead: Drive 1 mile west of the Big Oak Flat entrance station to Yosemite on Highway 120. Turn right (north) on Evergreen Road for about 7 miles. At Camp Mather turn right (northeast) on Hetch Hetchy Road. Pass through the park entrance station in about a mile, then continue on for 8 miles to where the road ends in a one-way loop. Partway around is the dam, and just beyond it, a parking area.

Special considerations: Even though there are bridges over several sections of Wapama Falls where the trail crosses below it, you may still be wading shin-deep through fast-moving water. Be prepared for wet feet and carry some sort of pack cover, even if only a plastic bag, because the spray can be heavy enough to soak your pack and its contents. At the height of snowmelt in spring, check with rangers before you begin to make sure you can get past the falls safely.

The Hike

Walk across the dam past some historical markers and on through a dark and dripping tunnel on an old gravel road lined with live oak, bay trees, and poison oak, along with dozens of species of wildflowers. Climb easily along the road for a while, then, at 0.9 mile, turn right toward the lake at a signed trail that cuts off from the road. The route rises and falls and curves back and forth past delicate little gardens, waterfalls, and pools while Kolana Rock broods darkly over the reservoir on the other side.

▶ Watch for congregations of all kinds of butterflies gathered at mud puddles or damp spots along the trail. These are young males sucking up water and minerals, biding their time until the females, who emerge later, appear. This behavior is called "puddling."

Rancheria Creek cascades into Hetch Hetchy Reservoir over Rancheria Falls.

Farther along, Tueeulala Falls tumbles down over the trail, where you will get your feet wet in early season, though by mid-June the creek that feeds it is dry. The trail continues along the cliff above the lake, climbing and descending for a short distance more until, at 2.5 miles, the spray and thunder of Wapama Falls make themselves felt. Pick your way across the several bridges that span the multiple strands of the falls, sometimes sloshing through deep water, sometimes bracing yourself against potentially dangerous torrents, sometimes strolling by with perfectly dry feet. The trail gains some elevation above the lake and the base of the falls, makes its way around Hetch Hetchy Dome, occasionally climbing or dropping on switchbacks to avoid various obstacles. Occasional patches of shady oak forest alternate with stretches of sunny, sweaty trudging until the trail crosses a shady, unnamed creek on a little bridge, rounds a corner, and crosses more substantial Tiltill Creek on a bigger one. Finally, after one last hot, shadeless climb, it tops out on a shoulder from which there is a good view of Rancheria Creek roaring down a series of water slides to the reservoir. About a quarter mile beyond, at 6.9 miles, a sign marks the turnoff to the camping area near the river on your right. This is such a popular spot that it is especially important to pitch your tent at least 100 feet from the creekside and practice zero-impact camping techniques. When you are ready, retrace your steps to the dam and the parking lot.

Miles and Directions

0.0   O'Shaughnessy Dam Trailhead.
0.9   Wapama Falls Trail cuts off to the right.
2.5   Wapama Falls.
6.9   Rancheria Falls Campground.
13.8 Return to trailhead.

Option: To visit the top of the Rancheria Falls, continue up the trail past the campground, keeping to the right at a junction with the trail to Tiltill Valley at about a quarter mile. Just around the corner, the bridge over the Rancheria Creek spans a rocky gorge where the stream is squeezed into the neck of a deep, narrow funnel that opens out just below the bridge, releasing water in a boiling, foaming rush down past the campground. This adds only about a half mile round-trip.

48 Lake Vernon and Tiltill Valley

Lake Vernon lies in a real subalpine setting at an elevation of only 6,568 feet, so this loop is a good way to get in a real High Sierra backpack while the higher country is still under snow. The wildflowers and waterfalls along the Hetch Hetchy Reservoir on the last leg of the trip are spectacular, there are Native American sites to investigate in Tiltill Valley, and good camping can be enjoyed at Rancheria Falls.

See map on page 212

Start: Trailhead at O'Shaughnessy Dam.
Distance: 26.7-mile loop.
Approximate hiking time: 2 to 4 days.
Difficulty: Moderate.
Seasons: Early May through early July and October.
Nearest facilities: Food and accommodations

at Evergreen Lodge near Camp Mather; phones, toilets, and water near the trailhead; gas at Crane Flat.
Permits: Available in advance or from the Hetch Hetchy entrance station.
Maps: USGS Hetch Hetchy Reservoir, Kibbie Lake, Lake Eleanor, and Tiltill Mountain quads.

Finding the trailhead: Drive 1 mile west of the Big Oak Flat entrance station to Yosemite on Highway 120. Turn right (north) onto Evergreen Road and drive about 7 miles. At Camp Mather turn right (northeast) onto Hetch Hetchy Road. Pass through the park entrance station in about a mile, then continue on for 8 miles to where the road ends in a one-way loop at O'Shaughnessy Dam and the parking area.

The Hike

Walk across the dam past some historical markers and on through a dark and dripping tunnel to emerge into sunlight on the old Lake Eleanor Road, lined with live oak, bay trees, and poison oak along with dozens of species of wildflowers. At 0.9 mile a trail cuts away from the road heading to the right toward the reservoir. Stay on the road and follow the long, partly shaded switchbacks to a junction with the trail to Miguel Meadow at 3.6 miles. Keep right (north) and ascend beneath pines and incense cedars to a more level stretch that winds through an open, rocky area lined with manzanita. Stay alert and watch the ducks to avoid losing the trail.

Reenter burned-over forest and climb past a couple of tiny emerald green meadows carpeted with white meadow foam and yellow monkeyflowers until you arrive at another junction heading back to Lake Eleanor at 6 miles, and keep right (north) again. Very soon you reach Beehive at 6.8 miles. It is a soggy and mosquito-ridden meadow with a piped spring protected by wood planks. (The water should be purified before drinking.) Another path goes west to Laurel Lake from here, but it has not yet recovered from a severe burn and is not very attractive. Keep right, heading northeast out of Beehive, gaining elevation steadily to reach yet another junction at 8.1 miles with the Jack Main Canyon trail heading northeast to the top of Moraine Ridge toward Wilma Lake. Follow the right fork for a time, then drop down an open rocky slope and cross over a low hump to enter the Lake Vernon basin at 10.3 miles. There is some beautiful camping to be found on broad flat rock slabs along the northwestern shore of the lake.

Leaving Lake Vernon, head south, crossing Falls Creek, the lake's outlet stream, on a bridge. The route now climbs above the lake basin and looks out over splendid High Sierra scenery—wild and open glacier-scoured white granite, dotted with junipers. In springtime, this section of trail reeks with the smell of onions. So many tiny, low-growing, almost transparent flowers sprout in the sandy soil at your feet that it's impossible to avoid stepping on some of them. The trail crosses over the top of this ridge, reenters forest, and hops a creek. It follows the ridge for a time, passes alongside a meadow, then swings left around its south end and crosses another creek. The route curves east and drops down the hot, south-facing slope through scratchy, overgrown ceanothus and manzanita for what seems like a long time before it once again reaches forest cover. Listen for the booming of male blue grouse announcing their territorial claims along this stretch. You are almost guaranteed to hear them in spring.

Continue the knee-jarring descent into Tiltill Valley and cross a creek. The trail sloshes along the north side of the soggy meadow, then rather abruptly turns south. A detour of a few yards eastward takes you to the only area near the meadow high and dry enough for camping. A big boulder at the upper end of the campsite has several bedrock mortars, smooth hollows in the rock where the native Miwok pounded their acorn meal.

Back in the meadow's center, a trail to Tilden Lake and beyond cuts off to the east at 17.1 miles. The path is extremely mushy at the south side of the meadow and there is no convenient way to get around it, but you can enjoy the lovely liquid song of red-winged blackbirds as you slosh along. Your boots will dry on the climb to the top of the ridge above the meadow. Pass through a notch and skirt a lovely little pond lined with azaleas and blooming with yellow pond lilies. There may be lots of mosquitoes too. Now you'll drop down hot dry switchbacks to meet a trail junction just above Rancheria Falls at 19.8 miles. Turn right (north) and head toward Hetch

Hetchy Reservoir. The Rancheria Creek camping area, marked by a sign, is the last place you can camp along this loop. Beyond the campground, the path switchbacks down to bridges across Tiltill Creek and a smaller, unnamed stream, then contours along the cliff above the reservoir to reach Wapama Falls at mile 24.2. You will probably be ready for the refreshing shower you'll get from the bridge beneath it. In little more than a half mile, wade the stream at the base of wispy Tueeulala Falls, and continue in and out of black and live oak forest to meet the junction at mile 25.8, where you once again pick up the Lake Eleanor Road. Turn left, and follow it back through the tunnel to the O'Shaughnessy Dam Trailhead.

Miles and Directions

0.0   O'Shaughnessy Dam Trailhead.

0.9   Lake Eleanor Road/trail junction.

3.6   Miguel Meadow junction.

6.0   Lake Eleanor cutoff.

6.8   Beehive.

8.1   Jack Main Canyon junction.

10.3   Lake Vernon.

17.1   Tiltill Valley.

19.8   Rancheria junction.

24.2   Wapama Falls.

25.8   Lake Eleanor Road/trail junction.

26.7   O'Shaughnessy Dam Trailhead.

49 Jack Main Canyon and Tilden Lake

This multiday loop hike has been included in the Hetch Hetchy section because it begins and ends there, but part of it extends into the remote north boundary country. Spring runoff in early season makes some sections of trail nearly impassible and many creek crossings extremely dangerous. On the other hand, if you wait too long, the beginning and end of the trip at the low elevations around Hetch Hetchy Reservoir can be hot and dry. Still, if the conditions are right, it's a great hike, with solitude guaranteed. Just be sure to check with the park service about trail conditions before setting out.

Start: Trailhead at O'Shaughnessy Dam.
Distance: 46.5-mile loop.
Approximate hiking time: 3 to 6 days.
Difficulty: Moderate to strenuous, depending on how fast you take it.
Seasons: Mid-July through September.
Nearest facilities: Food and accommodations at Evergreen Lodge near Camp Mather;

phones, toilets, and water near the trailhead; gas at Crane Flat.
Permits: Available in advance or from the Hetch Hetchy entrance station.
Maps: USGS Hetch Hetchy Reservoir, Kibbie Lake, Lake Eleanor, Tiltill Mountain, and Piute Mountain quads.

Finding the trailhead: Drive 1 mile west of the Big Oak Flat entrance station to Yosemite on Highway 120. Turn right (north) on Evergreen Road and drive about 7 miles. At Camp Mather, turn right (northeast) on Hetch Hetchy Road. Pass through the park entrance station in about a mile, then continue on for 8 miles more to where the road ends in a one-way loop. Partway around is the dam, and just beyond it, a parking area.

The Hike

Walk across the dam past some historical markers and on through a dark and dripping tunnel to emerge into sunlight on the old Lake Eleanor Road, lined with live oak, bay trees, and poison oak, along with dozens of species of wildflowers early in the year, though dry and dusty by midsummer. At 0.9 mile, a trail cuts away from the road heading to the right toward the reservoir. Stay on the road and follow the long, partly shaded switchbacks to a junction with the trail to Miguel Meadow at 3.6 miles. Keep right (north) and ascend beneath pines and incense cedars to a more level stretch that winds through an open rocky area lined with manzanita, where you must stay alert and watch the ducks to avoid losing the trail.

Reenter burned-over forest and climb past a couple of tiny meadows carpeted with white meadow foam and yellow monkeyflowers until you arrive at another junction heading back to Lake Eleanor at 6 miles, and keep right (north) again. Very soon you reach Beehive at 6.8 miles. It is a soggy and mosquito-ridden meadow with a piped spring protected by wood planks. The water should be purified before

Tilden Lake is a classic glacial finger lake.

drinking. Another path goes west to Laurel Lake. Keep right, heading northeast out of Beehive, gaining elevation steadily to reach the junction with the Jack Main Canyon trail at 8.1 miles. Keep left here and climb Moraine Ridge, part of which is shaded, part open, grassy, and waterless, with heavy sand underfoot that makes uphill progress tedious. Drop down off the toe of Moraine Ridge on a section of trail known as the Golden Stairs into Jack Main Canyon, and along the way enjoy a glimpse of one of the Branigan Lakes to the east. At the base of the stairs, meet Falls Creek, which drops into Hetch Hetchy Reservoir as Wapama Falls far below. It must be one of the most interesting and beautiful streams in Yosemite as it winds its way along the floor of Jack Main Canyon, cascading from pool to pool, widening out in lazy meanders, then roaring through narrow gaps in the canyon walls. There are plenty of good places to camp, the finest being on sunny rock slabs above one of the many small, unnamed lakes. The trail undulates over uneven ground that is sometimes very rocky, sometimes sloppy, sometimes completely underwater. At 15.1 miles, a trail heads off to the east to connect with the Pacific Crest Trail (PCT) in a little more than 2 miles. You can make a shorter loop using this route if you

Jack Main Canyon and Tilden Lake

don't have time for the longer one, or if the trail farther north at Wilma Lake is flooded.

To continue, keep left and ascend very gradually, passing through interesting narrow slots that have trapped snowmelt lakes that have no inlets or outlets. Pass to the west of a long, wide meadow just below Wilma Lake. You can't reach the lake directly from here, but must continue north to the junction with the Pacific Crest Trail at 18.1 miles, then cut back along the PCT to the south to reach the lakeshore. If the water is high, this section may be too deep and wide to negotiate.

Return to the main trail. Your trail and the PCT now coincide and continue north. Go through a gate and wander along the flat valley floor to 20 miles, where you leave the PCT again and turn right (east). Climb a ridge to meet the southern end of Tilden Lake at its outlet at 21.7 miles. Chittenden Peak squats beside the outlet. Tilden Lake is a classic glacial finger lake that has plenty of good camping on its southeast side. There are great views up the lake canyon, with Tower Peak at the far end. The trail follows the irregular shore for a while, then swings south through meadows and pools and climbs to meet the PCT again at 25.4 miles. Keep left here. The right fork goes back to Wilma Lake.

In a very short time, at 25.5 miles, leave the PCT as it goes east toward Stubblefield Canyon. Your trail goes right (southwest) dropping into a valley just west of main Tilden Canyon through more grassy, marshy meadows and ponds, then climbs to a junction with the trail back over to Jack Main Canyon at 28.1 miles. Just beyond this are good views back to Tower Peak and the surrounding wilderness. Descend very gradually now through the forest to the south until you reach a ridge where you descend more steeply over rocks through hot, open brush toward Tiltill Valley, which is now visible below with the Hetch Hetchy Reservoir beyond. At the end of a knee-knocking drop, splash through the meadow at Tiltill Valley to meet the trail back down to Rancheria Falls at 35.9 miles. Climb out of the basin, passing a very pretty lily pond. Drop down hot, dry switchbacks to meet a trail junction just above Rancheria Falls at 38.6 miles. Turn right (north) and head toward Hetch Hetchy Reservoir. The Rancheria Creek camping area, marked by a sign, is the last place camping is possible along this loop. Descend to cross Tiltill Creek on a bridge, then another little stream, and skirt the lake, bobbing up and down along the cliff above it to reach Wapama Falls at mile 44. You will probably be ready for the refreshing shower you might get from the bridge beneath it if it is early enough in the season to be flowing. A little more than a half mile beyond, wade or hop the stream at the base of gentler Tueeulala Falls and continue in and out of black and live oak forest to meet the trail junction at mile 45.6, where you once again pick up the Lake Eleanor Road. Turn left, and follow it back to the O'Shaughnessy Dam Trailhead.

Miles and Directions

0.0 O'Shaughnessy Dam Trailhead.

0.9 Lake Eleanor Road/trail junction.

3.6 Miguel Meadow junction.

6.0 Lake Eleanor cutoff.

6.8 Beehive.

8.1 Jack Main Canyon junction.

15.1 Jack Main Canyon.

18.1 Wilma Lake.

20.0 Tilden Creek crossing.

21.7 Tilden Lake outlet.

25.4 Wilma Lake junction.

28.1 Jack Main Canyon junction.

35.9 Tiltill Valley.

38.6 Rancheria Falls junction.

44.0 Wapama Falls.

45.6 Lake Eleanor Road/trail junction.

46.5 O'Shaughnessy Dam Trailhead.

The North Boundary Country

This is Yosemite at its wildest. It is part of the largest roadless area in California, and one of the largest in the United States. The average elevation here is lower than in other parts of Yosemite, though the northeastern crest has some high peaks. The topography away from the crest appears to be more rolling, too, but the hiking is no less strenuous. The glaciers that shaped the land have gouged a series of parallel canyons that make east-west hiking exhausting. There is more open rock and fewer extensive stands of forest because the recent (in geologic terms) glaciers have scoured away most of the soil. When the snow melts in spring these rocky canyons carry enormous volumes of water, at least partly because there is little soil to absorb it. Early in the year, even well into July, big sections of the trails may be completely submerged, and many stream crossings are high and dangerous. Trails are not as frequently patrolled or maintained, so you must be well prepared, must be skilled at route finding, and must take special pains to find out about trail conditions before you start.

The shorter hikes that begin near U.S. Highway 395 on the eastern border of the park are popular, since most pass through sections of the Hoover Wilderness, part of the Toiyabe and Inyo National Forests, which allow more commercial development than the National Park Service does. The forest service also stocks the hundreds of lakes with trout and permits hunting, so day hikers will meet lots of fishermen, and in fall, a few hunters. Hikers who have penetrated farther than a day's journey into the park from any of its borders, or those who have entered from one of the more remote trailheads to the north, however, will only meet other hardy souls like themselves and a few through-hikers on the Pacific Crest Trail.

All the hikes in this section begin off US 395 or the Tioga Road, Highway 120. Supplies and gas can be found in Lee Vining or Bridgeport on US 395, and in Tuolumne Meadows. Trailheads with small resorts like Mono Village, Saddlebag Lake, Lundy Lake, Virginia Pass, and Tioga Pass have cafes and limited groceries.

For hikes beginning outside Yosemite, get permits at the Mono Basin or Bridgeport USDA Forest Service ranger stations. They are good inside the park and are also subject to trailhead quotas.

50 Saddlebag Lake and 20 Lakes Basin

Saddlebag Lake is just outside Yosemite in the Hoover Wilderness and, like Lundy Canyon, is a favorite of Yosemite hikers. It is also a backdoor cross-country entrance into the park by way of McCabe Lakes. The region behind and including Saddlebag Lake is known as the 20 Lakes Basin, but is not identified by that name (or any other) name on the topo. The loop can be hiked in either direction but the views are better if you proceed counterclockwise. The lakes are stocked with trout and are simply swarming with anglers. The little resort near the trailhead operates a shuttle boat that will drop you off at the far end of the lake and pick you up later at whatever time you specify, if you are in a hurry. It is inexpensive and saves you 1.5 miles each way.

Start: Saddlebag Lake Trailhead east.
Distance: 8.3-mile loop.
Approximate hiking time: 4 to 6 hours.
Difficulty: Moderate.
Seasons: All summer; whenever Tioga Road is open; however, high water, wet meadows, and deep snow sometimes make travel difficult early in the season.

Nearest facilities: Cafe, store, and campground at Saddlebag Lake Resort.
Permits: None for a day hike. Available at the kiosk in the backpackers' parking lot at Saddlebag Lake, or from the Mono Basin visitor center just outside Lee Vining at Mono Lake.
Maps: USGS Dunderberg Peak and Tioga Pass quads.

Finding the trailhead: From Tioga Road (Highway 120) drive about a mile east of the Yosemite Park entrance and turn west onto Saddlebag Lake Road. Drive 2.5 miles over partly paved road to the south end of the lake. Follow the signs to the backpackers' parking lot near the wilderness permit kiosk or to the day-use parking area at the end of the road.

The Hike

Begin at the closed gate near the sign welcoming hikers to the basin and warning that campfires are prohibited. Skirt the eastern shore of the lake on broken red and black rock. While this entire basin is a veritable wonderland of wildflowers, this part of the trail is lined with sagebrush and pennyroyal and is exceptionally aromatic. Directly ahead lies the Shepherd Crest culminating in the sharp point of Sheep Peak, surprisingly white among the adjoining rusty crags. As you progress along Saddlebag's eastern shore, North Peak gradually appears from behind a nearby ridge; then even bigger Mount Conness, among the highest peaks in the park at 12,590 feet, is revealed. It shelters a small glacier at its base. A ranger station that looks like a little dollhouse surrounded by the round white heads of flowers known as ranger buttons stands at the end of the lake above the boat landing.

Just beyond the cabin, at 2.2 miles, the trail splits. Follow the right (north) fork and climb easily past the sign announcing the entrance to the Hoover Wilderness. Just beyond, to the right of the trail, is little Hummingbird Lake. Above it are a few

North Peak provides a backdrop for Shamrock Lake in the 20 Lakes Basin.

small campsites in the shelter of some whitebark pines. Cross the outlet from the lake over rather flimsy logs and continue climbing to Lundy Pass at 3.1 miles. Below soaring, rusty red-and-black cliffs lies Odell Lake, with an odd little round island in the middle. Descend to the northwestern shore of the lake, then follow its outlet down a steep, narrow, rocky gorge, crossing the creek partway down, to Helen Lake. This gorge holds some snow for most of the year, and in early season it may be too steep, icy, and dangerous to attempt.

The path around the eastern side of Helen Lake goes along a rocky and precipitous slope to the outlet, where a sign at 3.9 miles points the way to Lundy Canyon, straight ahead. Your route is to the left (west). Follow a use trail, not shown on the topo map, around the west side of the lake. It's quite distinct, and passes several little ponds, waterfalls, and meadows spangled with alpine wildflowers. Climb a beautifully ice-polished ridge and follow ducks to look out upon one of the prettiest views in the Sierra. Shamrock Lake below has an irregular, rocky shoreline and several picturesque islands, all trimmed with perfect arrangements of gnarled whitebark pine and brilliant magenta mountain pride penstemon. Beyond, North Peak provides a

Saddlebag Lake and 20 Lakes Basin

majestic backdrop. The trail descends round the west side of Shamrock Lake to another small unnamed lake. Here, a very short steep path drops down to the right to meet an old mining road running past Steelhead Lake at 4.9 miles. The road ends about 100 yards to the right at the abandoned Hess Mine.

The flat ridge above the mine between North and Sheep Peaks is a fairly easy cross-country route into Yosemite via McCabe Lakes. Your present route turns left, crossing an outlet from the lake on a log, and follows the road southward along the main outlet from Steelhead Lake. A low, flat isthmus separates Wasco from Saddlebag Lake, and several use trails leave the road to cross to the west side of the basin at 6.6 miles. Some of these fade out partway across the meadow, and some arrive at the creek connecting the two lakes, at a place where it is impossible to cross. Follow any (or none) of these paths to wherever you can ford easily and pick up the trail on the other side heading south along the western shore of Saddlebag Lake, then hike the rough, rocky path along the mountainside to the dam. You can cross on the top of the dam if the spillway is closed, or if it is open, follow a trail downstream and over a bridge to meet Saddlebag Lake Road, on which you turn left and proceed to your car.

Miles and Directions

0.0   Saddlebag Lake Trailhead.

2.2   North end of Saddlebag Lake, follow the right fork where the trail splits.

3.1   Cross Lundy Pass.

3.9   Helen Lake/Lundy Canyon junction, turn left.

4.9   Steelhead Lake.

6.6   North end Saddlebag Lake, keep right.

8.3   Saddlebag Lake Trailhead.

51 Lundy Canyon

Lundy Canyon is part of the Hoover Wilderness. It does not actually belong to Yosemite, but it can be used as a route into the park via a short cross-country connection. At any rate, it is well known to those who love Yosemite and is included here because it is the most beautiful canyon in the area, with the finest wildflower display, the most brilliant fall colors, and the greatest number of waterfalls. You can do it as an out-and-back day hike—just sample a short portion of the valley—or make a shuttle hike into 20 Lakes Basin if you can arrange a ride.

Start: Lundy Canyon Trailhead in the Lundy Campground.
Distance: 10.8 miles out and back.
Approximate hiking time: All day.
Difficulty: Strenuous.
Seasons: Summer through fall.

Nearest facilities: Lundy Lake Resort.
Permits: None for a day hike; backpacker permits are available at the Mono Basin visitor center, just outside Lee Vining at Mono Lake.
Map: USGS Dunderberg Peak quad.

Finding the trailhead: From U.S. Highway 395 take the Lundy Lakes turnoff 7 miles north of Lee Vining. Drive west 5 miles to the far end of Lundy Lake. When the road forks just below the lake, keep right. The left fork ends at the dam. Pass the tiny general store and continue for about a mile on a narrow bumpy road through a campground to where the road makes a one-way loop.

The Hike

Begin along the northeast slope of Lundy Canyon above Mill Creek on colorful red, black, and white rock. A very active population of beavers has dammed the lower part of the creek in several places, but eventually the slope becomes too steep and the stream too rapid for their dams as it drops over the first of several sets of waterfalls. The trail crosses the creek amid riotously blooming flower gardens under dense quaking aspen, whose brilliant golden foliage more than compensates for lack of blooms in late September.

Cross another branch of the creek on logs and come to the remains of an old trapper's cabin. Out in the open again, waterfalls flow down the cliffs on all sides of the canyon above the aspen groves. The low, contorted shapes of these trees hint of the violence of snow and rockfall that occur here in winter.

The trail now begins to climb the slope above the canyon. Ignore any apparent trails that cut away from the main route, and continue up and southwest, then due south, zigzagging up a very steep and rough, slaty slope. Partway to the top of the ridge, the trail meets Mill Creek and climbs close alongside it as it tumbles down a gully. The top of this gully holds snow until quite late in the year. If the trail is mostly snow covered or icy, do not continue upward without crampons or an ice axe. At

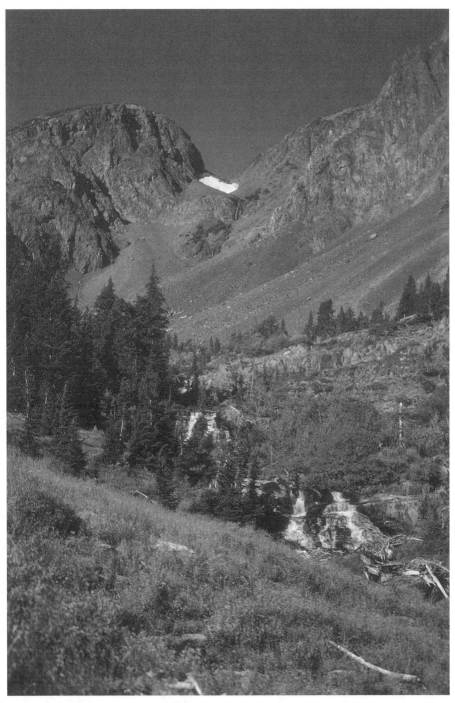

With its wildflowers, fall colors, and waterfalls, Lundy Canyon is among the most beautiful approaches to Yosemite from the east.

Lundy Canyon

To 395

CANYON

Lundy Lakes

START

LUNDY

Creek

Mill

INYO NATIONAL
FOREST

Mount
Scowden
11,180 ft.

Helen
Lake

Hypsometry

12,000

8000 **Elevation in Feet**

N

Kilometer

0   0.5   0.5

Mile

0

302,000

301,000

300,000

299,000

4,210,000

4,209,000

302,000

301,000

300,000

299,000

4,210,000

4,209,000

last, the trail tops a rise and enters the 20 Lakes Basin (though it is not named on the map). A very short distance farther, Mill Creek rushes through a narrow slot, beyond which lies Helen Lake. Beyond, North Peak rises above a permanent snowfield, and just behind it Mount Conness shades the Conness Glacier.

You can return this way, descending the rocky gully very cautiously, or you can continue on down into the basin, exploring the lakes and skirting big Saddlebag Lake, where you can leave a car or arrange to be picked up. There is camping in the upper part of Lundy Canyon as well as in the 20 Lakes Basin, but no fires are allowed.

52 Green Creek

The Green Creek drainage offers high drama and great photos because of its vivid red-and-white metamorphic rocks, intensely blue lakes, green forests, and in fall, golden aspen groves. It is a fairly steady uphill pull to the crest of the ridge, but there are plenty of excuses to stop and plenty of places to camp all the way up if you want to spend the night.

Start: Green Creek Trailhead.
Distance: 11.6 miles out and back.
Approximate hiking time: All day or overnight.
Difficulty: Strenuous as a day hike, moderate as a backpack.
Seasons: Fine hiking all summer; late September to mid-October for fall foliage.

Nearest facilities: Groceries, gas, phones, and accommodations in Bridgeport.
Permits: None for a day hike; available for overnights at the USDA Forest Service ranger station in Bridgeport.
Map: USGS Dunderberg Peak quad.

Finding the trailhead: From U.S. Highway 395, turn west on Green Creek Road 21 miles north of Lee Vining or 4.7 miles south of Bridgeport. Follow the dirt road for about 10 miles, just past the Green Creek Campground, to the parking area.

East Lake is the largest in the Green Creek drainage.

The Hike

The trail rambles alongside Green Creek through dense quaking aspen groves and lots of water-loving wildflowers at first, then climbs steeply beside a series of noisy cascades. A sign marks the entrance to the Hoover Wilderness as you continue to ascend steadily to a junction with the West Lake trail at 2 miles. Take the left fork south past the northwest corner of Green Lake, usually lined with anglers. The forest service stocks these lakes, but the park service does not plant trout anymore, so the fishing is more challenging beyond the Yosemite Park border. There are plenty of good campsites around the lake, but you'll have lots of neighbors.

Cross the stream connecting Green Lake to East Lake and climb the steep switchbacks alongside it, crossing again where it flows out of East Lake, largest in the basin, at 3.5 miles. There is a small, artificial dam that probably made the lake bigger than it was originally. There is plenty of camping near the dam. The trail follows the shoreline very closely for a time, then clambers over more open rocky ridges above the lake. Just beyond, beautiful little Nutter Lake appears below the trail at the base of a smooth rock outcrop, trimmed with red mountain heather in

Green Creek

START

To 395

Green Creek

RIDGE

N

Kilometer
0   1

Mile
0   1

MONUMENT

HUMBOLDT-TOIYABE
NATIONAL FOREST

West
Lake

West Fork

East Fork

Green
Lake

KAVANAUGH RIDGE

HOOVER
WILDERNESS
AREA

Gabbro
Peak
11,033 ft.

East
Lake

Hypsometry
12,500

8000
Elevation in Feet

Nutter
Lake

Gilman
Lake

Moat
Lake

Camiaca
Peak
11,739 ft.

Hoover Lakes

Summit Lake

YOSEMITE
NATIONAL
PARK

summer and scarlet Sierra bilberry in fall. After passing a small, unnamed pond, Gilman Lake appears down in a pocket to the left (east) at 4.5 miles. A faint, unmarked spur leads down to the lakeside. You will find more solitude here than at some of the other lakes, since it is off the trail.

Cross the Gilman Lake inlet very carefully. The rocks are smooth and slimy here and have soaked many a backpacker and gear. Ascend through a subalpine forest of lodgepole, whitebark pine, graceful, droopy mountain hemlock, and tall, straight, dignified silver pines. These last, with their reddish bark in more-or-less regular square plates, are widely scattered and relatively uncommon.

All but small patches of trees are left behind as the rocky path skirts the lakeshore of the lower Hoover Lake on one side and the steep, shaley base of the ridge on the other, at 5.8 miles. There are a few isolated camping sites in clumps of trees near the lakes, but for the most part, camping here is bleak and exposed. The two Hoover Lakes are separated by a narrow strip of broken rock beneath which you can hear water flowing from the upper to the lower lake. Return the way you came.

Miles and Directions

0.0   Green Creek Trailhead.

2.0   Green Creek/West Lake Trail junction.

3.5   East Lake.

4.5   Gilman Lake.

5.8   Hoover Lakes.

11.6   Return to Green Creek Trailhead.

53 Virginia Lakes Basin

This is a high-elevation, out-and-back hike through a cluster of timberline lakes. It is actually outside the Yosemite border, but it is a convenient and very scenic route to many more hikes in the north boundary country of the park and beyond.

Start: Virginia Lakes Trailhead.
Distance: 6.6 miles out and back.
Approximate hiking time: 3 to 6 hours.
Difficulty: Moderate.
Seasons: Summer through fall.

Nearest facilities: Store, cafe, lodge, and phone at the largest of the Virginia Lakes.
Permits: None for a day hike; available for a backpack from the USDA Forest Service ranger station in Bridgeport.
Map: USGS Dunderberg Peak quad.

Finding the trailhead: From U.S. Highway 395 at Conway Summit north of Mono Lake, take Virginia Lakes Road west for 6 miles. Beyond the pack station, the road forks. To the left is a small lodge, store, and cafe. To the right is the USDA Forest Service Trumbull Campground, and beyond that, the marked trailhead and hikers' parking lot.

The Hike

The trail begins climbing gradually around the north shore of Blue Lake. A long, cascading waterfall flowing from Cooney and Moat Lakes above feeds into it at the far end. There is nothing subtle about this scenery. While most of the basin containing the brilliant sapphire of the lake is gray granite, Dunderberg Peak to your right (north) is red, and Black Mountain to the left (south) is . . . you guessed it . . . black. White snow patches and green clumps of forest make this basin a favorite with color photographers.

The rocky slope beside Blue Lake is home to a colony of pikas, busy little earth-colored creatures related to rabbits, which scamper over the rocks of the high country all summer, cutting plant material to store in their burrows under the rubble for winter use. The bundles of grass they carry as they scurry over the talus makes them appear to have huge green mustaches. You can hear their sharp chirps of alarm as you

This Virginia Lake is the first in a series along Virginia Canyon.

approach, but they become invisible when immobile. If you stand quietly for a few minutes until they decide you are not dangerous, they will resume their activities.

As the trail climbs, it passes an old miner's log cabin, crosses the outlet from Moat Lake, then ascends through forest to the north shore of Cooney Lake. After gaining the shelf above the lake, it flattens out as it crosses a creek and winds through the open meadow basin containing the Frog Lakes, at 1.8 miles. The gnarled whitebark pines that mark timberline are left behind now as you climb toward the head of the canyon, passing one last stark unnamed lake before puffing up the few remaining steep switchbacks, sometimes through late-lying snowfields, to the pass at 3.3 miles. This pass is unnamed on the USGS topos, but is known as "Burro Pass" to locals. (There is another "real" officially named Burro Pass to the west near Matterhorn Peak, so don't get the two confused.) Whatever its name, it is actually just a broad, flat bench. Make sure to cross over to the west side for a look around before turning back or you will miss the dramatic multicolored panorama that includes the Sawtooth Range to the north behind Summit Lake. If you have come for only a day hike, return the way you came.

Virginia Lakes Basin

Miles and Directions

0.0 Virginia Lakes Trailhead.

1.8 Frog Lakes.

3.3 "Burro Pass."

6.6 Virginia Lakes Trailhead.

Option: Green Creek/Virginia Canyon Shuttle

If you can leave one vehicle, or get a ride to either the Green Creek or Virginia Lakes Trailhead, you can explore two spectacular canyons in one hike and avoid retracing your steps. Hike up the Virginia Lakes Trail to "Burro Pass" at 11,100 feet, then head northwest for 1 mile, down to the Summit Lake/Green Creek Trail junction. Turn right at the junction and drop down into Green Creek Canyon toward Hoover Lakes and finish at the Green Creek Trailhead. The total distance is a little more than 10 miles.

54 Matterhorn Canyon and the Sawtooth Range

This is a long semiloop shuttle hike beneath the spectacular Sawtooth Range, where you will cross three high passes and visit dozens of high country lakes while experiencing more solitude (except at the very beginning and end of the hike) than you'll find in most other regions of Yosemite.

Start: Barney Lake Trailhead in Mono Village.

Distance: 39.1-mile one-way shuttle.

Approximate hiking time: 5 to 7 days.

Difficulty: Moderate to strenuous, depending on how much time you take.

Seasons: All summer and early fall.

Nearest facilities: Groceries, cafe, campground, phones at Mono Village.

Permits: Required. Available from the USDA Forest Service ranger station in Bridgeport.

Maps: USGS Buckeye Ridge, Dunderberg Peak, Falls Ridge, Matterhorn Peak, and Twin Lakes quads.

Finding the trailhead: From Bridgeport turn west off U.S. Highway 395 onto Twin Lakes Road and follow it about 13 miles to its end at Mono Village. Supervised overnight parking is available for a flat rate of $7.00. Drive to the kiosk in front of the campground for a parking permit and directions to the backpackers' lot. Behind the kiosk look for the sign that reads BARNEY LAKE TRAIL. Leave a second car (or arrange to be picked up) at the Green Creek Trailhead, 4.7 miles south of Bridgeport, 10 miles southeast of US 395.

The Hike

Follow the trail directly through the campground on a road until you reach a meadow. Climb over a chain blocking the way, then turn right at a trail sign and leave the road. Pass through a forest of Jeffrey pine, then an aspen grove, then into the open,

You will find more solitude in Matterhorn Canyon beneath the Sawtooth Range than in other parts of Yosemite.

where the glorious panorama of Robinson, Eagle, Victoria, and Hunewill Peaks, as well as the Sawtooth Range, stretches out before you. In the foreground is a field of big, yellow mule ears, blue lupine, and in early season, purple irises. After passing the mouth of Little Slide Canyon coming in from the south, enter another aspen grove and climb moderate switchbacks up through flowery gardens. Cross several little runnels to reach Barney Lake at 4 miles. The lake is overused around its edges, but if you cross the outlet stream on logs, you will find beautiful campsites among the junipers above its eastern shore.

Skirt Barney Lake's west shore, watching for pikas in the rock piles and signs of beavers at the upper end of the swampy area at the head of the lake. Cross Robinson Creek and begin switchbacking uphill, sometimes through graceful mountain hemlocks, sometimes over open rock. At 6.3 miles, meet the junction with the Peeler Lake Trail, which goes off to the northwest. Your trail turns south, winds around a few big rocky outcrops, then drops into a basin, first passing a little pond with improbably blue-green water, then past the north edge of lower Robinson Lake. Camping here is usually too damp and buggy for comfort. The trail crosses an isthmus between the two lakes, climbs a few switchbacks, cuts through a gap where

Matterhorn Canyon and the Sawtooth Range

START

Hunewill Peak 11,713 ft.

HUMBOLDT - TOIYABE NATIONAL FOREST

Twin Lakes

Barney Lake

Kettle Peak 11,010 ft.

To Peeler Lake

Glacier Lake

Crown Lake

Blacksmith Creek

Horse Creek

SAWTOOTH RIDGE

Matterhorn Peak 12,264 ft.

Mule Pass

To Rock Island Pass

Finger Peaks 11,498 ft.

Burro Pass

YOSEMITE NATIONAL PARK

MATTERHORN CANYON

Whorl Mountain 12,029 ft.

Virginia Peak 12,001 ft.

Spiller Creek

Spiller Lake

Soldier Lake

VIRGINIA CANYON

Virginia Creek

To Benson Pass

Pacific Crest Trail

Miller Lake

Return Creek

YOSEMITE NATIONAL PARK

McCabe Lakes

Upper McCabe Lake

Summit Lake

East Lake

Gilman Lake

Virginia Lakes

West Lake

Green Lake

Hunewill Lake

Tamarack Lake

HOOVER WILDERNESS AREA

To 395

Saddlebag Lake

Virginia Lake

To Glen Aulin

Hypsometry

12,000

7000

Elevation in Feet

snow often lingers late in the season, then reaches Crown Lake at 8 miles. Backed by Crown Point, the lake is stunning, but the only camping nearby is at its north end on sandy spaces among the rocks.

The trail skirts Crown Lake for a short distance before switchbacking up the slope to the west, past little pocket meadows with tiny lakes and miniature gardens, to a junction with the Rock Island Pass Trail at 8.5 miles. Keep left as your trail curves gently southward and continue up a narrowing gully, often partly snow filled. Just below the top is another sparkling little lake. The trail flattens out a bit just before reaching 10,400-foot Mule Pass at 10.1 miles and entering Yosemite. The Sawtooth Ridge spreads out along the horizon with Matterhorn Peak at its far end. The trail descends, then rises to cross a low saddle, then drops down a gulch into the Piute Creek drainage, bottoming out at 9,400 feet. Follow the creek, climbing gently past numerous cascades through a carpet of dwarf bilberry, brilliant green in summer, glowing red in fall. There are several good campsites here along the creek.

Continue to climb moderately, heading straight for Matterhorn Peak until the sparse whitebark pine gives out altogether, the route curves south, and you easily cross Burro Pass at 12.8 miles. At 10,600 feet, this is the highest point on the route.

The trail descends along the west side of the big bowl at the head of Matterhorn Canyon, then eases down very gently alongside Matterhorn Creek past some spectacular avalanche areas—the velocity of the snow was so great here that trees were flattened all the way down one side of the canyon and halfway up the other. Be sure to glance backward now and then as you descend. The jagged Sawtooth Ridge on the horizon back at the head of the canyon is spectacular. There are small campsites for the first couple of miles in the canyon, but after you have passed Quarry Peak, the walls narrow and camping becomes more difficult.

You cross Matterhorn Creek three times before reaching the junction with the Pacific Crest Trail at 19 miles, then follow it almost due south, leaving the stream and climbing fairly steeply out of the canyon. The trail levels out just before a big meadow, at the far end of which lies Miller Lake at 20.5 miles. This is a good, shallow, warm lake for swimming, and there is good camping in the timber across the meadow from the trail.

From the lake, the route gently undulates, passing a couple more little ponds, goes through a gate, and makes a last steep, sandy climb out of the basin. Then it drops steeply on dusty switchbacks to cross Spiller Creek just before its confluence with Return Creek in Virginia Canyon at 24.8 miles. Now you leave the Pacific Crest Trail and walk up Virginia Canyon, gaining elevation very gradually, passing more avalanche chutes on the way. Cross to the east side of Return Creek one last time to find the Virginia Pass junction on the far side, at 28.8 miles. There is a small, mediocre campsite just upstream.

Now climb the steep, forested slope to Summit Pass at 29.9 miles, leaving Yosemite at the top. Skirt the northern shore of Summit Lake, which is very beautiful but often very windy. Since the shore is also quite fragile, camping is discouraged near the lake, though there are a few small, protected sites past its east end. The trail drops below the lake along a flowery creek, rock-hops over another shallow stream, and turns left (north), climbing a little until it meets the Green Creek Trail junction at 31.9 miles. Continue on down Green Creek to Hoover Lakes at 32.9 miles, passing between the two on a narrow strip of broken rock beneath which you can hear water flowing from the upper to the lower lake. Drop down to follow along the rim of the bowl containing Gilman Lake, crossing the slippery rocks at its inlet at 34.2 miles. Pass a small, unnamed pond, then pretty Nutter Lake, to reach East Lake, largest in the basin at 35.2 miles. There is plenty of camping near the dam at its outlet, as there is at Green Lake, just below, though you will have to share the shore with plenty of other campers and anglers. At mile 37.2, turn right (northeast) at a junction with the West Lake Trail, and reach the Green Creek Trailhead at 39.1 miles.

Miles and Directions

0.0 Barney Lake Trailhead.

4.0 Barney Lake, turn right to skirt its western shore.

6.3 Peeler Lake junction, turn left.

8.0 Crown Lake.

8.7 Rock Island Pass junction, turn left.

10.1 Cross Mule Pass (Yosemite Park boundary).

12.8 Cross Burro Pass.

19.0 Benson Pass Trail junction, keep left.

20.5 Miller Lake, trail turns sharply northeast.

24.8 Return Creek, turn left, up canyon.

28.8 Virginia Pass junction, keep right.

29.9 Summit Pass (Yosemite Park boundary).

31.9 Green Creek Trail, turn left.

32.9 Upper Hoover Lake.

34.2 Pass Gilman Lake.

35.2 Pass the eastern shore of East Lake.

37.2 Green Lake/West Lake junction, keep right.

39.1 Green Creek Trailhead.

55 Benson Pass–Northeast Yosemite Grand Tour

This extended backpack loop is probably the most challenging hike in the book. Not only is the distance long and the changes in elevation extreme (between 4,400 and 10,000 feet), but your window of opportunity is narrow. The high north country may still have lots of snow while the low point in Pate Valley can be hot. Still, for most of the way, you'll have solitude and a good sampling of remote Yosemite in all its variety.

Start: Glen Aulin Trailhead in Tuolumne Meadows.
Distance: 58-mile lollipop loop.
Approximate hiking time: 5 to 9 days.
Difficulty: Moderate to strenuous, depending on how much time you take.
Seasons: Summer through early fall.

Nearest facilities: Tuolumne Meadows.
Permits: Available in advance or from the wilderness center in Tuolumne Meadows.
Maps: USGS Dunderberg Peak, Falls Ridge, Matterhorn Peak, Ten Lakes, and Tioga Pass quads.

Finding the trailhead: From the west, follow Tioga Road (Highway 120) past the Tuolumne Meadows visitor center, store, cafe, and campground, all on your right. Just after crossing the bridge over the Tuolumne River, turn left (north) into the Lembert Dome parking area. From the east (Tioga Pass) follow the Tioga Road past the turnoff to the wilderness center on your left and continue about a hundred yards to the Lembert Dome parking area on your right. You can also ride the Tuolumne Meadows shuttle bus to Lembert Dome. Overnight parking is prohibited in the parking lot so you must park along the paved road parallel to Tioga Road. The road turns right at a closed gate where your hike begins.

The Hike

Go through the gate and follow the road (closed to vehicles) through the meadow, keeping right and climbing a small rise where the road splits. From the top of the rise, head toward the ramshackle log structure partially containing Soda Springs at mile 0.5. Just beyond is Parsons Lodge, a stone building with historical exhibits. The path splits at mile 0.6 and you turn right to a big GLEN AULIN trail sign where the trail meets the road a few yards beyond. Turn left and walk through flowery meadows and lodgepole forest on footing that is heavy and dusty from lots of horse and foot traffic. Ford Delaney Creek at mile 1.2. A trail heading north to Young Lakes cuts off to the right at mile 1.6, but your route stays left (northwest). In less than a mile, you emerge from behind a low ridge to behold the spectacular Cathedral Range with the Tuolumne River in the foreground. The next couple of miles along the trail offer one incredible photo-op after another. After passing through a short stretch of forest, climb around a low shoulder of rock and keep watch on your left for the Little Devil's Postpile, an unusual volcanic feature much younger than the surrounding rock.

Benson Pass–Northeast Yosemite Grand Tour

272,000

4,212,000

276,000

To
Seavey Pass

280,000

▲ Piute Mountain
10,541 ft.

Piute Creek

N

Sister
Lake

Benson
Lake

Smedberg
Lake

0   Kilometers   2

0   Miles   2

▲ Volunteer Peak
10,479 ft.

Rodgers
Lake

4,208,000

PLEASANT
VALLEY

Neall
Lake

▲ Pettit Peak
10,788 ft.

R O D G E R S   C A N Y O N

Rodgers Creek

4,204,000

Register Creek

PATE
VALLEY

Piute Creek

MUIR
GORGE

Tuolumne River

To
Hetchy Hetchy

G R A N D   C A N Y O N   O F   T H E   T U O L U M N E   R I V E R

4,200,000

Hypsometry

11,500

3500

Elevation in Feet

Ten
Lakes

4,196,000

Yosemite Creek

Grant
Lakes

Tuolumne Peak
10,845 ft.

To
May Lake

272,000

276,000

280,000

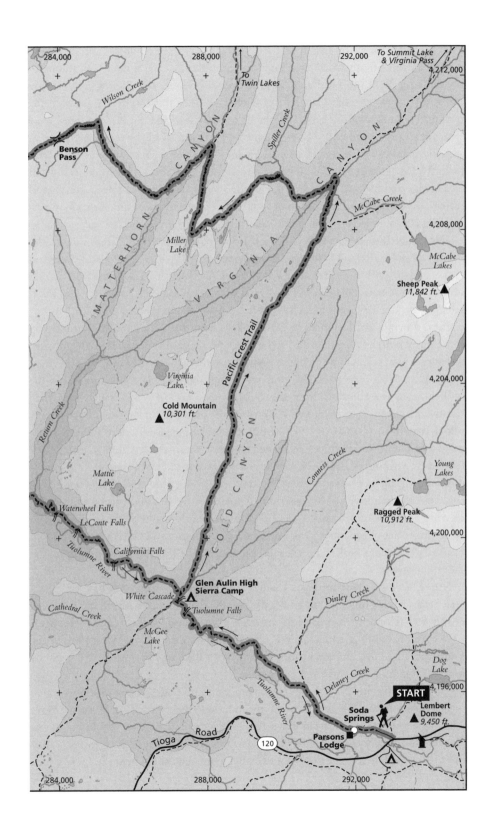

The trail turns sharply right and drops down a short, steep notch, and very soon reaches a pair of footbridges across the Tuolumne River at 3.5 miles. From this point on, the river picks up speed and cascades over a series of falls. As you descend, you can enjoy views up Cold Canyon to Matterhorn Peak and Mount Conness on the northern boundary of the park. The trail dives twice into and out of deep forest lined with Labrador tea and corn lily, then emerges again into sunlight on cobblestones or smooth granite marked with ducks. Finally it meets a junction with the May Lake/McGee Lake trail at 5 miles. A few more steep, slippery switchbacks lead down to a bridge and back to the other side of the river. Few hikers can resist the urge to stop on the bridge to snap a photo or simply gape at the frothy White Cascade splashing into a pool in front of the High Sierra Camp. You have come 5.2 miles.

Head northward across Cold Creek from the High Sierra Camp, still on the Pacific Crest Trail (PCT), partly through open forest, partly through meadow, up Cold Canyon, with Mount Conness at its head. The McCabe Lakes junction, at 12.2 miles, is not shown correctly on the topo, but if you stay left, following the PCT, you'll be on track. At 13.2 miles, keep left again, following Return Creek in Virginia Canyon downstream, dropping to cross Spiller Creek, then climbing fairly steeply up some dusty switchbacks. Pass through a gate, and make another sandy descent, cross a low rise, pass a couple of shallow ponds, then emerge into the meadow bordering Miller Lake. It's a nice warm lake for swimming, and there is good camping in the timber across the meadow from the trail. Leaving the lake, the trail swings back northward, crossing a shoulder with views to the Sawtooth Ridge, then drops steeply into Matterhorn Canyon at 19 miles, in a flowery meadow where there is more good camping. The Pacific Crest Trail makes a sharp dogleg here cutting back southwest, crossing Matterhorn Creek and following its broad meandering course downstream for more than a mile. The trail swings northwest, climbing along Wilson Creek, which it crosses several times before it turns west and climbs switchbacks to wide, grassy Benson Pass at mile 22.8. Descend fairly gradually from the pass and wade the outlet of Smedberg Lake at the edge of a meadow. The lake lies at the foot of blocky Volunteer Peak. There is good camping at the lake; the best sites are on the shore opposite the trail.

After leaving Smedberg Lake, reach a junction at the steep west base of Volunteer Peak at 26.5 miles. Here you leave the PCT, which cuts off westerly toward Seavey Pass. Continue south, climb an open grassy hump, and descend to Rodgers Lake at the base of flat-topped, red Regulation Peak, with pointed West Peak to the south. Continue descending a short spur to Neall Lake in a little hollow fringed by forest. Camping is best near the lake's outlet.

Soon after leaving Neall Lake, meet a junction in Rodgers Canyon at 30.1 miles, turn left (south) and follow along the meandering creek through a broad meadow. The grade steepens as you head down Rodgers Canyon toward the Tuolumne River Canyon. Eventually the trail swings west and leaves Rodgers Creek, your last source of water for awhile if the season is late. Cross a low saddle, then meet the Piute Creek junction at 34.9 miles. Turn left (west) and tighten your boots for the long, long, knee-bashing, toe-squashing descent to the river. As you lose elevation, the vegetation changes to ponderosa pine, incense cedar, and black oak in the places where there is still some tree cover, and it can become uncomfortably hot. At last you reach the cool green pools and refreshing cascades along the Tuolumne, at 39.5 miles, at the upper end of Pate Valley. Your route goes upstream to the left, but there is camping downstream in the lower part of the valley. Watch out for rattlesnakes in this low country.

From the upper end of Pate Valley, turn left (east) to follow the Tuolumne upstream, crossing Rodgers Creek on a bridge, then Register Creek over rocks at the base of a pretty cascade at mile 43.5. The trail now climbs steeply up out of the drainage of Register Creek, detouring over a smooth polished boulder above the steep impassable canyon walls of Muir Gorge. The trail remains above the river for a long up-and-down dry spell before rejoining its north shore again and following it gradually up through the Grand Canyon of the Tuolumne to cross the footbridge over Return Creek at 48.4 miles. Begin the switchbacks that take you up alongside the Tuolumne's most exciting section of cascades and falls, one after another, up stair-step after stair-step of roaring river, including the fabulous Waterwheels at mile 50.2, then LeConte and California Falls, and back up to Glen Aulin High Sierra Camp at mile 52.8, where you retrace your steps to the trailhead.

Miles and Directions

0.0 Glen Aulin Trailhead.

0.5 Soda Springs.

1.2 Ford Delaney Creek.

1.6 Young Lakes Trail junction, keep left.

3.5 Cross the twin bridges.

5.0 McGee Lake Trail junction, turn sharp right, downhill.

5.2 Glen Aulin High Sierra Camp.

12.2 McCabe Lakes junction, stay left.

13.2 Virginia Canyon/Return Creek, hairpin turn to the left (south) then sharp north again at Miller Lake.

19.0 Matterhorn Canyon, another sharp left turn (south).

22.8 Benson Pass.

26.5 Rodgers Lake junction, keep straight ahead (south).

30.1 Rodgers Canyon, turn left.

34.9 Piute Creek, turn left.

39.5 Pate Valley, turn left, upstream along the Tuolumne.

43.5 Cross Rodgers, then Register Creeks.

48.4 Cross Return Creek.

50.2 Waterwheel Falls.

52.8 Glen Aulin High Sierra Camp.

58.0 Glen Aulin Trailhead.

56 McCabe Lakes

This out-and-back overnight hike takes you to Upper and Lower McCabe Lakes in their beautiful cirque at the base of Sheep Peak by way of Green Creek, just outside the northeast boundary of Yosemite. If you prefer, you can begin and end the hike within the park by way of Glen Aulin High Sierra Camp.

Start: Green Creek Trailhead.
Distance: 30.4 miles out and back.
Approximate hiking time: 2 to 4 days.
Difficulty: Moderate.
Seasons: Summer through early fall.
Nearest facilities: Gas, groceries, and phones in Lee Vining and Bridgeport.

Permits: Available in advance or from the USDA Forest Service ranger station in Bridgeport.
Maps: USGS Dunderberg Peak, Tioga Pass, Matterhorn Peak, and Falls Ridge quads.

Finding the trailhead: From U.S. Highway 395, turn west on Green Creek Road 21 miles north of Lee Vining or 4.7 miles south of Bridgeport. Follow the dirt road for about 10 miles, just past the Green Creek Campground, to the parking area.

The Hike

The trail rambles alongside Green Creek through dense quaking aspen groves and lots of water-loving wildflowers at first, then climbs steeply beside a series of noisy cascades. A sign marks the entrance to the Hoover Wilderness as you continue to ascend steadily to a junction with the West Lake Trail at 2 miles. Take the left fork south past the northwest corner of Green Lake, usually lined with anglers. There are plenty of good campsites around the lake, but you'll have lots of neighbors.

Cross the stream connecting Green Lake to East Lake and climb the steep switchbacks alongside it, crossing again where it flows out of East Lake, largest in the

Pikas, or rock rabbits, are abundant in the high country.

basin at 3.5 miles. There is a small, artificial dam that probably made the lake bigger than it was originally. There is plenty of camping near the dam. The trail follows the shoreline very closely for a time, then clambers over more open rocky ridges above the lake. Just beyond, beautiful little Nutter Lake appears below the trail at the base of a smooth rock outcrop, trimmed with red mountain heather in summer and scarlet Sierra bilberry in fall. After passing a small, unnamed pond, Gilman Lake appears down in a pocket to the left (east) at 4.5 miles. A faint, unmarked spur leads down to the lakeside. You will find more solitude here than at some of the other lakes, since it is off the trail. Cross the Gilman Lake inlet carefully on slippery rocks. Ascend through a subalpine forest of lodgepole, whitebark pine, graceful mountain hemlock, and tall, dignified silver pines.

All but small patches of trees are left behind as the rocky path skirts the lakeshore of the lower Hoover Lake on one side of the steep, shaley base of the ridge at 5.8 miles. The two Hoover Lakes are separated by a narrow strip of broken rock. Beneath this you can hear water flowing from the upper to the lower lake under your feet, as the trail follows this narrow isthmus to the north side of the upper lake. There are a few isolated camping sites in clumps of trees near the lakes, but for the most part, camping here is bleak and exposed. The trail crosses the inlet to the upper lake and toils up a sunny slope to a junction with the Virginia Lakes Trail at 6.2 miles. Continue to the right up to a flower-filled gully along a gurgling creek to Summit Lake. The views here are stupendous, and this seems a natural place to camp, but it is usually very windy, and the few sheltered spots among the whitebark pines are car-

McCabe Lakes

- **292,000** · 294,000 · 296,000 · 298,000 · 300,000
- 4,222,000
- HUMBOLDT - TOIYABE NATIONAL FOREST
- **START**
- To 395
- N
- 0 Kilometers 2
- 0 Miles 2
- 4,219,000
- West Lake
- Green Lake
- HOOVER WILDERNESS AREA
- 4,216,000
- East Lake
- Nutter Lake
- Gilman Lake
- Hoover Lakes
- Soldier Lake
- Summit Lake
- 4,213,000
- YOSEMITE NATIONAL PARK
- VIRGINIA CANYON
- Creek
- Return
- Excelsior Mountain 12,446 ft.
- Shepherd Lake
- 4,210,000
- To Matterhorn Canyon
- McCabe
- Creek
- Upper McCabe Lake
- McCabe Lakes
- **Hypsometry**
- 12,500
- 8000
- **Elevation in Feet**
- 4,207,000
- To Glen Aulin
- **Sheep Peak** 11,842 ft.
- **North Peak** 12,242 ft.
- 292,000 · 294,000 · 296,000 · 298,000 · 300,000

peted with very fragile and slow-growing vegetation, easily trampled and destroyed. Much of the area near the lake is closed to camping. Continue on along the north shore of the lake to a sign that marks the Yosemite boundary at Summit Pass, at 7.2 miles, the highest point on this hike. From here, switchback steeply downhill into Virginia Canyon and arrive at the Virginia Pass Trail junction at Return Creek at 8.2 miles. You can make a detour to Virginia Pass by turning right (north) and following Return Creek upstream, then scrambling up a steep slope to the pass, an extra 1.6 miles each way.

To continue on to McCabe Lakes, cross the creek and follow the trail to the left. A mediocre campsite can be found just off the trail to the right. You can usually rock-hop the creek, but there is a big log to cross on downstream if the water is high. Soon the forest opens as you very gradually descend along Return Creek, passing massive Excelsior Peak on your left. The slopes above the canyon for the next couple of miles have been scarred by repeated avalanches. Notice how, in some cases, the force was so great that trees were flattened not only down the side of the slope but also across the canyon floor and even a short distance up the other side. The height of the new little trees in the avalanche path gives a hint of how recently the last slide occurred.

The trail eventually nears the creek, where it flows over sculpted granite in picturesque cascades and falls. There are come campsites nearby. It's a great place for lunch, a snack, a nap, or a swim. Just beyond is the junction with the Pacific Crest Trail (PCT) at 12.2 miles. Turn left (south) here and follow the PCT for a short distance, climbing steeply. At a junction at 13.2 miles, turn left (east) leaving the PCT. Continue climbing, more gently now, up a wooded slope through an occasional meadow to Lower McCabe Lake, with Sheep Peak as its backdrop, at 15.2 miles. There is good camping on both sides of the outlet. Be sure to pitch your tent away from the lakeside to avoid trampling. You can scramble to Upper McCabe for better views by following the green slope to the west uphill along an inlet stream to an intermediate small lake, then cross the low ridge to the northwest to reach the largest of the lakes. Return the way you came.

Miles and Directions

0.0 Green Creek Trailhead.

2.0 Green Creek/West Lake Trail junction.

3.5 East Lake.

4.5 Gilman Lake.

5.8 Upper Hoover Lake.

6.2 Green Creek/Virginia Lakes trail junction.

7.2 Summit Pass (Yosemite Park boundary).

8.2 Return Creek.

12.2 Pacific Crest Trail junction.

13.2 McCabe Lakes junction.

15.2 Lower McCabe Lake.

30.4 Return to Green Creek Trailhead.

Option: McCabe Lakes via Tuolumne Meadows

To get to McCabe Lakes without leaving Yosemite at all, you can start at the Glen Aulin Trailhead in Tuolumne Meadows, hike to Glen Aulin High Sierra Camp, then continue all the way up Cold Canyon to the lakes. The distance out-and-back is approximately the same as that from Green Creek, about 30 miles. If you can arrange a car shuttle or get a ride, you can also hike to the lakes from one trailhead and return to the other.

57 Piute Mountain–Peeler Lake Loop

An alternative to the Matterhorn Canyon semiloop, this extended hike makes a complete circle through the heart of the north boundary country, beginning and ending at Twin Lakes just outside Bridgeport, so a car shuttle is not necessary.

Start: Barney Lake Trailhead in Mono Village.
Distance: 48.7-mile loop.
Approximate hiking time: 5 to 8 days.
Difficulty: Moderate to strenuous, depending on how much time you take.
Seasons: Summer through early fall.
Nearest facilities: Groceries, cafe, campground, and phones can be found at Mono Village; gas is available in Bridgeport.
Permits: Require; available in advance or from the USDA Forest Service ranger station in Bridgeport.
Maps: USGS Buckeye Ridge, Dunderberg Peak, Falls Ridge, Matterhorn Peak, Piute Mountain, and Twin Lakes quads.

Finding the trailhead: From Bridgeport, turn west off U.S. Highway 395 onto Twin Lakes Road and follow it about 23 miles to its end at Mono Village. Supervised overnight parking is available for a flat rate of $7.00. Drive to the kiosk in front of the campground for a parking permit and directions to the backpackers' lot.

Piute Mountain–Peeler Lake Loop

The Hike

Follow the trail/road directly through the campground until you reach a meadow. Climb over a chain blocking the way, then turn right at a trail sign and leave the road. Pass through a forest of Jeffrey pine, then an aspen grove, then into the open, where the glorious panorama of Robinson, Eagle, Victoria, and Hunewell Peaks as well as the Sawtooth Range stretch before you. In the foreground is a field of big, yellow mule ears, blue lupine, and in early season, purple irises. After passing the mouth of Little Slide Canyon coming in from the south, enter another aspen grove and climb moderate switchbacks up through flowery gardens, crossing several little runnels and reaching Barney Lake at 4 miles. The lake is overused around its edges, but if you cross the outlet stream on logs, you will find beautiful campsites among the junipers above its eastern shore.

Skirt Barney Lake's west shore, watching for pikas in the rock piles and signs of beaver at the upper end of the swampy area at the head of the lake. Cross Robinson Creek and begin switchbacking uphill, sometimes through graceful mountain hemlocks, sometimes over open rock. At 6.3 miles, meet the junction with the Peeler Lake Trail going off to the northwest. Your trail turns south, winds around a few big rocky outcrops, then drops into a basin, first passing a little pond with improbably blue-green water, then the north edge of lower Robinson Lake. Camping here is usually too damp and buggy for comfort. The trail crosses an isthmus between the two lakes, climbs a few switchbacks, cuts through a gap where snow often lingers late in the season, then reaches Crown Lake at 8 miles. Backed by Crown Point, the lake is stunning, but the only camping nearby is at its north end on sandy spaces among the rocks.

The trail skirts Crown Lake for a short distance before switchbacking up the slope to the west, past little pocket meadows with tiny lakes and miniature gardens to a junction with the Rock Island Pass Trail at 8.5 miles. Keep left as your trail curves gently southward and continue up a narrowing gully, often partly snow filled. Just below the top is another sparkling little lake. The trail flattens out a bit just before reaching 10,400-foot Mule Pass, at 10.1 miles, and entering Yosemite. The Sawtooth Range spreads out along the horizon with Matterhorn Peak at its far end. The trail descends, then rises to cross a low saddle, then drops down a gulch into the Piute Creek drainage, bottoming out at 9,400 feet. Follow the creek, climbing gently past numerous cascades through a carpet of dwarf bilberry, brilliant green in summer, glowing red in fall. There are several good campsites here along the creek.

Continue to climb moderately, heading straight for Matterhorn Peak, until the sparse whitebark pines give out altogether, the route curves south, and you easily cross Burro Pass at 12.8 miles. At 10,600 feet, this is the highest point on the route. The trail descends along the west side of the big bowl at the head of Matterhorn Canyon, then eases down very gently alongside Matterhorn Creek past some spectacular avalanche chutes. There are small campsites for the first couple of miles in the canyon, but after you have passed Quarry Peak, the walls narrow and camping becomes more difficult. You cross Matterhorn Creek three times before reaching the junction with the Pacific Crest Trail (PCT) at 19 miles. The PCT makes a sharp dogleg here, and you follow to the right (southwest), crossing Matterhorn Creek and continuing downstream for more than a mile. The trail swings northwest climbing along Wilson Creek now, which it must cross several times before it turns west and climbs switchbacks to wide, grassy Benson Pass. Descend gradually and wade across the inlet of Smedberg Lake at the edge of a meadow, backed by blocky Volunteer Peak. There is good camping at the lake, but the best is on the shore opposite the trail.

Leaving Smedberg, reach a junction at the base of Volunteer Peak at 26.5 miles. Now make a short climb through forest to another junction at 27.1 miles, and turn right (north) toward Benson Lake, dropping down to cross then follow the stream connecting Smedberg and Benson Lakes. Leave the stream to cross a rocky shoulder and descend to a boggy flat blooming with corn lilies, onions, wild geraniums, and other water-loving flowers, to meet the spur trail to the lake at 30.1 miles. This is a big lake in a beautifully ice-polished rocky bowl. It is surprisingly popular for such a remote spot, probably because of its good camping and beautiful beach at the end nearest the trail.

Leaving the lake, the trail climbs up open manzanita-covered slopes heading toward the pointed beacon of Piute Mountain, directly ahead. Near the peak, it swings northeast, climbs more steeply along the cascading stream, then levels out beside the first of several little lakes near Seavey Pass, a rather long, open ridge studded with shining domes and tarns. A short distance down the north side of Seavey Pass, the Pacific Crest Trail leaves your route and heads off down Kerrick Canyon, at 33.5 miles. Turn right and begin climbing easily along Rancheria Creek, which you soon cross in a meadow tinged pale lavender in July with shooting stars and little elephant heads. Continue upward out of the meadow through a beautiful rocky gorge that opens once again into another wide, sandy grassy area. Arndt Lake, just off the trail to the east, feeds this meadow and its several little ponds.

Meet the Buckeye Pass junction at 38.7 miles. Walk northward along the edge of Kerrick Meadow, then turn right at a junction at 39.7 miles, toward Peeler Lake, at whose northwest shore you leave Yosemite at 40.2 miles. There is good camping and lots of human activity at this lake beneath the scenic backdrop of Crown Point.

Cross the inlet stream and climb around a rock ridge, then drop, winding through rocks, to a junction with the Robinson Lakes trail, at 40.7 miles. Here you turn left (northeast) and descend switchbacks to Barney Lake at 44.7 miles. Then retrace your steps to Twin Lakes and the trailhead.

Miles and Directions

0.0   Barney Lake Trailhead.

4.0   Barney Lake, turn right to skirt its western shore.

6.3   Peeler Lake junction, turn left.

8.0   Crown Lake.

8.7   Rock Island Pass junction, turn left.

10.1   Cross Mule Pass (Yosemite Park boundary).

12.8   Cross Burro Pass.

19.0   Pacific Crest Trail junction, keep right.

25.5   Wade inlet to Smedberg Lake.

26.5   Rodgers Lake junction.

27.1   Benson Lake junction, turn right.

30.1   Benson Lake spur.

33.5   Kerrick/Rancheria junction, turn right.

38.7   Buckeye Pass junction.

39.7   Peeler Lake junction, turn right.

40.2   Peeler Lake.

40.7   Robinson Creek junction, turn left.

48.7   Barney Lake Trailhead at Twin Lakes.

Two Famous Trails

The John Muir and Pacific Crest Trails traverse some of the most spectacular high country anywhere. Both pass through Yosemite and for a time become one and the same. The John Muir Trail follows the crest of the Sierra Nevada for roughly 211 miles between Yosemite Valley, at a mere 4,000 feet, and Mount Whitney, at around 14,500 feet in Sequoia National Park. It begins in Yosemite at Happy Isles, swings northeast to pass through Tuolumne Meadows, then turns south to leave the park at Donohue Pass. The trail was scouted by Theodore Solomons and named in honor of John Muir, who did so much to preserve the wild country of the Sierra Nevada for the public to enjoy. Congress appropriated the funds to being the trail in 1915, and it was completed in 1938.

The entire trail takes anywhere from three to six weeks to finish, although the Yosemite section takes only a few days. It is enjoyable in either direction, but I describe it here beginning at Happy Isles. In this direction you do have more uphill, but starting low gives you a chance to adjust to higher elevations gradually. There is no trailhead at Donohue Pass, so if you plan to hike only the Yosemite section, you will have to divide it into two parts: Tuolumne to Donohue Pass, and Tuolumne to Yosemite Valley (or vice versa).

The Pacific Crest Trail (PCT), dedicated in 1993, is part of the National Trails System authorized by Congress in 1968. It begins at the Mexican border and runs through the most scenic parts of the western states for 2,650 miles to the Canadian border. Hiking the entire trail takes a long summer season, but in about two weeks you can sample one of its finest sections as it goes through Yosemite from Donohue Pass in the south to Dorothy Lake Pass on the northern park border.

Most PCT through-hikers begin in Mexico and hike north, following the summer snowmelt to reach Canada in fall. They usually reach the northern part of Yosemite by June, and frequently find the deep snow and swift, high river crossings challenging, or at worst, impossible. The Yosemite section is described here in the usual south-to-north direction, but wait until mid-July for the most rewarding, least frustrating experience. The Pacific Crest Trail Association has lots of good information about current trail conditions and trip planning. You can contact them at 5325 Elkhorn Boulevard 256, Sacramento, CA 95842; (916) 349–2109; or check online at www.pcta.org.

58 The John Muir Trail

Start: John Muir Trailhead at Happy Isles.
Distance: 34.3 miles one way.
Approximate hiking time: 4 to 6 days.
Difficulty: Moderate.
Seasons: Summer through early fall.

Nearest facilities: Yosemite Village and Tuolumne Meadows.
Permits: Required. Apply in advance.
Maps: USGS Half Dome, Koip Peak, Merced Peak, Tenaya Lake, and Vogelsang Peak quads.

Finding the trailhead: Leave your car in the backpackers' lot east of Curry Village and ride the shuttle bus to Happy Isles, or follow the signs along the footpath to Happy Isles.

The Hike

The trail climbs gently on an eroded asphalt path through black oak and ponderosa pine forest among enormous lichen-draped boulders. In about a half mile, across the thundering Merced on your right, watch for 370-foot Illilouette Fall tucked back in its deeply cut gorge in the Panorama Cliff. The trail now steepens briefly, then suddenly descends to the Vernal Fall Bridge at 0.8 mile. Upstream, Vernal Fall is perfectly framed by maple, alder, and various conifers as it drops 317 feet over the lower step of the Giant Staircase.

Cross the bridge to the south side of the river and turn left (upstream). Pass a lateral trail on the right for horses only that leads back to the stables, then pass the turnoff to the Mist Trail on the left. The John Muir Trail switchbacks relentlessly uphill, but there are plenty of excuses to stop and rest on the way. To the northeast across the river gorge, the rounded backside of Half Dome comes into view along with Mount Broderick, Liberty Cap, and finally, 594-foot Nevada Fall. Beyond the excellent viewpoint at Clark Point, where a lateral trail cuts over to the Mist Trail, pass beneath a dripping rock overhang decorated with delicate hanging gardens of ferns, columbines, and monkeyflowers. At 3.3 miles, the Panorama Trail leading back to Glacier Point joins this one from the right (south). The trail drops a bit, hops a couple of little creeks, then emerges into a wide sunny expanse of smooth granite at the top of Nevada Fall. Here, at 3.5 miles, amid crowds of humans and panhandling squirrels, cross to the north shore of the river on a footbridge. There is an outhouse here, and just beyond, the junction with the upper end of the Mist Trail. Continue upstream, climbing the well-defined trail over inlaid rocks. The way soon levels out and passes from sunlight into shade, and the Merced changes from a rushing, raging torrent to become quiet, dark, and deep.

At 4.3 miles, the John Muir Trail cuts off to the left to reach busy Little Yosemite Valley at mile 4.8, your first camping opportunity. From the campground, climb the well-beaten path toward Half Dome along with the crowd of hikers heading for the summit. The Half Dome Trail junction is at 5.3 miles. Turn right (east), and at 5.8

From the John Muir Trail, Echo Peak and its neighbors look like the spine of the world.

miles, keep right again at the Sunrise Lakes junction and ascend along Sunrise Creek. At 7.7 miles, meet a junction with a lateral trail to Echo Valley. Keep left (north) here, and very soon arrive at a second junction, at 7.8 miles, where the John Muir Trail turns right (east). Climb gently, then steeply to a ridgetop where there are views of the Cathedral Range, then descend to the big meadow and Sunrise High Sierra Camp at 12.3 miles. There is a backpackers' camping area here, and some emergency supplies. Now follow the trail eastward at first, then northward, skirting the meadow's edge to meet the trail to Merced Lake at 13.2 miles. Continue straight ahead into the forest, cross Echo Creek, then skirt the creek on its east side through aptly named Long Meadow. Veer northwest and climb toward Columbia Finger, rounding its base and reaching an open, rocky saddle. Here, one of those awe-inspiring Yosemite vistas bursts upon you. The grand, sweeping, sculptured granite of Cathedral Peak, Echo Peak, and Matthes Crest looks like the spine of the world. Descend the hillside to the meadow below Cathedral Peak. At the end of the meadow, the trail drops over Cathedral Pass, revealing another knock-your-socks-off view. The spire of Cathedral Peak rises above a green meadow filled with flowers and the impossibly blue Upper Cathedral Lake, embellished with windblown pines and backdropped by the park's

The John Muir Trail

4,190,000

300,000

Dana Fork

Lyell Fork Tuolumne River

LYELL CANYON Pacific Crest Trail

John Muir Trail

Donohue Pass

4,180,000

Mount Lyell
13,114 ft.

Ireland
Lake

Evelyn
Lake

N

Rafferty Creek

Vogelsang
Lake

Bernice
Lake

Kilometers

Miles

0

4

4

300,000

TUOLUMNE MEADOWS

Tuolumne
Meadows
Visitor Center

Elizabeth
Lake

CATHEDRAL

Vogelsang High
Sierra Camp

Echo Creek

Fletcher Creek

Emeric
Lake

Lewis Creek

Washburn
Lake

290,000

290,000

Trail

John Muir

Cathedral
Lakes

Merced Lake High
Sierra Camp

Merced
Lake

120

Tioga Road

Tenaya
Lake

Sunrise High
Sierra Camp

Sunrise Creek

Merced River

LITTLE YOSEMITE VALLEY

May Lake
High Sierra
Camp

May
Lake

Double
Falls

TENAYA CANYON

Tenaya Creek

Merced

Little Yosemite
Valley

280,000

280,000

120

Snow Creek

Half
Dome
8,836 ft.

START

LITTLE YOSEMITE

Yosemite Creek

4,190,000

4,180,000

Happy
Isles

northern ranges. Descend the pass and cross the marshy meadow to Upper Cathedral Lake at 16.3 miles.

Drop down through forest to a spur trail to Lower Cathedral Lake at mile 16.8. The lower lake is a half mile to the west and is well worth a detour since Cathedral Peak is seen head-on from the lakeside and appears as a single, needlelike spire. From the lower lake cutoff the trail rounds the end of the ridge on which Cathedral Peak is perched, then descends through forest to a junction with the trail to Tuolumne Meadows, just after crossing Budd Creek and before reaching the Tioga Road at 20.7 miles.

The trail passes behind the visitor center, Tuolumne Village, and the Tuolumne Meadows Campground, in case you need supplies or information. It passes several junctions leading to the Tioga Road and the other facilities to the north, then passes the rear entrance to the campground, the Elizabeth Lake Trailhead, and a second campground turnoff at 22.4 miles. Follow along the north shore of the Lyell Fork of the Tuolumne River until you meet a junction where the Pacific Crest Trail (PCT) joins the John Muir Trail (JMT) at 23.1 miles near the Tuolumne Meadows Lodge.

Follow the PCT/JMT southeast to a footbridge over the Dana Fork, ignoring the cutoff back to the lodge. Cross the bridge then turn left and follow the river upstream, pausing to enjoy the wildflower gardens along the shore. Ignore another cutoff to the left toward Gaylor Lakes just a short distance beyond. The route bends slightly to the right, crosses a low rise alongside a marshy area, and reaches the twin bridges over the Lyell Fork at 24.7 miles. This is surely one of the most sublime vistas in Yosemite, with the clear turquoise river winding toward you through the green meadow. Soon after you leave the twin bridges, another path leads back to the Tuolumne Meadows Campground, but you keep left on the John Muir Trail through lodgepole forest and over open rock to 25.4 miles, where the Rafferty Creek Trail heads uphill to the right, toward Vogelsang. Cross the bridge over the creek on your left and continue through forest and meadows until a glorious view of Lyell Canyon opens up and you rejoin the Tuolumne River, which you will now be following almost all the way to its headwaters, the Lyell Glacier, tucked beneath the shaded crest of Mount Lyell, the highest peak in Yosemite at 13,114 feet.

At 27.7 miles, keep left at a fork with another trail to Vogelsang. Just beyond the point where Kuna Creek drops down from the Kuna Crest to join the Lyell Fork from the east, the trail begins to climb, winding among avalanche debris. Views of the river snaking away to the north down the canyon get better and better as you gain elevation. Cross the river on a bridge and arrive at Lyell Base Camp. It's a busy place used by climbers preparing to tackle the mountain. There are plenty of good campsites here, and plenty of bears.

The trees begin to disappear as you climb beyond the camp, and from here on you get superb views up the canyon to the peaks and glaciers. One of the finest of these is from the outlet of a little lake at the end of a flowery meadow. This outlet can be tricky to cross at high water. Just past this crossing, there is a rocky little rise sheltered by whitebark pines that could be used as a last, and simply exquisite, campsite before the pass. Climb another little rise, turn left (east) and cross the outlet of another tarn, not as difficult as the last one. Now work your way up over open granite, negotiating snow patches that often remain until midsummer, to Donohue Pass and the Yosemite Park boundary at 11,000 feet. Beyond, the John Muir and Pacific Crest Trails descend through an open rocky basin toward Rush Creek in the Ansel Adams Wilderness.

Miles and Directions

0.0 Happy Isles Trailhead.

0.8 Cross the Vernal Fall Bridge.

3.3 Panorama Trail junction, keep left.

3.5 Top of Nevada Fall, cross the bridge.

4.8 Little Yosemite Valley.

5.3 Half Dome Trail junction, turn right.

5.8 Sunrise Lakes Trail junction, turn right again.

7.7 Echo Valley Trail junction, keep left.

7.8 Sunrise High Sierra Camp Trail, turn right.

12.3 Sunrise High Sierra Camp.

13.2 Merced Lake Trail junction, continue straight ahead.

16.3 Upper Cathedral Lake.

20.7 Tuolumne Meadows Trail junction near Tioga Road, turn right.

22.4 Turnoff to Tuolumne Meadows Campground.

23.1 John Muir Trail and Pacific Crest Trail meet.

24.7 Twin bridges over the Lyell Fork.

25.4 Rafferty Creek Trail junction, turn left across the bridge.

27.7 Vogelsang High Sierra Camp cutoff, keep left.

34.3 Donohue Pass.

59 The Pacific Crest Trail

Start: Yosemite Park boundary at Donohue Pass.

Distance: 79.4 miles one way.

Approximate hiking time: 6 to 10 days.

Difficulty: Strenuous.

Seasons: Summer and early fall.

Nearest facilities: Tuolumne Meadows.

Permits: Required in advance.

Maps: USGS Koip Peak, Vogelsang Peak, Tioga Pass, Tenaya Lake, Falls Ridge, Matterhorn Peak, Piute Mountain, Tiltill Mountain, and Tower Peak quads.

Finding the trailhead: This hike is described from border to border of Yosemite. There are no trailheads at either end. The only road the trail crosses is at Tuolumne Meadows.

The Hike

From Donohue Pass at 11,000 feet, work your way down over open granite, negotiating snow patches that often remain until midsummer, crossing the outlet of a little tarn, and descending to the outlet of a second tarn where the ford can be tricky at high water. There is a small, exquisite campsite near the ford facing Mount Lyell, the highest peak in the park at 13,114 feet, and its glacier. The forest begins to thicken as you wind your way down to Lyell Base Camp, on the other side of a bridge at 2.7 miles. It's a busy place with lots of good campsites and lots of bears. Wind down through avalanche debris to the long, blooming meadow along the meandering Lyell Fork to a junction at mile 6.8, where a trail coming down from Vogelsang High Sierra Camp joins this one. The trail continues alongside the river for a time, then gradually swings away from it to make its way through forest and meadow, then back into forest to meet Rafferty Creek. Cross it on a bridge to find a junction with another route to Vogelsang at mile 11.1. Turn right. Ignore a side trail that cuts off to the left toward the Tuolumne Meadows Campground and swing right to reach the twin bridges over the Tuolumne at mile 11.7, where you will find one of the most sublime vistas in Yosemite. Leaving the bridges, head north over the dusty trampled trail to the JOHN MUIR TRAIL sign at a road across from which is the Dog Lake parking lot. Ignore several spur trails that cut off to your right toward Gaylor Lakes and the Tuolumne Meadows Lodge, keeping left. Turn right only when you can see the sign and the road at mile 12.4.

Walk along this secondary road heading west until it meets the Tioga Road. Continue west along the Tioga Road for less than a half mile until you can see the Lembert Dome parking lot on the north side. Cross Tioga Road to the parking lot, turn left (west) and continue along the road that parallels Tioga Road to the Glen Aulin Trailhead. It begins at the closed gate at 13 miles. Go through the gate and follow the road (closed to vehicles) through the meadow, keeping right and climbing a small rise where the road splits. From the top of the rise, head toward the ramshackle log structure partially containing Soda Springs at mile 13.5. Just beyond is

Dorothy Lake Pass above Dorothy Lake is the destination for this section of the Pacific Crest Trail.

Parsons Lodge, a stone building with historical exhibits. There the path splits; you turn right to a big GLEN AULIN TRAIL sign, then turn left. Walk through flowery meadows and lodgepole forest on footing that is heavy and dusty from lots of traffic. Ford Delaney Creek at mile 14.2, then ignore a trail that cuts off to the right toward Young Lakes at mile 14.4. In less than a mile you emerge from behind a low ridge to behold the spectacular Cathedral Range with the Tuolumne River in the foreground. After passing through a short stretch of forest, climb around a low shoulder of rock and keep watch on your left for the Little Devil's Postpile, an unusual volcanic feature much younger than the surrounding rock.

The trail turns sharply right and drops down a short, steep notch, and very soon reaches a pair of footbridges across the Tuolumne at mile 16.3. From this point on, the river picks up speed and cascades over a series of falls. It dives into and out of deep forest lined with Labrador tea and corn lily twice, then emerges again into sunlight on cobblestones or smooth granite marked with ducks. Finally it meets a junction with the McGee Lake Trail at 17.8 miles. A few more steep, slippery switchbacks lead down to a bridge and back to the other side of the river. Few hikers can resist the urge to stop on the bridge to snap a photo or simply gape at the frothy White

Cascade splashing into a pool in front of the Glen Aulin High Sierra Camp. You have come 18 miles.

Head northward across Cold Creek from the High Sierra Camp, partly through open forest, partly through meadow, up Cold Canyon, with Mount Conness at its head. The McCabe Lakes junction, at 25 miles, is not shown correctly on the topo, but if you stay left, following the Pacific Crest Trail (PCT), you'll be on track. At 26 miles, keep left again, following Return Creek in Virginia Canyon downstream, dropping to cross Spiller Creek, then climbing fairly steeply up some dusty switchbacks. Pass through a gate and make another sandy descent, cross a low rise, pass a couple of shallow ponds, then emerge into the meadow bordering Miller Lake. It's a nice warm lake for swimming and there is good camping in the timber across the meadow from the trail. Leaving the lake, the trail swings back northward, crossing a shoulder with views to the Sawtooth Ridge, then drops steeply into Matterhorn Canyon at 30.8 miles in a flowery meadow where there is more good camping. The PCT makes a sharp dogleg here, cutting back southwest, crossing Matterhorn Creek and following its broad meandering course downstream for more than a mile. The trail swings northwest, climbing along Wilson Creek, which it crosses several times before it turns west and climbs switchbacks to wide, grassy Benson Pass at mile 40.4. Descend fairly gradually from the pass and wade the outlet of Smedberg Lake at the edge of a meadow. The lake lies at the foot of blocky Volunteer Peak. There is good camping at the lake; the best sites are on the shore opposite the trail.

After leaving Smedberg Lake, reach a junction at the steep west base of Volunteer Peak at 52.5 miles. The fork continues south, but the PCT heads westerly toward Seavey Pass. You meet a second Seavey Pass junction at 53.1 miles. Head north toward Benson Lake, dropping down to cross, then follow the stream connecting Smedberg and Benson Lakes. Leave the stream to cross a rocky shoulder and descend to a boggy flat blooming with corn lilies, onions, wild geraniums, and more, to meet the spur trail to Benson Lake at 55.5 miles. This is a big lake in a beautifully ice-polished rocky bowl. It is surprisingly popular for such a remote spot, probably because of its good camping and beautiful beach at the end nearest the trail.

Leaving the lake, the trail climbs up open manzanita-covered slopes heading toward the pointed beacon of Piute Mountain directly ahead. Near the peak it swings northeast, climbs more steeply along the cascading stream, then levels out beside the first of several little lakes to Seavey Pass, a rather long, open ridge studded with shining domes and tarns. A short distance down the north side of the pass, reach a junction with Kerrick Canyon at 58.9 miles.

Turn left (west) down the shady floor of Kerrick Canyon, pass an avalanche chute, and proceed to the junction with the Bear Valley Trail, at 62.5 miles. Switchback up out of the gully and follow a roller-coaster route, then drop down steeply into the next valley, wading Thompson and Stubblefield Creeks in Stubblefield Canyon, then labor your way up and down over Macomb Ridge. Finally, cross Tilden Creek and meet the Tilden Canyon/Wilma Lake junction at 68.2 miles. Turn

The Pacific Crest Trail

right (north) here and proceed a very short distance to a second junction at 68.3 miles, toward Wilma Lake. The trail follows very close to the southwest shore of the lake and crosses a short stream that connects the lake to Falls Creek. Through much of July this is a soggy morass, and earlier in the year it may be so deeply flooded that it is impossible.

Once on the west side of Falls Creek, turn right (north) at the junction at 70.3 miles. Soon you pass through a gate and wander along the flat valley floor to 72.2 miles, where a trail cuts off to the right (east) to the shore of Tilden Lake. A visit to this lake is worth a detour, and there is good camping at the southwest shore of this long, narrow finger of water, with Tower Peak above its far end.

Back on the Pacific Crest Trail, continue north, passing Chittenden Peak, then a pretty waterfall, and level out to follow miles of grassy meadow. Pass briefly through forest, then into the even wider expanse of Grace Meadow. Ascend out of the meadow at its north end to reach the Dorothy Lake/Bond Pass junction at 78.7 miles. Turn right (east) here and skirt Dorothy Lake in its broad meadow to reach the park boundary at Dorothy Lake Pass, at 79.4 miles.

Miles and Directions

0.0 Donohue Pass.

2.7 Lyell Base Camp.

6.8 Vogelsang High Sierra Camp junction.

11.1 Rafferty Creek bridge.

11.7 Twin bridges over the Tuolumne.

12.4 Dog Lake parking lot.

13.0 Glen Aulin Trailhead.

13.5 Soda Springs.

14.2 Ford Delaney Creek.

14.4 Young Lakes Trail junction.

16.3 Twin bridges.

17.8 McGee Lake Trail junction.

18.0   Glen Aulin High Sierra Camp.

25.0   McCabe Lakes junction.

26.0   Return Creek.

30.8   Matterhorn Canyon.

40.4   Benson Pass.

52.5   Smedberg Lake junction.

53.1   Seavey Pass junction.

55.5   Spur trail to Benson Lake.

58.9   Kerrick Canyon.

62.5   Bear Valley Trail.

68.2   Tilden Canyon/Wilma Lake junction.

68.3   Second Wilma Lake junction.

70.3   Jack Main Canyon.

72.2   Tilden Lake Junction.

78.7   Dorothy Lake/Bond Pass junction.

79.4   Dorothy Lake Pass.

Trail Finder

Backcountry Lakes

Waterfalls

Alpine Country, Ridges, Passes, and Plateaus

18 Vogelsang High Sierra Camp

36 Lyell Fork and Donohue Pass

37 Mono Pass and Parker Pass

40 Ten Lakes

45 Gaylor Lakes

50 Saddlebag Lake and 20 Lakes Basin

51 Lundy Canyon

55 Benson Pass–Northeast Yosemite Grand Tour

56 McCabe Lakes

57 Piute Mountain–Peeler Lake Loop

Really Flat Trails with No Hills

1 East Valley Floor

2 West Valley Floor

5 Mirror Lake–Tenaya Canyon Loop

26 Wawona Meadow

32 Tenaya Lake

Trails for Day Hikers Only—No Backpacking Allowed

1 East Valley Floor

2 West Valley Floor

3 Glacier Point via the Four Mile Trail

4 Happy Isles to the Top of Nevada Fall

5 Mirror Lake–Tenaya Canyon Loop

8 Taft Point and the Fissures

9 Sentinel Dome

10 McGurk Meadow

12 The Panorama Trail–Glacier Point to Nevada Fall

16 Tuolumne Grove

23 Mariposa Grove of Big Trees

26 Wawona Meadow

32 Tenaya Lake

35 Elizabeth Lake

39 Lukens Lake

41 Soda Springs and Parsons Lodge

42 Dog Lake

43 Lembert Dome

45 Gaylor Lakes

46 Wapama Falls

Trails to Avoid if You Want Solitude

1 East Valley Loop

3 Glacier Point via the Four Mile Trail

4 Happy Isles to the Top of Nevada Fall

5 Mirror Lake–Tenaya Canyon Loop

6 Yosemite Falls

7 Half Dome

17–22 All High Sierra Camps

23 Mariposa Grove of Big Trees

32 Tenaya Lake

34 Cathedral Lakes

35 Elizabeth Lake

36 Lyell Fork and Donohue Pass

41 Soda Springs and Parsons Lodge

42 Dog Lake

43 Lembert Dome

50 Saddlebag Lake and 20 Lakes Basin

Early Season (Before July) Trails

1 East Valley Floor

2 West Valley Floor

5 Mirror Lake–Tenaya Canyon Loop

23 Mariposa Grove of Big Trees

24 Chilnualna Fall

26 Wawona Meadow

46 Wapama Falls

47 Rancheria Falls

48 Lake Vernon and Tiltill Valley

Wildflowers

1 East Valley Floor

2 West Valley Floor

10 McGurk Meadow

26 Wawona Meadow

39 Lukens Lake

41 Soda Springs-Parsons Lodge

27 Ostrander Lake

34 Cathedral Lakes

36 Lyell Fork

46 Wapama Falls

47 Rancheria Falls

49 Jack Main Canyon and Tilden Lake

51 Lundy Canyon

Wildlife (especially bears)

4 Happy Isles to the Top of Nevada Fall

10 McGurk Meadow

Hiker's Checklist

Always make and check your own checklist!

If you've ever hiked into the backcountry and discovered that you've forgotten an essential, you know that it's a good idea to make a checklist and check the items off as you pack so that you won't forget the things you want and need. Here are some ideas:

Clothing

  dependable rain parka
  rain pants
  windbreaker
  thermal underwear
  shorts
  long pants or sweat pants
  wool cap or balaclava
  hat
  wool shirt or sweater
  jacket or parka
  extra socks
  underwear
  lightweight shirts
  T-shirts
  bandana(s)
  mittens or gloves
  belt

Footwear

  sturdy, comfortable boots
  lightweight camp shoes

Bedding

  sleeping bag
  foam pad or air mattress

ground sheet (plastic or nylon)
dependable tent

Hauling
backpack and/or day pack

Cooking
1-quart container (plastic)
1-gallon water container for camp use (collapsible)
backpacking stove and extra fuel
funnel
aluminum foil
cooking pots
bowls/plates
utensils (spoons, forks, small spatula, knife)
pot scrubber
matches in waterproof container

Food and Drink
cereal
bread
crackers
cheese
trail mix
margarine
powdered soups
salt/pepper
main course meals
snacks
hot chocolate
tea
powdered milk
drink mixes

Photography
camera and film
filters
lens brush/paper

Miscellaneous
sunglasses
map and compass
toilet paper
pocketknife
sunscreen

good insect repellent
lip balm
flashlight with new batteries and a spare bulb
candle(s)
first-aid kit
your FalconGuide
survival kit
small garden trowel or shovel
water filter or purification tablets
plastic bags (for trash)
soap
towel
toothbrush
fishing license
fishing rod, reel, lures, flies, etc.
binoculars
waterproof covering for pack
watch
sewing kit

Further Reading

Barrett, S.A., and E. W. Gifford. *Miwok Material Culture.* Yosemite: Yosemite Natural History Association, 1933.

Browning, Peter. *Place Names of the Sierra Nevada.* Berkeley: Wilderness Press, 1991.

Gaines, David. *Birds of the Yosemite Sierra.* Oakland: California Syllabus Press, 1977.

Grater, Russell K. *Discovering Sierra Mammals.* Yosemite: Yosemite Natural History Association and Sequoia Natural History Association, 1978.

Harmon, Will. *Leave No Trace.* Guilford, Conn.: Globe Pequot Press, 1997.

Harvey, H. Thomas, Howard S. Shellhammer, and Ronald E. Stecker. "Giant Sequoia Ecology." *Scientific Monograph Series No. 12.* Washington, D.C.: U.S. Department of the Interior, 1980.

Huber, N. King. "The Geologic Story of Yosemite National Park." *U.S. Geological Survey Bulletin 1595.* Washington, D.C.: U.S. Department of the Interior, 1987.

Johnson, Verna R. *Sierra Nevada.* Boston: Houghton Mifflin Company, 1970.

Paruk, Jim. *Sierra Nevada Tree Finder.* Yosemite Association, 1997.

Preston, Gilbert. *Wilderness First Aid.* Guilford, Conn.: Globe Pequot Press, 1997.

Sax, Joseph L. *Mountains without Handrails.* Ann Arbor: University of Michigan Press, 1980.

Schneider, Bill. *Bear Aware.* Guilford, Conn.: Globe Pequot Press, 2004.

Schneider, Bill and Russ. *Backpacking Tips.* Guilford, Conn.: Globe Pequot Press, 2005.

Storer, Tracy I., and Robert L. Usinger. *Sierra Nevada Natural History.* Berkeley: University of California Press, 1966.

Swedo, Suzanne. *Wilderness Survival.* Guilford, Conn.: Globe Pequot Press, 1998.

Torres, Steven. *Lion Sense.* Guilford, Conn.: Globe Pequot Press, 2005.

Weeden, Norman. *A Sierra Nevada Flora.* Berkeley: Wilderness Press, 1996.

Whitney, Stephen. *The Sierra Nevada: A Sierra Club Naturalist's Guide.* San Francisco: Sierra Club Books, 1979.

Wiese, Karen. *Sierra Nevada Wildflowers.* Guilford, Conn.: Globe Pequot Press, 2000.

Woodmencey, Jim. *Reading Weather.* Guilford, Conn.: Globe Pequot Press, 1998.

Zwinger, Ann H., and Beatrice E. Willard. *Land Above the Trees.* New York: Harper & Row, 1972.

About the Author

Suzanne Swedo has taught natural science seminars for the Yosemite Association in Yosemite National Park for twenty years. During the same period, she has conducted wilderness survival, outdoor skills, and natural history outings as founder and director of W.I.L.D., an international and domestic adventure travel company. She has also led nature and wilderness trips for various educational organizations including the University of California Extension, the National Outings Program of the Sierra Club, Wilderness Institute, Pacific Wilderness Institute, and Outdoor Adventures. She has demonstrated wilderness skills in the ten-week television series *Alive and Well*, and served as a survival consultant for Warner Brothers Television. Her writings on travel and the outdoors have appeared in publications such as the *Los Angeles Examiner* and *California Magazine*. Other FalconGuides are *Wilderness Survival, Hiking California's Golden Trout Wilderness,* and *Best Easy Day Hikes Yosemite National Park*.